Charting the AI Transition in Education and Business Environments

This book delineates a comprehensive framework designed to ultimately assist organizations as they navigate the critical juncture—often termed the inflection point—in adopting generative Artificial Intelligence (AI). Addressing the exigent shift in organizational strategy mandated by Industry 4.0, and urging a transition from mere digital transformation to what is being progressively understood as "generative transformation," it fills a conspicuous lacuna in both academic and practical discourses by presenting a timely synthesis of research, empirical studies, and case analyses. The authors utilize an interdisciplinary methodology, bridging the epistemological divide between the technological intricacies of generative AI and its effective implementation within institutional frameworks. Reorienting the focus of organizational leaders from a simplistic replacement paradigm to one of technological-human augmentation, it works toward a prescriptive blueprint for enabling organizations to adopt generative AI without compromising their most valuable asset: human intellectual and emotional capital. Fostering interdisciplinary dialog among academics, industry professionals, and policymakers, it fills a critical gap in current discourses and serves as a catalyst for future research and collaboration.

James Hutson is Professor and Department Head of Art History, AI, and Visual Culture at Lindenwood University, USA.

TJ Rains is Vice President of Information Technology and Chief Information Officer at Lindenwood University, USA.

Routledge Research in Digital Education and Educational Technology

This series provides a forum for established and emerging scholars to discuss the latest debates, research and practice in the field of digital education and educational technology globally, including distance and open learning.

Overcoming Challenges in Online Learning
Perspectives from Asia and Africa
Edited by Areej ElSayary and Abdulrasheed Olowoselu

The New Digital Education Policy Landscape
From Education Systems to Platforms
Edited by Cristóbal Cobo and Axel Rivas

Digitalization and Digital Competence in Educational Contexts
A Nordic Perspective from Policy to Practice
Edited by Sara Willermark, Anders D. Olofsson and J. Ola Lindberg

Learning, Teaching, and Social Media
A Generational Approach
Andrew McWhirter

Designing Learning with Digital Technologies
Perspectives from Multimodality in Education
Edited by Fei Victor Lim and Mercedes Querol-Julián

Charting the AI Transition in Education and Business Environments
Navigating the Generative Inflection Point for Industry 4.0 Success
James Hutson and TJ Rains

For more information about this series please visit: https://www.routledge.com/Routledge-Research-in-Education/book-series/RRDEET

Charting the AI Transition in Education and Business Environments

Navigating the Generative Inflection Point for Industry 4.0 Success

James Hutson and TJ Rains

Routledge
Taylor & Francis Group
NEW YORK AND LONDON

First published 2025
by Routledge
605 Third Avenue, New York, NY 10158

and by Routledge
4 Park Square, Milton Park, Abingdon, Oxon, OX14 4RN

Routledge is an imprint of the Taylor & Francis Group, an informa business

Library of Congress Cataloging-in-Publication Data
Names: Hutson, James, author. | Rains, TJ, author.
Title: Charting the AI transition in education and business environments : navigating the generative inflection point for industry 4.0 success / James Hutson and TJ Rains.
Other titles: Charting the artificial intelligence transition in education and business environments
Description: New York, NY : Routledge, 2025. | Series: Routledge research in digital education and educational technology | Includes bibliographical references and index.
Identifiers: LCCN 2024033799 (print) | LCCN 2024033800 (ebook) | ISBN 9781032844664 (hardback) | ISBN 9781032844725 (paperback) | ISBN 9781003512813 (ebook)
Subjects: LCSH: Artificial intelligence--Educational applications. | Artificial intelligence in business.
Classification: LCC LB1028.43 .H87 2025 (print) | LCC LB1028.43 (ebook) | DDC 370.285/63--dc23/eng/20240821
LC record available at https://lccn.loc.gov/2024033799
LC ebook record available at https://lccn.loc.gov/2024033800

ISBN: 978-1-032-84466-4 (hbk)
ISBN: 978-1-032-84472-5 (pbk)
ISBN: 978-1-003-51281-3 (ebk)

DOI: 10.4324/9781003512813

Typeset in Times New Roman
by SPi Technologies India Pvt Ltd (Straive)

This book is dedicated to our families, whose unwavering support and encouragement have been the cornerstone of our journey. To our parents, we express deep gratitude for instilling in us a thirst for knowledge and the determination to pursue our passions. Your belief in our abilities and unwavering support have propelled us forward.

To our spouses and partners, we extend heartfelt appreciation for standing by our side throughout the long hours of research and writing. To our children, we are grateful for your inspiration and the joy you bring to our lives. Your presence reminds us of the importance of our work and motivates us to strive for excellence. To our extended families, friends, and loved ones, we thank you for your encouragement, words of wisdom, and unwavering belief in our abilities.

In particular, James Hutson would like to thank his wife Piper and children Bishop and Aurora. TJ Rains would like to thank his family, Aisha, Jules, Emaline, and Alison for their patience, understanding, and unwavering support.

Your support has been a source of strength and inspiration. We acknowledge the sacrifices you have made and the understanding you have shown, allowing us the time and space to pursue our scholarly endeavors. This book stands as a testament to your love and support. With deepest appreciation and heartfelt gratitude, we dedicate this work to our families.

Contents

Tables

About the Authors

Dr. James Hutson has academic and professional expertise residing in the domain of generative artificial intelligence (GAI), bolstered by his many contributions to the intersecting fields of neurohumanities, neurodiversity, immersive realities, and educational gamification. With a Ph.D. in Artificial Intelligence from Capitol Technology University and a Master of Arts in Leadership from Lindenwood University, his educational background offers a multifaceted lens through which he explores the complexities of AI adoption in institutional settings. Commencing his academic odyssey with a Bachelor of Arts in Art from the University of Tulsa, followed by a Master of Arts in Art History from Southern Methodist University and a Ph.D. in Art History from the University of Maryland, College Park, Dr. Hutson has cultivated a rich interdisciplinary profile. Since embarking on his academic career in 2006, he has donned various roles, spanning pedagogical to administrative, across five esteemed universities. These positions include Chair of Art History, Assistant Dean of Graduate and Online Programs, and most recently, Lead XR Disruptor and Department Head of Art History and Visual Culture. Of particular significance is his scholarly oeuvre, which is marked by an extensive array of research articles, monographs, and case studies focusing explicitly on generative AI. Additionally, Dr. Hutson has authored several seminal books examining the multifaceted applications of artificial intelligence in both the educational sector and cultural heritage preservation.

Dr. TJ Rains, CIO and VP, is an expert in digital transformation and institutional AI implementation. He serves as the Vice President for Information Technology and Chief Information Officer at Lindenwood University, where he plays a pivotal role in guiding institutional strategy and technology governance. He holds advanced degrees in Information Technology and a Ph.D. in Organizational Leadership. Rains' expertise includes IT governance, enterprise resource planning (ERP), data analytics, project management, and digital transformation. His work exemplifies a commitment to integrating technology with business and academic objectives in higher education, enhancing student experience and operational efficiencies. Rains' expertise extends to applied artificial intelligence, where he has engaged in initiatives to integrate AI-driven solutions into various aspects of university operations, enhancing efficiencies and core infrastructure for executive decision support. With a distinguished record of successful leadership in higher education and scholarly contributions to national and international technology and leadership conferences, Rains' work is primarily situated at the intersection of technology, education, change leadership, and strategic innovation.

Preface

As we find ourselves navigating through the aftermath of a significant inflection point with generative artificial intelligence (GAI), this book is designed as a playbook for leaders at the forefront of technological adoption in both industry and education. It is written in a straight forward fashion in order to demystify the complexities of integrating GAI into our daily operations and strategies. The co-authors, TJ Rains and James Hutson, bring to the table a diverse set of experiences, perspectives, and skills that complement each other in addressing the multifaceted challenges and opportunities presented by GAI.

TJ Rains, serving as a CIO and VP, has spearheaded numerous digital transformation initiatives, leveraging AI-driven solutions to enhance operations across various institutions. His expertise lies in navigating the practical implications of technology integration, from strategic planning to execution. On the other side, James Hutson offers a unique blend of administrative insight and faculty experience, having directed research on the institutional adoption of emergent technologies such as Extended Reality (XR) and AI. Together, their collaborative efforts shed light on actionable approaches for stakeholders across the educational and industrial spectrum as we edge into the Fifth Industrial Revolution.

Within the pages of this book, readers will be led through the nuanced landscape of GAI adoption within various institutional settings. The narrative weaves together various proven strategies, insights, and case studies aimed at maximizing the potential of existing assets, emphasizing the critical nature of selecting the appropriate tools for GAI integration. These tools, ranging from development platforms to advanced analytics applications, are pivotal for institutions looking to harness GAI and machine learning (ML) models for financial analytics and beyond.

In the realm of digital innovation, a prevailing theme of this book is the critical role of "platforming" as a strategic approach that institutions must adopt to achieve agility and adaptability within a rapidly evolving technological marketplace. This platforming approach does not merely represent a shift in the tools and technologies employed but signifies a profound transformation in organizational processes and strategies. Unlike prior technological advancements such as cloud computing or mobile technology, which primarily altered the technological landscape, the advent of generative AI heralds a new era of change management. This transformative phase is characterized by these advanced tools not only enhancing existing processes but fundamentally redefining them.

Institutions that effectively harness the capabilities of generative AI will find that they are not just adopting new technology, but are re-engineering their entire operational frameworks. This encompasses a shift from traditional methods to more dynamic, AI-driven processes that leverage deep analytics, enhance decision-making, and ultimately, transform institutional and business practices. This change management is crucial as it extends beyond the technological dimension, requiring a holistic approach that includes cultural shifts, training for new competencies, and rethinking strategic objectives to fully capitalize on the benefits of GAI.

The strategic integration of GAI thus paves the way for innovative solutions that are tailored to meet the dynamic needs of both educational and business environments. By focusing on change management as the core of digital transformation, institutions are better prepared to navigate the complexities of the current technological epoch, ensuring sustainability and success in the Industry 4.0 landscape.

Through case studies, including the exploration of Microsoft A5 customers' early access to the Co-Pilot platform, the book highlights how secured, AI-enhanced environments are revolutionizing the way faculty and staff engage with technology in educational settings. These environments provide a glimpse into the future of AI in education, where secured, interactive platforms like Co-Pilot become commonplace, enhancing the teaching and learning experience.

Furthermore, the book delves into the importance of differentiating AI solutions to cater specifically to the varied needs of students and administrative operations. The focus on developing student-centered, assistant-based models underscores a commitment to enhancing the educational journey through AI.

Guidance is also provided on establishing a robust IT management and governance framework, essential for fostering a productive relationship between AI technologies and business stakeholders. This framework is supported by a wealth of resources, templates, and blueprints aggregated from AI research centers and online marketplaces, designed to streamline the strategy-to-governance process and mitigate security and privacy risks.

The book also presents insights gleaned from interviews with executives and CIOs, shedding light on how AI is impacting organizational value streams. These discussions reveal the varied challenges and approaches institutions face, dependent on their resources and the type of institution, and underscore the transformative potential of AI across different sectors.

Legal considerations and cultural impacts are not overlooked; the book addresses the complexities of AI deployment within legal frameworks, advocating for transparency and openness. It explores the reluctancy some institutions face in sharing their policies and strategies, emphasizing the need for a candid dialog about the hurdles encountered when scaling AI solutions.

This playbook not only acts as a guide for institutional change but also as a reflection on the executive leadership behaviors critical for supporting transformation in the post-pandemic era, particularly from an organizational development perspective. Through real-world examples, including the integration of AI technologies, the book illustrates the varied landscape of GAI adoption, offering a lens through which leaders can view and shape their own strategies.

We invite leaders, strategists, and innovators in technology adoption to explore these pages, hoping to ignite a dialog that spans across disciplines and industries. For those interested in contributing further to this conversation or seeking advice on their GAI journey, feel free to reach out and join us in shaping the future of education and business in the age of artificial intelligence.

Welcome to the transition. Welcome to the future.

The AI tool Claude 2.5 from Anthropic was employed to summarize article PDFs, thereby facilitating the organization of information for the literature review. Subsequently, the authors reworded these summaries to ensure coherence and integration within the final version of the book, adhering to academic standards and enhancing the overall narrative quality of the book.

Acknowledgments

The authors express profound appreciation to the myriad of individuals and institutions whose contributions and unwavering support have been pivotal in the genesis and fruition of this tome. At the vanguard of acknowledgment stands Dr. John Porter, whose innovative leadership in aligning the adoption of emergent technologies like AI with educational initiatives has left an indelible mark on this work's evolution.

Acknowledgment is due to Dr. Kathi Vosevich, Dean of the College of Arts and Humanities, for her steadfast encouragement and support of the research culminating in this publication. Vosevich's guidance and confidence in the authors' academic endeavors have been fundamental in sculpting the contours of this volume.

The authors extend their gratitude to the research team responsible for composing this manuscript and acknowledge the critical insights and contributions of various colleagues and co-authors from ancillary projects. James Hutson extends thanks to Professors Ben Fulcher, Jeremiah Ratican, Joe Weber, Ben Scholle, and Dr. Trent Olsen, alongside MFA student Morgan Harper-Nichols. As well, Drs. Daniel Plate and Emily Barnes were instrumental in shaping many of the sections and the direction. TJ Rains wishes to thank the amazing administration, faculty, staff, and students of Lindenwood University for the depth of experience garnered from serving and supporting the diverse needs of our community.

The authors also convey their deep appreciation to the administrative leaders at all of the institutions that participated in the study for their relentless support and dedication to creating an environment conducive to academic excellence and scholarly exploration. The leadership, encompassing Presidents, Provosts, and Deans at these institutions, has been instrumental in providing the necessary guidance and resources for this research and writing project.

Furthermore, those that provided insight into their experiences as leaders in industry and education, we are indebted and thank you for your invaluable time and efforts in helping others navigate this unpredictable time.

Finally, the authors are thankful for the insights and constructive feedback from colleagues and fellow researchers throughout this project. Their contributions have significantly enriched the work and helped to refine the ideas encapsulated within this volume.

1 Introduction

The Generative Inflection Point

1.1 Defining Generative AI: Scope and Potential

In this era, marked distinctly as the Fourth Industrial Revolution or Industry 4.0, educational and industry technology professionals find themselves at the nexus of unprecedented change. This transformative period, characterized by the integration of digital, physical, and biological technologies, is reshaping the very fabric of society and the global economy (Schwab, 2017). Within this context, the emergence of generative artificial intelligence (GAI) represents a pivotal advancement, heralding new potentials and challenges for institutions worldwide. GAI, distinguished from its predecessors by its ability to create new, original content through learned data inputs, stands at the forefront of this technological frontier. Its capabilities extend far beyond simple task automation, venturing into realms previously considered the exclusive domain of human creativity. This progression from rule-based systems to sophisticated models capable of engaging in human-like interactions underscores a significant leap in an unprecedented evolution.

In fact, the rapid ascent of GAI into the technological and societal forefront is underscored by staggering statistics, heralding a transformative era across industries and everyday life. McKinsey's research reveals that 75% of professionals foresee GAI instigating "significant or disruptive change" within their fields over the next three years, highlighting the anticipation of profound industry shifts (McKinsey, 2024). Remarkably, OpenAI CEO Sam Altman reports that ChatGPT, a flagship GAI application, engages 100 million weekly users, evidencing the technology's mass adoption (Kearns, 2023). This surge in usage is mirrored in Salesforce's finding that 86% of IT leaders predict a dominant role for GAI in their organizations, indicating a widespread expectation for GAI to reshape IT and data management practices (Yao, 2023).

Furthermore, the GAI market is projected to expand by $180 billion in the next eight years, signifying the economic potential and investment magnetism of GAI technologies. Amidst this growth, generational divides

DOI: 10.4324/9781003512813-1

emerge, with 70% of Generation Z employing GAI, reflecting a trust in its decision-making support, contrasting with older generations' hesitancy (Marr, 2024). This demographic shift suggests a future where the influence of the technology permeates decision-making, creativity, and information consumption, reshaping content creation to the extent that 90% of online content could be AI-generated by 2026, as forecasted by the European Union Law Enforcement Agency (Cyber Security, 2024). These statistics not only illustrate the current impact of GAI, but also forecast its expanding role in shaping future digital landscapes and societal norms.

Historically, humanity's major revolutions—agricultural, industrial, and informational—have each ushered in radical shifts in societal organization, economic structures, and employment landscapes. For instance, the transition from nomadic lifestyles to settled agricultural communities marked the dawn of civilization, fundamentally altering human existence (Braidwood, 1960). Similarly, the Industrial Revolution catalyzed mass urbanization and the development of new work forms, profoundly impacting social dynamics (Deane, 1979). The Information Age, propelled by the advent of computers and the internet, transitioned the economy from industry-based to knowledge-oriented, again transforming how and where work is conducted (Castells, 2010).

The current technological revolution, driven by AI and the Internet of Things (IoT), necessitates a reevaluation of educational and industry practices to harness these advancements effectively. For educational institutions, this involves a critical assessment and realignment of curriculum, pedagogical approaches, and learning outcomes to equip students with the skills required in a rapidly changing job market. Similarly, industry leaders are tasked with navigating the integration of GAI into existing operational frameworks, balancing innovation with legal and financial considerations and workforce implications. This would (and continues to) prove challenging for reasons that have arisen over the past year.

Following the rapid and widespread adoption of AI, specifically OpenAI's ChatGPT-3 in February 2023, there were high expectations for an immanent "AI Gold Rush," anticipated to bring significant advancements, particularly in the industry (Rudolph, Tan, & Tan, 2023). Educational institutions were not far behind in recognizing the potential of this technological wave, signaling their readiness to embrace AI innovations as early as Spring 2023. Studies involving K-12 teachers across the nation highlighted their willingness to integrate AI into their teaching methodologies (Woodruff, Hutson, & Arnone, 2023), and similar sentiments were echoed in higher education surveys (McDonald et al., 2024). However, despite these positive inclinations, the anticipated surge in AI adoption did not materialize as expected by the fiscal year reporting in July 2023 (Schrager, 2023). A key obstacle for both industry and educational sectors was the concern over using public models, which posed a risk of exposing sensitive or proprietary data (Gupta et al., 2023). Additionally, there was a lack of internal expertise to develop customized solutions in the form of bespoke, closed institutional models (Vial et al., 2023). This hesitance persisted until we reached another pivotal moment, indicating a shift in the approach toward AI integration within these institutions.

This chapter, therefore, aims to provide a foundational understanding of generative AI's scope, potential, and implications for the future workplace to overcome these initial barriers. It advocates for a strategic, informed approach to AI adoption, emphasizing the need for institutions to remain agile and responsive to the ongoing technological evolution. By situating GAI within the historical continuum of technological revolutions, the narrative highlights the importance of adaptability, lifelong learning, and ethical stewardship as we navigate the complexities of this new digital era. Through an examination of generative AI's impact on education and industry, this initial discussion sets the stage for a deeper exploration of strategies, challenges, and opportunities presented by AI technologies. The goal is to equip technology professionals with the insights and tools necessary to lead their organizations through the transformative currents of the Fourth Industrial Revolution, fostering environments that leverage AI's capabilities to enhance human potential rather than supplant it.

1.2 From Machine Learning to Generative Models: An Evolutionary Path

As the Information Age unfolded during the Third Industrial Revolution, it became evident that societal adaptation to technological change was not only possible but could become a standard facet of modern professional life. Yet, the pace at which change occurred during this era was markedly slower compared to the rapid transformations witnessed in today's digital landscape. A pivotal moment in this evolution was in 1974, when computer scientists Vint Cerf and Robert Kahn developed TCP/IP, laying the groundwork for what would become the Internet, a global network for sharing information (Townes, 2012). This innovation set the stage for subsequent breakthroughs that would further democratize access to information and fundamentally alter communication practices.

The creation of the World Wide Web (WWW) by Tim Berners-Lee in 1989 introduced a system that allowed users to access a network of interlinked hypertext documents via the Internet, marking the first instance of the Internet being accessible through a graphical interface (McPherson, 2009). This development significantly eased the process of finding information online, a convenience that was further enhanced by the launch of the Google search engine in 1998 (Kobayashi & Takeda, 2000). The advent of social media platforms, such as Facebook in 2004, and the release of the first iPhone in 2007, epitomized the shift toward an era where information was accessible anywhere and at any time, facilitated by the ubiquity of smartphones and the emergence of social networking sites (Gikas & Grant, 2013).

The progression into the 2010s heralded the advent of the IoT, characterized by interconnected networks of physical devices, vehicles, home appliances, and other items embedded with electronics, software, and sensors. This innovation allowed for the collection and exchange of data between objects, creating "smart" systems and laying the foundation for the development of smart cities (Minoli, 2013; Zanella et al., 2014). The transformative impact of IoT, which bridges the physical and digital worlds, underscores the profound ways in which technology continues to reshape human activities, from work and leisure to communication and urban living.

Through these milestones, the Information Age has facilitated an unprecedented integration of technology into daily life, illustrating the dynamic interplay between technological advancements and societal adaptation. As we navigate the complexities of the Fourth Industrial Revolution, marked by the emergence of generative AI and other disruptive technologies, it is imperative to draw lessons from past transitions. Understanding the trajectory of technological evolution from the inception of the Internet to the IoT and beyond provides valuable insights for educational and industry leaders tasked with guiding their institutions through the ongoing digital transformation.

In the backdrop of the digital transformation that marks our current era, a silent yet profound shift toward an "algorithmic culture" has taken place, profoundly influencing our daily routines, professional lives, and the broader decision-making processes that govern our societies. This shift, primarily driven by advancements in artificial intelligence (AI) and machine learning (ML), has woven algorithms into the fabric of daily existence, impacting sectors ranging from business and education to governance. Hannah Fry, in her insightful book *Hello World: Being Human in the Age of Algorithms* (2018), delves into the essence of this phenomenon, highlighting the criticality of comprehending the various types of algorithms, their functionalities, applications, and the styles of learning they employ, to fully grasp their societal impacts.

Fry categorizes algorithms into four functional groups based on their operational purposes: prioritization, classification, association, and filtering. Each category plays a distinct role in processing and managing information:

Prioritization algorithms serve to rank data or tasks according to specified criteria, aiding in organizing items or activities by importance, urgency, or relevance to the user's past interactions.

Classification algorithms are designed to segregate data into predefined categories, aiding in organizing information into manageable groups based on shared characteristics.

Association algorithms seek to uncover relationships between varied data points, enabling the identification of patterns or trends such as consumer behavior in purchasing.

Filtering algorithms work to screen and exclude data based on predetermined criteria, enhancing the relevance and quality of the information presented to the user.

Moreover, Fry distinguishes algorithms into two broader paradigms: rule-based (RB) and ML algorithms. RB algorithms, known for their directness and transparency, operate on clear, predefined instructions developed by experts. These algorithms have found application in numerous fields, from medical diagnostics to financial decision-making systems. Conversely, ML algorithms are defined by their capacity to learn and adapt from data, improving their functionality over time through a process akin to reinforcement learning. This adaptability has seen ML algorithms deployed in diverse applications, including image recognition, natural language processing, and personalized recommendations.

This delineation between RB and ML algorithms further enriches our understanding of the algorithmic culture permeating modern life. While RB algorithms offer clarity and ease of comprehension, ML algorithms, though sometimes opaque and considered "black boxes," bring unmatched flexibility and adaptiveness to the table, making them ideally suited for navigating the complexities of today's dynamic environments. Through Fry's analysis, it becomes evident that the proliferation of algorithmic culture, while presenting challenges, notably in transparency and interpretability, also offers unprecedented opportunities for innovation and efficiency across all sectors of society.

Grasping the intricacies of how algorithms learn is pivotal to understanding the algorithmic culture that increasingly orchestrates our daily interactions and decision-making processes. Hristova et al. (2021) delineate three primary learning modalities for algorithms: supervised, unsupervised, and reinforcement learning, each defining a unique approach to algorithmic learning and application. In supervised learning, algorithms undergo training with labeled data, allowing them to make predictions or decisions when presented with new, unlabeled data. This process involves the algorithm learning the correlation between input data and the provided labels, enabling it to apply these learned relationships to predict outcomes accurately. Conversely, unsupervised learning challenges algorithms to discern patterns and structures within data without the guidance of labeled examples. The objective here is for the algorithm to independently uncover significant relationships within the data. Reinforcement learning adopts a trial-and-error approach, where the algorithm learns optimal behaviors through rewards or penalties, iteratively refining its strategies to maximize rewards over time.

These learning paradigms underscore a transition from algorithms being explicitly told the correct answer, as in supervised learning, to discovering solutions independently, either by identifying underlying patterns in data or through experiential learning and adaptation.

The ascendancy of algorithmic culture promises numerous advantages, particularly in enhancing efficiency and objectivity within decision-making processes. Algorithms, capable of parsing and analyzing extensive datasets, can unearth insights and patterns beyond human detection (Lepri et al., 2018). This computational objectivity, if the algorithms are trained on unbiased data, holds the promise of equitable outcomes across various domains, including recruitment, financial services, and healthcare (Kordzadeh & Ghasemaghaei, 2022). Moreover, the personalization capabilities of algorithms can significantly improve access to information, customizing content delivery to meet individual needs and preferences (Gran, Booth, & Bucher, 2021).

However, the integration of algorithms into societal frameworks is not without its challenges. The opacity of algorithmic decision-making processes, often described as "black-box" models, complicates the identification and correction of biases, potentially perpetuating or exacerbating discrimination and inequality (Saltelli et al., 2008; Angwin et al., 2016; Dwork & Roth, 2014). Furthermore, an overreliance on algorithmic systems risks diminishing human critical thinking and decision-making capacities, suggesting a need for a balanced approach to technology use that preserves human agency (Zerilli et al., 2019). The delicate balance between the benefits of instant access to information and the preservation of privacy and autonomy remains a contentious issue in the digital age, as algorithms increasingly influence our perceptions, interactions, and societal norms (Alvarado & Waern, 2018; Diakopoulos, 2019; Eslami et al., 2015; Feezell, Wagner, & Conroy, 2021; Gillespie, 2014; Khan et al., 2020; Powers, 2017). This complex, sometimes ambivalent relationship with technology underscores the need for critical engagement with algorithmic culture, advocating for transparency, accountability, and equitable practices in the development and deployment of AI and ML systems.

1.3 Revisiting Early AI Predictions: Expectations versus Reality

In the realm of science fiction, like the plot of *The Terminator* (1984), visions of an AI-driven apocalypse have captured the public imagination for decades. These narratives, while enthralling, have painted a picture of a future where AI's emergence leads to catastrophic outcomes for humanity. Yet, as we navigated past the fictional dates of these apocalyptic scenarios, reality unfolded quite differently. The dawn of the new millennium did not witness the rise of machines against humanity; instead, the integration of AI into our daily lives has been marked by significant advancements and challenges far removed from the cataclysmic fears of old. Despite this, the apprehension surrounding AI and its implications for the future of work remains pervasive, reflecting a deep-seated anxiety about technological displacement that, as Aoun (2017) observes, surpasses even the fear of death for many.

The definition of AI is a subject of considerable debate among experts and laypersons alike, with opinions diverging on what constitutes AI (Cremer, 2021; Ermakova & Frolova, 2021; Monett & Lewis, 2018; Wang, 2019). This lack of consensus stems partly from the rapid evolution of the field, which spans a broad spectrum of technologies from ML and natural language processing (NLP) to computer vision, robotics, and beyond. To some, AI might symbolize an autonomous entity—a robot or "The AI"—yet, more accurately, AI is understood as machines' emulation of human intelligence. These systems are designed to replicate and sometimes exceed human capacities in areas such as speech recognition, visual perception, language translation, and decision-making. The backbone of AI technology lies in sophisticated algorithms and statistical models that empower these systems to learn from data, identify patterns, and execute predictive analyses. AI can be categorized into two primary types: narrow or weak AI, which is engineered for specific tasks, and general or strong AI, which embodies the versatility and adaptability to undertake a wide array of activities typically requiring human intellect (Allen, 2019). Despite the fears often associated with AI, the reality is that most current applications of the technology fall into the category of narrow AI, developed to enhance efficiency and productivity in various sectors rather than to supplant human agency.

At the same time, predictive models concerning the development and evolution of AI in industry also overestimated the immediate impact the technology would have and were predicated on the limitations on capabilities pre-generative AI. The application of AI technologies across various sectors was anticipated to drive significant shifts in operational efficiency, product development, and customer engagement strategies. For instance, Bughin et al. (2018) predicted that AI would contribute up to $15.7 trillion to the global economy by 2030, with productivity and personalization enhancements being the primary value drivers. This projection underscored the planned transformative potential of AI in redefining industry standards and competitive landscapes. In the manufacturing sector, for example, predictive models emphasized the role of AI in optimizing production processes through predictive maintenance, real-time monitoring, and supply chain optimization. Schwab (2017) discussed the potential impact on manufacturing, where AI-driven systems were expected to significantly reduce downtime, enhance quality control, and streamline logistics. The finance industry offers another illustrative example of expected evolutionary paths. Predictive analytics, algorithmic trading, and robo-advisors represented key areas where AI was to reshape financial services (Chui et al., 2018). These technologies, it was touted, would enable more accurate risk assessment, personalized investment strategies, and automated trading decisions, contributing to both increased market stability and customer satisfaction. But new research is revealing the timeline of our modeling needs to be adjusted.

For instance, the study by Ho et al. (2024) brings to light the extraordinary pace at which algorithms for pre-training language models have improved, far surpassing the incremental hardware gains outlined by Moore's Law. The computation required to reach a set performance threshold in language models has halved approximately every 8 months since the advent of deep learning—a rate substantially faster than previously imagined. This acceleration has major implications for industries such as manufacturing and finance, where the anticipated benefits of AI, including predictive maintenance and algorithmic trading, may be realized sooner and more profoundly than initially predicted. The oversight in early models can be attributed to a lack of foresight regarding the scalable nature of AI technologies and the substantial impact of computational advancements. As the study suggests, the contributions from scaling models and innovations in training algorithms have propelled AI capabilities at a pace that was difficult to predict. The evolution of architectures like the transformer and the significant role of increased computational power in driving performance improvements underscore a new era of AI development that outstrips earlier expectations. In essence, while earlier predictive models laid the groundwork for understanding AI's potential impact, the reality of its development, characterized by the rapid progress in algorithmic efficiency, opens new frontiers for AI applications across industries. This realization not only revises expectations but also calls for an adaptive approach to integrating AI into strategic planning and operations, acknowledging the dynamic nature of technological advancement.

The speed of the technological advancements and speed of adoption have seen early wins for some. In fact, early adopters of GAI are witnessing significant gains in efficiency across various operational facets, with productivity and strategic planning at the forefront of transformation. At a recent Wharton conference, various experts underscored the potential to revolutionize managerial decision-making by enhancing value generation (Tambe & Snyder, 2024). Prasanna Tambe, for instance, a professor at Wharton, highlighted the prowess of the tools in processing the vast expanses of unstructured data that constitute the majority of new information within enterprises. This capability is particularly valuable in extracting actionable insights from communications platforms and project management tools, which are traditionally underutilized at the decision-making juncture. Tambe also pointed to the substantial potential for generative tools to distill complex data into understandable factors for managers, aiding in more accurate predictions and strategic insights. At the same time, Scott Snyder, emphasized GAI as a pivotal force in redefining enterprise operations. He drew parallels between the impact of the pandemic on digital acceleration and GAI's potential to similarly catalyze organizational change. In this context, businesses are advised to adopt a measured approach toward adoption, prioritizing specific applications that align with strategic objectives while ensuring robust data protection and ethical considerations. This strategy involves iterative rollouts, performance-based incentives, and fostering a culture of innovation and risk-taking, particularly in human resources, to fully harness its potential.

1.4 Overcoming Adoption Barriers: Technical and Societal Hurdles

The discussions surrounding AI consistently emphasize its significant impact on the future of work, education, and social life. The AI100 study by Stanford University (Littman et al., 2022) projects AI to contribute approximately $13 trillion to the global economy by 2030, while simultaneously displacing an estimated 800 million jobs due to AI and automation advancements (Hutson et al., 2022). These predictions, circulating for the past decade, have spurred early planning stages across various sectors, including industry, business, education, and government, to navigate the forthcoming disruptions thoughtfully.

The automotive industry, as highlighted by Miguel et al. (2022), is experiencing a significant transformation driven by electrification, automation, and new mobility paradigms, reshaping vehicle usage and manufacturing processes. This evolution is prompting a reevaluation of business models, regulatory environments, and supply chain dynamics, alongside profound implications for employment and the broader economic landscape. Similarly, organizations are confronting the operational and workforce challenges posed by AI's increasing pervasiveness. A report by Accenture Federal Services (2018) underscored the necessity for entities to tackle the ethical, societal, and workforce considerations of AI deployment (Liu & Murphy, 2020). In the realm of education, the dialogue has extended to the integration of emerging technologies within curricula, ensuring that educators are equipped to incorporate technology in teaching effectively and ethically (Burbules, Fan, & Repp, 2020).

Moreover, the advent of AI and the IoT introduces new privacy and security concerns for government sectors. Officials are tasked with addressing the ethical, legal, and policy ramifications of these technologies, necessitating the development of frameworks for their responsible utilization (Omolara et al., 2022; Wirtz, Weyerer, & Sturm, 2020). However, preparations for AI integration, particularly in education, remain nascent, with many leaders previously believing there was more time to adapt (Hutson et al., 2022). The latter half of 2022 marked a pivotal moment in the acceleration of generative AI's influence, as seen with the introduction of technologies like ChatGPT, DALLE-3, and Stable Diffusion. These innovations have significantly disrupted traditional paradigms in art, advertising, marketing, and education, igniting debates over the use of "AI Art" and catalyzing the emergence of new markets for NFTs (Ansari, 2022a; Hazucha, 2022). The launch of ChatGPT-3 (November 2022), in particular, demonstrated the capacity of these new tools to generate original content and engage in conversational interactions, challenging existing information retrieval models and content creation processes (DelSignore, 2022; Francke & Alexander, 2019; Murphy, 2022; Sherry, 2022). With the release of more and more powerful models by OpenAI, Anthropic, and Google, the urgency for cross-sectoral readiness to embrace AI's transformative potential has never been more critical.

The question of job security and automation looms large in the minds of many, challenging the notion that certain tasks are inherently human and immune to technological advancements. The evolving capabilities of AI, from art generation to voice replication, signal a departure from previous assumptions about the non-replicability of human-centric jobs. Technologies like generative AI and deepfake have showcased their potential to replace even the most creative and interpersonal roles, leaving society to grapple with the implications of these advancements on the future workforce. The impact of AI and automation on employment has been a subject of extensive study and debate. A seminal analysis conducted by the University of Oxford projected that up to 47% of jobs were at risk of computerization, particularly those involving routine tasks with minimal demands for creativity or human interaction (Frey & Osborne, 2017). However, this prediction has undergone revisions, acknowledging the indispensable role of human judgment in supervising and correcting AI technologies to prevent errors and biases (Mok & Zinkula, 2023). Holzinger et al. (2023) advocate viewing emerging technologies as tools that enhance productivity rather than substitutes for human labor. This perspective aligns with the broader understanding that while certain sectors may experience disruption, the advent of automation does not necessarily herald widespread unemployment.

The Great Resignation of 2022 further complicates the narrative of job loss due to automation. Despite historic levels of job departures, the motivations behind these resignations were attributed to factors such as low wages, limited advancement opportunities, and a lack of respect in the workplace rather than the fear of being replaced by machines (Ansari, 2022b; Deloitte, 2021). This underscores the multifaceted nature of workforce dynamics and the importance of addressing job quality and employee satisfaction. In response to the challenges posed by automation, the focus has shifted toward preparing the workforce for future roles. The World Economic Forum (2023) emphasizes the importance of adapting to change and re-skilling for jobs that leverage human capabilities beyond what robots can achieve. This approach necessitates a reevaluation of educational curricula to incorporate training that equips individuals with the skills needed to thrive alongside AI and ML technologies.

AI in education (AIEd) has already shown promise in enhancing learning outcomes, increasing accessibility, and personalizing educational experiences (Holzinger et al., 2023). The future of AIEd includes interactive education accessible anytime and anywhere, personalized AI mentors, and mass personalization catering to individual learning preferences. Despite these potential benefits, there remains hesitation among educators to embrace AI, driven by misconceptions and the perceived need to overhaul traditional teaching methods.

1.5 Ethical Considerations and Societal Impact

The urgency for educational reform in response to the advancements in AI and ML has never been more pronounced than in the current era, marked by rapid technological evolution and unforeseen global challenges. Joseph Aoun's *Robot-Proof: Higher Education in the Age of Artificial Intelligence* (2018) presented a compelling argument for the transformation of higher education to better prepare students for a job market in continuous flux due to AI developments. Aoun's critique of traditional education models, which heavily focus on specialized knowledge, underscores the necessity for a paradigm shift toward cultivating "human skills" like creativity, critical thinking, and communication—skills that AI is less likely to supplant.

Moreover, Aoun emphasizes the importance of lifelong learning, advocating for educational frameworks that equip students with the ability to adapt to new technologies and job market shifts over the course of their careers. His call to action for higher education to pivot toward developing learners who can innovate and create in the face of AI advancements is increasingly relevant, particularly in light of the minimal progress made toward interdisciplinary curriculum development in the years following his publication.

However, the predictions and data underpinning *Robot-Proof's* strategies face scrutiny due to their reliance on pre-pandemic estimates of job automation. The assertion that 4.4 million jobs would emerge in the information technology sector by 2024 (U.S. Bureau of Labor Statistics, 2018) was upended by the loss of an estimated 130,000 jobs in just the first month of 2023—a consequence of the accelerated capabilities of AI and ML technologies that surpassed expectations. Aoun's vision that creation and innovation would form the cornerstone of future economic activities and human endeavors seemed prescient, highlighting that tasks once considered uniquely human, including sophisticated white-collar roles, could be automated.

Yet, Aoun reassured readers that the essence of human creativity—literature, art, and music birthed from human imagination—would remain untouched by machines. This prediction has been challenged by the recent emergence and rapid adoption of AI-generative content in creative industries, overturning the assumption that manual, blue-collar jobs would be the first to face automation. The disruptive impact of AI on the technology sector, exemplified by significant layoffs and strategic shifts toward AI-focused operations by major companies like Google, indicates a broader susceptibility across various fields previously deemed "robot-proof."

The automation of tasks in caregiving, culinary arts, and even artisanal crafts through robotics and AI technologies reveals the expansive reach of automation beyond initial expectations. This reality prompts a reevaluation of assumptions about the security of certain job sectors and underscores the imperative for educational systems to evolve rapidly. Embracing an educational model that fosters creativity, adaptability, and lifelong learning is crucial for preparing students to navigate the complexities of a future where AI and automation are omnipresent. The challenge now lies in implementing these educational reforms swiftly and effectively to align with the pace of technological change and the evolving demands of the global job market.

1.6 Embracing AI: Toward a Collaborative Future

The COVID-19 pandemic has served as a watershed moment for both industry and higher education, revealing both vulnerabilities and opportunities within the sectors. As Cameron, Fogarty-Perry, and Piercy (2022) have documented, the year 2023 witnessed the closure of several small, private, non-profit, and underfunded regional institutions, signaling a significant shift in the landscape of higher education. Concurrently, departments and majors rooted in the arts and humanities experienced dwindling enrollment numbers, leading to their reduction or elimination—a trend that not only undermines support for these disciplines but also diminishes the breadth of a well-rounded education (Magness & Mitchell, 2022; Massey, 2020). The financial challenges imposed by the pandemic were compounded by a rapid transition to online learning. This shift, while necessary, resulted in lost revenue from tuition and campus facilities and highlighted preparedness gaps in delivering quality online education (Mishra, Gupta, & Shree, 2020). Despite these hurdles, universities that adopted online or hybrid formats in response to the pandemic found that student demand sustained these models post-pandemic, suggesting a permanent transformation in the delivery of higher education (Singh, Steele, & Singh, 2021).

However, amidst these challenges, the pandemic catalyzed a surge in research and development across various industries, particularly in XR, AI, ML, and neural networks. This wave of innovation helped society navigate through unprecedented social changes, enhancing remote education, work, and healthcare (Brem, Viardot, & Nylund, 2021). Notably, the adoption of VR technologies like the Oculus Quest 2, investments in UAVs and drones, and the expansion of telemedicine services exemplify how technological advancements have enabled continued productivity and operational continuity during the pandemic (He, Zhang, & Li, 2021; Aabid et al., 2022; Patel, Hamdan, & Donahue, 2022).

In response to the technological and social changes ushered in by the pandemic, the education sector has made significant strides in integrating emerging technologies to support learning in a constrained environment. The necessity to maintain educational continuity prompted a swift adoption of video conferencing platforms and LMS, while the use of VR and AR technologies gained traction to provide immersive learning experiences despite physical distancing requirements (Doi, Lucky, & Rubin, 2022; Siakalli et al., 2022; Garzón, 2021). Moreover, AI and ML technologies have emerged as pivotal tools in personalizing learning, enabling educational institutions to develop tailored learning plans that accommodate individual student needs, preferences, and pacing. Warrier, John, and Warrier (2021) highlight the potential of AI and ML to revolutionize education by providing personalized recommendations and feedback, thereby enhancing the quality and accessibility of education (Ciolacu et al., 2023).

The adoption of emerging technologies, particularly generative AI, is poised to profoundly influence both the educational sector and industry, necessitating a comprehensive approach to digital transformation that includes retooling, reskilling, and reevaluating teaching and assessment methodologies (Rof, Bikfalvi, & Marques, 2022; Pavlik, 2023). The post-pandemic era has underscored the importance of preparing for a workforce increasingly integrated with AI and ML, driving higher education institutions to integrate AI concepts into their curricula. This integration spans from introducing courses on AI ethics (Cath et al., 2018), programming (Yang & Evans, 2019), and applications (Zawacki-Richter et al., 2019), to aligning traditional subjects like mathematics and computer science with AI's relevance, even for non-specialists (Cooper, 2022).

Beyond imparting technical knowledge, there's a growing consensus on the need to cultivate soft skills such as critical thinking, creativity, and problem-solving abilities. These competencies are crucial for students and workers alike to navigate an algorithm-driven culture effectively, fostering meaningful engagement with AI technologies (Bühler, Jelinek, & Nübel, 2022; Greenstein, 2012; Chen et al., 2023). Additionally, addressing the ethical and social ramifications of AI's proliferation becomes paramount, emphasizing an education that prepares individuals to contribute responsibly to an AI-integrated society (Schiff, 2022; Zhang et al., 2022).

The transformation extends to assessment strategies, moving away from traditional exams toward performance and project-based evaluations that more accurately reflect students' proficiency in a rapidly evolving technological landscape (Carvalho et al., 2022; Babitha & Sushma, 2022; Krajcik et al., 2023; Palladino & Shepard, 2023). This shift is crucial for all educational stakeholders, from administrators to students, as it underscores the agility and adaptability required to thrive in an AI-enhanced future.

Educational administrators are tasked with strategically implementing AI technologies, aligning them with institutional goals, and ensuring ethical use and data privacy (Li & Gu, 2023). Faculty members, on the other hand, are vital in weaving AI into their disciplines and staying abreast of technological advances to enrich their teaching and research (Rensfeldt & Rahm, 2023). This demands a culture that values and incentivizes ongoing professional development and cognitive flexibility. Support staff will be instrumental in facilitating the use of AI within educational settings, providing necessary technical assistance and resources while also adapting their skills to remain competitive in an AI-driven job market (Kaliraj & Devi, 2023). Students, as digital natives, are uniquely positioned to influence the integration of AI in education, advocating for training and resources that reflect their needs and perspectives as future users and innovators of AI technology (Milton & Al-Busaidi, 2023).

Future-proofing academia, akin to retrofitting a steam engine for the digital age, emerges as a critical endeavor amidst the accelerating pace of technological advancements. The traditionally slow-moving nature of academic institutions—characterized by protracted curriculum updates, the meticulous pace of research, the arduous journey to tenure, and the gradual evolution of academic committees and policies—stands in stark contrast to the rapid evolution of the digital world (Antony et al., 2022). This dichotomy raises the question of whether incremental changes are sufficient or if a more radical transformation of the academic model is warranted.

Kellner and Gennaro (2022) argue for a comprehensive reevaluation of the existing academic framework, noting that traditional educational paradigms are increasingly misaligned with the demands of a workforce that prizes technological fluency and adaptability. The advent of sophisticated technologies, including algorithms and ML, underscores the necessity for academia to adapt, ensuring students are equipped with the skills and knowledge pertinent to navigating a tech-centric job market (Ter Beek, Wopereis, & Schildkamp, 2022).

However, the path to integrating these technological advancements within academic settings is fraught with challenges, notably more so than in industry, due to a complex web of regulatory, legal, and institutional barriers. These constraints impede the swift adoption of innovative teaching methodologies, interdisciplinary research initiatives, and the inclusion of cutting-edge technologies in the curriculum. Despite these obstacles, the imperative to overhaul the academic model remains paramount. To foster an educational environment that is both responsive and relevant to the demands of the digital age, academic institutions must cultivate a culture of agility and embrace a forward-thinking approach to curriculum development, research, and governance.

The necessity of involving all stakeholders in the conversation surrounding institutional transformation, whether in education or industry, cannot be overstated. The dynamic nature of today's technological landscape demands an inclusive approach to change, one that considers the perspectives, needs, and contributions of each constituent group within the organization. As underscored by Ford (2015), successful transformation initiatives are characterized by their ability to engage stakeholders at all levels, fostering a sense of ownership and commitment to the change process. This inclusive strategy ensures that the transition not only reflects the collective vision but also addresses the unique challenges and opportunities faced by different groups within the institution.

In the context of industry, the involvement of employees, middle management, and leadership is crucial for navigating the complexities of digital transformation. Employees, being at the forefront of operational processes, possess invaluable insights into the practical implications of technological integration (Martínez-Peláez et al., 2023). Middle management plays a pivotal role in mediating between strategic objectives and operational realities, ensuring the alignment of transformation efforts with day-to-day activities (Kane et al., 2015). Leadership, on the other hand, provides the vision and support necessary to drive change, allocating resources and setting policy directions that facilitate a conducive environment for innovation (Hess et al., 2016).

Similarly, in the educational sector, collaboration among students, faculty, staff, and administration, in partnership with IT departments, is essential for achieving meaningful and sustainable transformation. Students, as the primary beneficiaries of educational services, offer unique perspectives on learning needs and technological preferences, making their involvement critical for designing student-centered learning experiences (Selwyn, 2016). Faculty and staff, with their expertise in pedagogy and operational support, are instrumental in implementing and sustaining technological innovations in teaching and learning (Ertmer & Ottenbreit-Leftwich, 2010). Administration and IT departments provide the strategic planning, infrastructure, and technical support necessary to actualize these initiatives, ensuring they are aligned with institutional goals and capabilities (Brown et al., 2020).

Adopting a bottom-up approach to transformation, in tandem with strong leadership support, ensures a holistic and participatory process. This dual strategy not only enhances the effectiveness of change initiatives but also promotes a culture of continuous learning and adaptability within the organization. By fostering open communication, collaboration, and shared responsibility, institutions can navigate the challenges of digital transformation more effectively, leveraging the collective expertise and creativity of their constituents. This comprehensive engagement is critical for realizing the full potential of technological advancements, ensuring that both education and industry can thrive in an increasingly digital world (Westerman, Bonnet, & McAfee, 2014; Hess et al., 2016).

1.7 Overview of the Book

Chapter 1 of this book has set the stage for a comprehensive exploration into the profound changes and challenges presented by the advent of AI across various sectors, particularly in education and industry. As we delve deeper into the subsequent chapters, we will further examine the nuances of these transformations, seeking to provide insights, strategies, and frameworks that can aid organizations and institutions in navigating the complexities of the digital age.

Chapter 2: Digital Transformation: Bridging Industry and Education will trace the origins and evolution of digital transformation, highlighting key milestones in information technology that have reshaped the landscapes of both industry and education. It will explore how the progression from the Internet to big data has set the stage for Industry 4.0 and discuss the strategic role of data science in garnering insights to drive forward-thinking decisions.

Chapter 3: Generative Transformation in the Age of Industry 4.0 will delve into the fundamentals of generative AI, examining its role as a catalyst in the ongoing Industry 4.0 revolution. This chapter will investigate future trends, drawing lessons from case studies of both success and failure, and evaluate tools for assessing readiness and resilience, alongside the economic implications of investments and returns in generative AI.

Chapter 4: Strategic Leadership and Governance will focus on the pivotal role of leadership in implementing AI strategies and the importance of long-term strategic planning for AI integration. It will cover models for AI governance, the balancing act between risk and reward in navigating the AI landscape, and the significance of aligning AI initiatives with organizational goals, emphasizing the value of external expertise in AI integration.

Chapter 5: Organizational Culture and Skill Development will explore how cultivating an AI-ready culture and addressing the psychological dimensions of AI adoption are essential for fostering a conducive environment for technological innovation. It will discuss strategies for skill development, employee engagement with AI, and the efficacy of various professional development initiatives.

Chapter 6: Conclusion: Embracing the AI Future will reflect on the journey of AI from unmet expectations to the current reality, anticipating the challenges and rewards that lie ahead. It will chart new research directions, offer policy recommendations for navigating the generative AI era, and underscore the importance of leadership in steering toward the next technological frontier.

As this book unfolds, it becomes evident that identifying and involving all stakeholders in the transformation process—be it in education or industry—is essential. A collaborative approach, combining bottom-up and top-down strategies, is necessary to harness the full potential of AI. By fostering dialogue and cooperation among students, faculty, staff, administration, employees, middle management, and leadership, organizations can ensure a more inclusive, adaptive, and successful transition into the AI-enhanced future. This holistic engagement is vital for aligning policy, professional development, and fiscal resources with the evolving needs and opportunities presented by AI and digital technologies.

References

Aabid, A., Parveez, B., Parveen, N., Khan, S. A., & Shabbir, O. (2022). A case study of unmanned aerial vehicle (drone) technology and its applications in the COVID-19 pandemic. *Journal of Mechanical Engineering Research and Developments*, *45*, 70–77.

Accenture. (2018). *The rise of artificial intelligence: Opportunities and challenges*. Accenture. AI, A. I. (2022). The fourth industrial revolution. *Presented at the American Psychological Association in Minneapolis*, *4*, 6.

Allen, B. (2019). Machine learning with deep neural nets artificially augmenting my intelligence in a narrow but occasionally superhuman kind of way. *Journal of the American College of Radiology*, *16*(10), 1480–1481.

Alvarado, O., & Waern, A. (2018, April). Towards algorithmic experience: Initial efforts for social media contexts. In *Proceedings of the 2018 chi conference on human factors in computing systems, Montréal, Canada* (pp. 1–12).

Angwin, J., Larson, J., Mattu, S., & Kirchner, L. (2016). Machine bias. In *Ethics of data and analytics* (pp. 254–264). Auerbach Publications.

Ansari, S. (December 7, 2022a). Recognizing the risks of job automation in 2023. *HR Tech Series*. Retrieved from: https://techrseries.com/ai-automation/recognizing-the-risks-of-job-automation-in-2023/

Ansari, T. (October 30, 2022b). How AI transformed the art world in 2022. *Analytics India Magazine (AIM)*. Retrieved from: https://analyticsindiamag.com/how-ai-transformed-the-art-world-in-2022/

Antony, J. S., Cauce, A. M., Gangone, L. M., & Nicola, T. P. (Eds.). (2022). *The college president handbook: A sustainable and practical guide for emerging leaders*. Harvard Education Press.

Aoun, J. E. (2017). *Robot-proof: Higher education in the age of artificial intelligence*. MIT Press.

Babitha, M. M., & Sushma, C. (2022). Trends of artificial intelligence for online exams in education. *International Journal of Early Childhood Special Education*, *14*(01), 2457–2463.

Braidwood, R. J. (1960). The agricultural revolution. *Scientific American*, *203*(3), 130–152.

Brem, A., Viardot, E., & Nylund, P. A. (2021). Implications of the coronavirus (COVID-19) outbreak for innovation: Which technologies will improve our lives?. *Technological Forecasting and Social Change*, *163*, 120451.

Brown, M., McCormack, M., Reeves, J., Brooks, D. C., & Grajek, S. (2020). *The state of innovation in higher education: A survey of academic administrators*. Louisiana State University and the EDUCAUSE Center for Analysis and Research.

Bughin, J., Seong, J., Manyika, J., Chui, M., & Joshi, R. (2018). *Notes from the AI Frontier: Applications and value of deep learning*. McKinsey Global Institute.

Bühler, M. M., Jelinek, T., & Nübel, K. (2022). Training and preparing tomorrow's workforce for the fourth industrial revolution. *Education Sciences*, *12*(11), 782.

Burbules, N. C., Fan, G., & Repp, P. (2020). Five trends of education and technology in a sustainable future. *Geography and Sustainability*, *1*(2), 93–97.

Cameron, M., Fogarty-Perry, B., & Piercy, G. (2022). The impacts of the COVID-19 pandemic on higher education students in New Zealand. *Journal of Open, Flexible and Distance Learning*, *26*(1), 42–62.

Carvalho, L., Martinez-Maldonado, R., Tsai, Y. S., Markauskaite, L., & De Laat, M. (2022). How can we design for learning in an AI world?. *Computers and Education: Artificial Intelligence*, *3*, 100053.

Castells, M. (2010). The information age. *Media Studies: A Reader*, *2*(7), 152.

Cath, C., Wachter, S., Mittelstadt, B., Taddeo, M., & Floridi, L. (2018). Artificial intelligence and the 'good society': The US, EU, and UK approach. *Science and Engineering Ethics*, *24*, 505–528.

Chen, Y., Jensen, S., Albert, L. J., Gupta, S., & Lee, T. (2023). Artificial intelligence (AI) student assistants in the classroom: Designing chatbots to support student success. *Information Systems Frontiers*, *25*(1), 161–182.

Chui, M., Harrysson, M., Manyika, J., Roberts, R., Chung, R., Nel, P., & van Heteren, A. (2018). *Notes from the AI Frontier: Insights from hundreds of use cases*. McKinsey Global Institute.

Ciolacu, M. I., Mihailescu, B., Rachbauer, T., Hansen, C., Amza, C. G., & Svasta, P. (2023). Fostering engineering education 4.0 paradigm facing the pandemic and VUCA world. *Procedia Computer Science*, *217*, 177–186.

Cooper, T. (2022). *Ancestors and Algorithms: Ethnocomputing AI with African & African Diasporic Heritage* (Doctoral dissertation).

Cremer, C. Z. (2021). Deep limitations? Examining expert disagreement over deep learning. *Progress in Artificial Intelligence*, *10*, 449–464.

Cyber Security (February 6, 2024). Artificial intelligence: The acceleration of technology and how to prepare. *Inzpire*. Retrieved: https://www.inzpire.com/news/artificial-intelligence-the-acceleration-of-technology-and-how-to-prepare#:~:text=Lawmakers%20and%20law%20enforcers%20are,be%20synthetically%20generated%20by%202026

Deane, P. M. (1979). *The first industrial revolution*. Cambridge University Press.

DelSignore, P. (December 23, 2022). The new age of creative AI began in 2022. *Medium*. Retrieved from: https://medium.com/predict/the-new-age-of-creative-ai-began-in-2022-ece07bb93350

Deloitte (2021). The Deloitte global 201 millennial and gen Z survey. *Deloitte*. Retrieved: July 31, 2024. https://www.deloitte.com/global/en/about/people/social-responsibility/millennialsurvey-2021.html

Diakopoulos, N. (2019). *Automating the news: How algorithms are rewriting the media*. Harvard University Press.

Doi, C., Lucky, S., & Rubin, J. E. (2022). Open educational resources in the time of COVID-19: Two case studies of open video design in the remote learning environment. *KULA*, *6*(1), 1–15.

Dwork, C., & Roth, A. (2014). The algorithmic foundations of differential privacy. *Foundations and Trends® in Theoretical Computer Science*, *9*(3–4), 211–407.

Ermakova, E. P., & Frolova, E. E. (2021). Using artificial intelligence in dispute resolution. In *Smart technologies for the digitisation of industry: Entrepreneurial environment* (pp. 131–142). Springer.

Ertmer, P. A., & Ottenbreit-Leftwich, A. T. (2010). Teacher technology change: How knowledge, confidence, beliefs, and culture intersect. *Journal of Research on Technology in Education*, *42*(3), 255–284.

Eslami, M., Rickman, A., Vaccaro, K., Aleyasen, A., Vuong, A., Karahalios, K., … & Sandvig, C. (2015, April). "I always assumed that I wasn't really that close to [her]" Reasoning about Invisible Algorithms in News Feeds. In *Proceedings of the 33rd annual ACM conference on human factors in computing systems*, Seoul Republic of Korea (pp. 153–162).

Feezell, J. T., Wagner, J. K., & Conroy, M. (2021). Exploring the effects of algorithm-driven news sources on political behavior and polarization. *Computers in Human Behavior*, *116*, 106626.

Ford, J. (2015). Stakeholder engagement in the digital age. *Management Communication Quarterly*, *29*(3), 471–476.

Francke, E., & Alexander, B. (2019). The potential influence of artificial intelligence on plagiarism a higher education perspective. In *Proc European conference on the impact of artificial intelligence and robotics. EM Normandie Business School, Oxford*, pp. 131–140.

Frey, C. B., & Osborne, M. A. (2017). The future of employment: How susceptible are jobs to computerisation? *Technological Forecasting and Social Change*, *114*, 254–280.

Garzón, J. (2021). An overview of twenty-five years of augmented reality in education. *Multimodal Technologies and Interaction*, *5*(7), 37.

Gikas, J., & Grant, M. M. (2013). Mobile computing devices in higher education: Student perspectives on learning with cellphones, smartphones & social media. *The Internet and Higher Education*, *19*, 18–26.

Gillespie, T. (2014). The relevance of algorithms. *Media Technologies: Essays on Communication, Materiality, and Society*, *167*(2014), 167.

Gran, A. B., Booth, P., & Bucher, T. (2021). To be or not to be algorithm aware: A question of a new digital divide?. *Information, Communication & Society*, *24*(12), 1779–1796.

Greenstein, L. M. (2012). *Assessing 21st century skills: A guide to evaluating mastery and authentic learning*. Corwin Press.

Gupta, M., Akiri, C., Aryal, K., Parker, E., & Praharaj, L. (2023). *From ChatGPT to ThreatGPT: Impact of generative ai in cybersecurity and privacy*. IEEE Access.

Hazucha, B. (2022). Artificial intelligence and cultural production: Possible impacts on creativity and copyright law. *Available at SSRN 4028106*.

He, W., Zhang, Z. J., & Li, W. (2021). Information technology solutions, challenges, and suggestions for tackling the COVID-19 pandemic.

Hess, T., Matt, C., Benlian, A., & Wiesböck, F. (2016). Options for formulating a digital transformation strategy. *MIS Quarterly Executive*, *150*(2), 123–139.

Ho, A. Besiroglu, T., Erdil, E. Owen, D., Rahman, R., Guo, Z., Atkinson, D., Thompson, N. & Sevilla, J. (2024). Algorithmic progress in language models. *arXiv:2403.05812*.

Holzinger, A., Keiblinger, K., Holub, P., Zatloukal, K., & Müller, H. (2023). AI for life: Trends in artificial intelligence for biotechnology. *New Biotechnology 74* (25), 16–24.

Hristova, S., Hong, S., Slack, J. D., Hristova, S., Hong, S., & Slack, J. D. (2021). Introduction: In the presence of algorithms. *Algorithmic Culture How Big Data and Artificial Intelligence Are Transforming Everyday Life*, 1–14.

Hutson, J., Jeevanjee, T., Vander Graaf, V., Lively, J., Weber, J., Weir, G., … & Edele, S. (2022). Artificial intelligence and the disruption of higher education: Strategies for integrations across disciplines. *Creative Education*, *13*(12), 1–28.

Kaliraj, P., & Devi, T. (2023). Innovating higher education 4.0 in the era of industry 4.0. In *Industry 4.0 technologies for education* (pp. 1–10). Auerbach Publications.

Kane, G. C., Palmer, D., Phillips, A. N., Kiron, D., & Buckley, N. (2015). *Strategy, not technology, drives digital transformation*. MIT Sloan Management Review and Deloitte University Press.

Kearns, S. (November 6, 2023). OpenAI says ChatGPT clocks 100M active users weekly. *Hyperbeast*. Retrieved: https://hypebeast.com/2023/11/openai-chatgpt-100-million-active-users-weekly

Kellner, D., & Gennaro, S. (2022). Critical theory and the transformation of education in the new millennium. In *The Palgrave handbook on critical theories of education* (pp. 21–45). Springer International Publishing.

Khan, W., Ghazanfar, M. A., Azam, M. A., Karami, A., Alyoubi, K. H., & Alfakeeh, A. S. (2020). Stock market prediction using machine learning classifiers and social media, news. *Journal of Ambient Intelligence and Humanized Computing*, *13*, 3433–3456.

Kobayashi, M., & Takeda, K. (2000). Information retrieval on the web. *ACM Computing Surveys (CSUR)*, *32*(2), 144–173.

Kordzadeh, N., & Ghasemaghaei, M. (2022). Algorithmic bias: Review, synthesis, and future research directions. *European Journal of Information Systems*, *31*(3), 388–409.

Krajcik, J., Schneider, B., Miller, E. A., Chen, I. C., Bradford, L., Baker, Q., … & Peek-Brown, D. (2023). Assessing the effect of project-based learning on science learning in elementary schools. *American Educational Research Journal*, *60*(1), 70–102.

Lepri, B., Oliver, N., Letouzé, E., Pentland, A., & Vinck, P. (2018). Fair, transparent, and accountable algorithmic decision-making processes: The premise, the proposed solutions, and the open challenges. *Philosophy and Technology*, *31*, 611–627.

Li, S., & Gu, X. (2023). A risk framework for human-centered artificial intelligence in education. *Educational Technology & Society*, *26*(1), 187–202.

Littman, M. L., Ajunwa, I., Berger, G., Boutilier, C., Currie, M., Doshi-Velez, F., … & Walsh, T. (2022). Gathering strength, gathering storms: The one hundred year study on artificial intelligence (AI100) 2021 study panel report. *arXiv preprint arXiv:2210.15767*.

Liu, X. M., & Murphy, D. (2020). A multi-faceted approach for trustworthy AI in cybersecurity. *Journal of Strategic Innovation and Sustainability*, *15*(6).

Magness, J., & Mitchell, M. M. (2022). Religious studies & the imagined boundaries of the humanities. *Daedalus*, *151*(3), 166–179.

Marr, B. (January 29, 2024). 10 mind-blowing generative AI stats everyone should know about. *Forbes*. Retrieved: https://www-forbes-com.cdn.ampproject.org/c/s/www.forbes.com/sites/bernardmarr/2024/01/29/10-mind-blowing-generative-ai-stats-everyone-should-know-about/amp/

Martínez-Peláez, R., Ochoa-Brust, A., Rivera, S., Félix, V. G., Ostos, R., Brito, H., … & Mena, L. J. (2023). Role of digital transformation for achieving sustainability: mediated role of stakeholders, key capabilities, and technology. *Sustainability*, *15*(14), 11221.

Massey, J. W. (2020). *The Challenges of Neoliberalism to the Democratic Promises of Higher Education* (Doctoral dissertation, The University of North Carolina at Greensboro).

McDonald, N., Johri, A., Ali, A., & Hingle, A. (2024). Generative artificial intelligence in higher education: Evidence from an analysis of institutional policies and guidelines. *arXiv preprint arXiv:2402.01659*.

McKinsey Global Institute (July 26, 2024). Generative AI and the future of work in America. Retrieved: https://www.mckinsey.com/mgi/our-research/generative-ai-and-the-future-of-work-in-america

McPherson, S. S. (2009). *Tim Berners-Lee: Inventor of the world wide web*. Twenty-First Century Books.

Miguel, P. M. D., De-Pablos-Heredero, C., Montes, J. L., & García, A. (2022). Impact of dynamic capabilities on customer satisfaction through digital transformation in the automotive sector. *Sustainability*, *14*(8), 4772.

Milton, J., & Al-Busaidi, A. (2023). New role of leadership in AI era: Educational sector. In *SHS web of conferences* (Vol. *156*, p. 09005). EDP Sciences.

Minoli, D. (2013). *Building the internet of things with IPv6 and MIPv6: The evolving world of M2M communications*. John Wiley & Sons.

Mishra, L., Gupta, T., & Shree, A. (2020). Online teaching-learning in higher education during lockdown period of COVID-19 pandemic. *International Journal of Educational Research Open*, *1*, 100012.

Mok, A. & Zinkula, J. (February 2, 2023). ChatGPT may be coming for our jobs. Here are the 10 roles that AI is most likely to replace. *Insider*. Retrieved from: https://www.businessinsider.com/chatgpt-jobs-at-risk-replacement-artificial-intelligence-ai-labor-trends-2023-02?amp=#amp_tf=From%20%251%24s&aoh=16754252090476&csi=0&referrer=https%3A%2F%2Fwww.google.com

Monett, D., & Lewis, C. W. (2018). Getting clarity by defining artificial intelligence—A survey. In *Philosophy and theory of artificial intelligence 2017* (pp. 212–214). Springer International Publishing.

Murphy, B. P. (15 December, 2022). Is Lensa AI stealing from human art? An expert explains the controversy. *Science Alert*. Retrieved: https://www-sciencealert-com.cdn.ampproject.org/c/s/www.sciencealert.com/is-lensa-ai-stealing-from-human-art-an-expert-explains-the-controversy/amp

Omolara, A. E., Alabdulatif, A., Abiodun, O. I., Alawida, M., Alabdulatif, A., & Arshad, H. (2022). The internet of things security: A survey encompassing unexplored areas and new insights. *Computers & Security*, *112*, 102494.

Palladino, J., & Shepard, L. A. (2023). Authentic assessment embedded in project-based learning. *Schools of opportunity: 10 research-based models for creating equity*, 67. Teachers College Press.

Patel, S., Hamdan, S., & Donahue, S. (2022). Optimising telemedicine in ophthalmology during the COVID-19 pandemic. *Journal of Telemedicine and Telecare*, *28*(7), 498–501.

Pavlik, J. V. (2023). Collaborating with ChatGPT: Considering the implications of generative artificial intelligence for journalism and media education. *Journalism & Mass Communication Educator 78* (1), 84–93.

Powers, E. (2017). My news feed is filtered? Awareness of news personalization among college students. *Digital Journalism*, *5*(10), 1315–1335.

Rensfeldt, A. B., & Rahm, L. (2023). Automating teacher work? A history of the politics of automation and artificial intelligence in education. *Postdigital Science and Education*, *5*(1), 25–43.

Rof, A., Bikfalvi, A., & Marques, P. (2022). Pandemic-accelerated digital transformation of a born digital higher education institution. *Educational Technology & Society*, *25*(1), 124–141.

Rudolph, J., Tan, S., & Tan, S. (2023). War of the chatbots: Bard, Bing Chat, ChatGPT, Ernie and beyond. The new AI gold rush and its impact on higher education. *Journal of Applied Learning and Teaching*, *6*(1).

Saltelli, A., Ratto, M., Andres, T., Campolongo, F., Cariboni, J., Gatelli, D., ... & Tarantola, S. (2008). Introduction to sensitivity analysis. In *Global sensitivity analysis. The primer*, 1–51. Wiley.

Schiff, D. (2022). Education for AI, not AI for education: The role of education and ethics in national AI policy strategies. *International Journal of Artificial Intelligence in Education*, *32*(3), 527–563.

Schrager, A. (November 3, 2023). The tech gold rush is over. Where's the next one? *Bloomberg*. Retrieved: https://www.bloomberg.com/opinion/articles/2023-11-03/the-tech-gold-rush-is-over-the-search-for-the-next-gold-rush-is-on?embedded-checkout=true

Schwab, K. (2017). *The fourth industrial revolution*. Currency.

Selwyn, N. (2016). *Digital technology and the contemporary university: Degrees of digitization*. Routledge.

Sherry, B. (2022). 3 Limits to artificial intelligence's creativity (and how to solve them): Here's what you need to know about harnessing A.I. technology to be more creative. *Inc*. Retrieved: https://www.inc.com/ben-sherry/3-limits-to-artificial-intelligences-creativity-and-how-to-solve-them.html

Siakalli, M., Mousoulidou, M., Christodoulou, A., Savvidou, A., & Kouppa, K. (2022). Secondary education and COVID-19. *Encyclopedia*, *2*(1), 409–427.

Singh, J., Steele, K., & Singh, L. (2021). Combining the best of online and face-to-face learning: Hybrid and blended learning approach for COVID-19, post vaccine, & post-pandemic world. *Journal of Educational Technology Systems*, *50*(2), 140–171.

Tambe, P. & Snyder, S. (February 20, 2024) How early adopters of gen AI are gaining efficiencies. *Knowledge at Wharton*. Retrieved: https://knowledge.wharton.upenn.edu/article/how-early-adopters-of-gen-ai-are-extracting-efficiencies/

Ter Beek, M., Wopereis, I., & Schildkamp, K. (2022). Don't wait, innovate! Preparing students and lecturers in higher education for the future labor market. *Education Sciences*, *12*(9), 620.

Townes, M. (2012). The spread of TCP/IP: How the Internet became the Internet. *Millennium*, *41*(1), 43–64.

U.S. Bureau of Labor Statistics (2018). U.S. Bureau of Labor Statistics 2018. Retrieved July 31, 2024: https://www.bls.gov/opub/mlr/2018/

Vial, G., Cameron, A. F., Giannelia, T., & Jiang, J. (2023). Managing artificial intelligence projects: Key insights from an AI consulting firm. *Information Systems Journal*, *33*(3), 669–691.

Wang, P. (2019). On defining artificial intelligence. *Journal of Artificial General Intelligence*, *10*(2), 1–37.

Warrier, U., John, M., & Warrier, S. (2021). Leveraging emotional intelligence competencies for sustainable development of higher education institutions in the new normal. *FIIB Business Review*, *10*(1), 62–73.

Westerman, G., Bonnet, D., & McAfee, A. (2014). *Leading digital: Turning technology into business transformation*. Harvard Business Review Press.

Wirtz, B. W., Weyerer, J. C., & Sturm, B. J. (2020). The dark sides of artificial intelligence: An integrated AI governance framework for public administration. *International Journal of Public Administration*, *43*(9), 818–829.

Woodruff, K., Hutson, J., & Arnone, K. (2023). Perceptions and barriers to adopting artificial intelligence in K-12 education: A survey of educators in fifty states. In Mistretta, S. ed, *Reimagining education - The role of e-learning, creativity, and technology in the post-pandemic era*. IntechOpen. https://doi.org/10.5772/intechopen.1002741 https://www.intechopen.com/online-first/1171043

World Economic Forum (January 16–20, 2023). *World Economic Forum Annual Meeting*. Retrieved July 31, 2024: https://www.weforum.org/events/world-economic-forum-annual-meeting-2023/

Yang, S., & Evans, C. (November, 2019). Opportunities and challenges in using AI chatbots in higher education. In *Proceedings of the 2019 3rd international conference on education and e-learning*, Tokyo, Japan (pp. 79–83).

Yao, D. (2023). Salesforce survey: 86% of IT leaders see key role for generative AI. *AI + Business*. July 20, 2023. Retrieved: https://aibusiness.com/nlp/salesforce-survey-86-of-it-leaders-see-key-role-for-generative-ai

Zanella, A., Bui, N., Castellani, A., Vangelista, L., & Zorzi, M. (2014). Internet of things for smart cities. *IEEE Internet of Things Journal*, *1*(1), 22–32.

Zawacki-Richter, O., Marín, V. I., Bond, M., & Gouverneur, F. (2019). Systematic review of research on artificial intelligence applications in higher education–where are the educators?. *International Journal of Educational Technology in Higher Education*, *16*(1), 1–27.

Zerilli, J., Knott, A., Maclaurin, J., & Gavaghan, C. (2019). Algorithmic decision-making and the control problem. *Minds and Machines*, *29*, 555–578.

Zhang, H., Lee, I., Ali, S., DiPaola, D., Cheng, Y., & Breazeal, C. (2022). Integrating ethics and career futures with technical learning to promote AI literacy for middle school students: An exploratory study. *International Journal of Artificial Intelligence in Education*, *33*, 1–35.

2 Digital Transformation in Industry and Education

2.1 The Origins of Digital Transformation

Digital transformation represents a foundational shift in how organizations leverage technology to fundamentally alter business and operational models, presenting an indispensable pathway toward innovation, competitiveness, and efficiency. The importance of digital transformation in today's global landscape cannot be overstated, as it not only enhances organizational agility but also caters to evolving customer expectations, ensuring sustainability in an increasingly digital economy. The digital transformation journey is crucial for several reasons. First, it enables businesses to stay competitive in a fast-paced market environment. Organizations that embrace digital technologies can streamline operations, reduce costs, and increase efficiency, thereby gaining a competitive edge (Westerman, Bonnet, & McAfee, 2014). In the realm of education, digital transformation facilitates the adoption of innovative teaching and learning methodologies, expanding access to education and enabling personalized learning experiences (Selwyn, 2016).

Second, digital transformation is pivotal for customer and student engagement. In the business sector, leveraging digital channels allows for the creation of more meaningful and personalized customer experiences, fostering loyalty and satisfaction (Lemon & Verhoef, 2016). Similarly, in education, the integration of digital tools and platforms can significantly enhance student engagement and motivation, leading to improved learning outcomes (Bates, 2015).

Moreover, digital transformation is essential for data-driven decision-making. The ability to collect, analyze, and act on data insights allows organizations to make informed strategic decisions, optimizing performance and driving growth (Davenport, 2013). In educational institutions, data analytics can inform curriculum design, pedagogical strategies, and student support services, ensuring that educational offerings are aligned with learner needs and market demands (Daniel, 2015).

DOI: 10.4324/9781003512813-2

Additionally, digital transformation fosters innovation by providing organizations with the tools and methodologies to explore new business models and services. This capacity for innovation is critical for addressing emerging challenges and opportunities in both the business and educational landscapes (Bharadwaj et al., 2013). Furthermore, the digital transformation imperative is underscored by the need for resilience and adaptability in the face of disruptions, such as the global COVID-19 pandemic. Organizations with robust digital infrastructures were better equipped to pivot to remote operations, maintain continuity, and quickly adapt to changing circumstances (Kane et al., 2020).

The origins of digital transformation trace back to the advent of computing technology, marking a significant shift in how information is processed, stored, and communicated. This transformation began in the mid-20th century, with the development of the first electronic computers. These machines, originally designed for specific tasks such as code-breaking and calculations, laid the groundwork for the broader application of digital technology in various sectors (Campbell-Kelly & Aspray, 2004). The invention of the transistor in 1947 was pivotal in miniaturizing and enhancing the performance of electronic devices, thereby accelerating the pace of digital innovation (Riordan & Hoddeson, 1997). By the 1970s and 1980s, the introduction of personal computers (PCs) and the subsequent development of the internet revolutionized the way individuals and organizations interacted with digital technology. The PC democratized access to computing power, allowing for the widespread adoption of digital tools across industries and laying the foundation for the digital workplace (Ceruzzi, 2003).

The internet, emerging from a network of computers initially designed for research and military communication, evolved into a global platform for information exchange, collaboration, and commerce (Leiner et al., 2009). These technological advancements set the stage for what is now known as "digital transformation," a process that extends beyond mere digitization (converting analog information into digital format) to fundamentally change how businesses operate and deliver value to customers. As highlighted by Westerman, Bonnet, and McAfee (2014), digital transformation encompasses the integration of digital technology into all areas of a business, resulting in fundamental changes to how businesses operate and how they deliver value to customers. Digital transformation in business is a dynamic process that reshapes the way organizations operate and engage with their customers. This transformation is driven by the integration of digital technologies across all facets of business, resulting in fundamental changes to operations, customer interactions, and value delivery.

In the context of education, digital transformation has similarly redefined the landscape, making learning more accessible, engaging, and personalized than ever before. This shift toward digital integration encompasses a broad spectrum of innovative strategies and technologies that are fundamentally altering the educational landscape, offering unprecedented opportunities for educators and learners alike. The adoption of learning management systems (LMS), online course materials, and digital collaboration tools represents a shift toward a more flexible, accessible, and student-centered approach to education (Selwyn, 2016). But unlike industry, these developments in education occurred largely over the past two decades, and with marked barriers to adoption, not least among them institutional culture within education. The following short review of IT innovation makes clear that these advances were already well-established in industry long before broadly integrating into academia.

The journey of digital transformation encompasses a series of meticulously structured steps that guide organizations through the intricate process of integrating digital technologies into all areas of their operations (Table 2.1). This transformative journey not only revolutionizes how businesses operate and deliver value to customers but also necessitates a cultural shift that challenges organizations to continually challenge the status quo, experiment, and get comfortable with failure. These steps, as outlined by Team Kissflow (2024) have become the bedrock upon which every significant digital evolution, such as the advent of mobile technology and cloud computing, is built upon.

Table 2.1 Seven Key Steps to Digital Transformation

Step	*Description*	*Key actions*	*Outcome*
1 **Assess current digital state**	Evaluate current digital capabilities and performance levels.	Survey internal users and consumers; benchmark against industry leaders.	Understanding of where the organization currently stands in its digital journey.
2 **Identify and analyze the gap**	Determine the difference between the current state and desired future state.	Examine business operations, technology stack, and customer experience gaps.	Clear understanding of necessary changes and priorities for digital transformation.
3 **Define main objectives**	Establish clear goals for the digital transformation effort.	Decide on objectives like improving customer experience, efficiency, or reducing operational costs.	A set of targeted outcomes that the digital transformation aims to achieve.

(*Continued*)

Table 2.1 (Continued)

Step	*Description*	*Key actions*	*Outcome*
4 **Create digital transformation strategy**	Develop a comprehensive plan that aligns with business goals and addresses identified gaps.	Align goals with business state, set a budget, prepare for organizational change, choose technology.	A roadmap for achieving digital transformation objectives with specific initiatives.
5 **Build a team**	Assemble a team to drive and support digital transformation efforts.	Include IT specialists, data professionals, marketers, financial analysts, security advisors, etc.	A dedicated team equipped to implement and manage the digital transformation strategy.
6 **Take initiatives and track them**	Implement digital transformation initiatives in manageable, trackable segments.	Start with specific strategies like digitizing processes or adopting digital collaboration platforms.	Progressive steps toward overall digital transformation, with each initiative moving the organization closer to its goals.
7 **Measure the progress**	Continuously evaluate the success of digital transformation efforts.	Use feedback, customer satisfaction ratings, digital adoption levels, and ROI on digital investments as metrics.	Insight into the effectiveness of the transformation efforts and areas for improvement or adjustment.

The initial step involves a thorough assessment of the organization's current digital state. This foundational phase requires an honest evaluation of existing digital capabilities, performance levels, and technological assets. By understanding where they currently stand, organizations can better plan their digital transformation journey with a clear perspective. Following this, identifying and analyzing the gap between the current digital state and the desired future state is crucial. This step illuminates the disparities within business operations, technological infrastructures, and customer engagement strategies that need bridging. It is in understanding these gaps that organizations can articulate the "why" behind their digital transformation endeavors.

Defining the main objectives for digital transformation is the third step. It necessitates a clear articulation of what digital transformation means for the organization and what it aims to achieve. Objectives may range from improving customer experience and internal collaboration to increasing efficiency and reducing operational costs. Setting these goals provides direction and purpose to the digital transformation efforts. The creation of a digital transformation strategy marks the fourth step. This strategy is a comprehensive plan that encompasses the assessment of the current digital state, the gaps identified, and the objectives set. It is a blueprint that guides the organization through its digital makeover, ensuring that every technological adoption or process innovation aligns with the overarching business goals.

Building a team dedicated to achieving digital transformation objectives constitutes the fifth step. This team is a blend of visionaries, technologists, data analysts, and business strategists who drive the digital transformation from the front. Their collective expertise and collaborative efforts are pivotal in navigating the complexities of digital transformation. Taking initiatives and tracking them form the sixth step. It involves breaking down the digital transformation strategy into manageable projects or initiatives that can be monitored and measured. This segmented approach allows for agility and adaptability, ensuring that the organization can respond to challenges and opportunities as they arise during the transformation process.

Finally, measuring the progress of digital transformation initiatives is essential. This seventh step involves setting clear metrics and key performance indicators to evaluate the success of digital transformation efforts. Through continuous monitoring and evaluation, organizations can glean insights into what works, what doesn't, and where adjustments are necessary. These steps have become standardized as they offer a structured approach to navigating the complexities of digital transformation. Whether it is adapting to mobile technology, leveraging cloud computing, or embracing any new digital innovation, these steps provide a roadmap that helps organizations systematically transform their operations, culture, and customer experiences in the digital era. This methodical approach ensures that digital transformation is not just about technological adoption but about creating a sustainable, agile, and forward-looking organization ready to thrive in an ever-evolving digital landscape.

2.2 Digital Milestones: From the Internet to Big Data

The journey from the inception of the internet to the era of big data represents a remarkable trajectory of digital milestones that have fundamentally transformed the landscape of information and communication technologies. This evolution has not only revolutionized the way data is generated, stored, and analyzed but has also had profound implications for both industry and education. The internet, initially conceptualized as a network for sharing information among research institutions and defense agencies, became publicly accessible in the early 1990s. This pivotal moment, as described by

Leiner et al. (2009), marked the beginning of an unprecedented expansion of digital connectivity, facilitating the global exchange of information. As noted, the creation of the World Wide Web by Tim Berners-Lee in 1989 further democratized access to information, making it possible for people worldwide to connect, communicate, and share data on an unparalleled scale (Berners-Lee et al., 1994).

The proliferation of digital content and the advent of e-commerce platforms in the late 1990s and early 2000s signified the next phase of digital evolution, where the internet became a critical medium for business operations and consumer transactions. The introduction of search engines, notably Google, revolutionized information retrieval, making it easier to navigate the vast amounts of data available online (Brin & Page, 1998). As digital technologies continued to advance, the mid-2000s witnessed the rise of social media platforms such as Facebook and Twitter, which transformed communication patterns and social interactions. These platforms facilitated the creation and sharing of user-generated content, leading to an exponential increase in data production (Kaplan & Haenlein, 2010). The concept of big data emerged as a response to the burgeoning volume, velocity, and variety of data generated by digital activities. Big data refers to datasets that are so large or complex that traditional data processing applications are inadequate to deal with them (Manyika et al., 2011). The ability to harness big data has unlocked new potentials for predictive analytics, personalized services, and decision-making processes in both the private and public sectors.

In education, the digital milestones from the internet to big data have paved the way for e-learning platforms, virtual classrooms, and online resources, expanding access to education and enabling personalized learning experiences. The analysis of educational big data has offered insights into student learning patterns, contributing to more effective teaching strategies and improved educational outcomes (Picciano, 2012). These digital milestones signify a continuous journey of innovation and transformation, highlighting the critical role of digital technologies in shaping modern society. The progression from the internet to big data underscores the importance of adapting to technological advancements to leverage the opportunities they present for enhancing operational efficiency, fostering knowledge creation, and facilitating learning and development.

2.3 The Current Landscape: Industry and Educational Systems

The 2024 AI Index Report (HAI, 2024) presents an illuminating snapshot of the landscape of artificial intelligence, revealing its broadening impact on society and pinpointing several critical trends. One of the standout findings is AI's differential performance across tasks: while it excels in image classification and language understanding, surpassing human benchmarks, it struggles with more complex cognitive challenges like high-level mathematics and commonsense reasoning. This dichotomy highlights the nuanced capabilities of AI, where its strengths can significantly enhance certain operations while remaining limited in others. Another major theme is the economic aspect of AI development, where the industry continues to dominate AI innovation, producing 51 notable machine learning models compared to academia's 15. This trend is coupled with soaring costs, as exemplified by OpenAI's GPT-4 and Google's Gemini Ultra, which required immense financial investments of approximately $78 million and $191 million, respectively for training.

On the geopolitical front, the United States remains a leader in AI development, significantly outpacing other regions like the European Union and China. This dominance is reflective of the strategic emphasis the United States places on advancing AI technologies, shaping the global dynamics of technological innovation. Additionally, 2023 marked a significant year for AI-related regulations in the United States, with a sharp increase to 25 new regulations, illustrating a growing focus on managing AI's integration into society responsibly. Meanwhile, investment trends in AI reveal a specific enthusiasm for generative AI, with funding nearly octupling to $25.2 billion, signaling robust market confidence in its future applications.

Public perception and the societal impact of AI also feature prominently in the report's findings. There is a significant increase in global awareness and apprehension regarding AI's potential impact, with surveys indicating that 66% of people now believe AI will dramatically affect their lives in the near future, up from 60% the previous year. This growing concern is paralleled by a lack of standardization in AI responsibility evaluations, where disparate benchmarks used by major developers like OpenAI and Google complicate the systematic assessment of AI models' risks and limitations. These insights underscore the necessity for educational systems to evolve, integrating AI training that aligns with these emerging trends and preparing students for a future deeply intertwined with AI, ensuring they are capable of navigating its benefits and challenges effectively.

The current landscape of both industry and educational systems is increasingly characterized by the pervasive influence of digital technologies, signifying a transformative shift toward more interconnected, efficient, and innovative practices. In the realm of industry, this digital era has ushered in advanced operational models, where data analytics, AI, and cloud computing redefine the boundaries of productivity, customer engagement, and competitive strategy. Concurrently, educational systems are witnessing a parallel evolution, as digital tools and platforms revolutionize teaching methodologies, learning environments, and access to knowledge. This chapter delves into the intricacies of the current digital landscape, exploring how the integration of digital technologies is reshaping industry and education.

It highlights the challenges and opportunities presented by this digital convergence, examining the role of technological advancements in driving systemic change and preparing individuals for a future that is increasingly digital. Through a detailed exploration of the current state of digital transformation, this section aims to provide insights into how organizations and educational institutions can navigate the complexities of the digital age, leveraging technology to foster innovation, inclusivity, and resilience in the face of rapid change.

The examples provided highlight various aspects of digital transformation, illustrating how businesses leverage technology to enhance efficiency, customer experience, and market competitiveness. Mobile applications represent a significant shift in customer engagement and operational efficiency. Companies across industries have developed mobile apps to offer personalized services, streamline transactions, and provide instant access to information and support (Wright et al., 2019). This mobile-centric approach aligns with consumer expectations for convenience and accessibility, enabling businesses to maintain a continuous connection with their audience. The concept of constant connectivity has become integral to modern business practices. Seamless connectivity across platforms and devices ensures that teams can collaborate effectively regardless of location, enhancing productivity and facilitating remote work environments (Fernandez-Vidal et al., 2022). This interconnectedness also extends to customer interactions, enabling businesses to provide cohesive experiences across various digital channels.

Digital processes for loan approvals exemplify the transformation in the financial services sector. Implementing digital systems for instant loan approvals not only improves operational efficiency but also significantly enhances the customer experience by reducing waiting times and simplifying procedures (Puschmann, 2017). This digital approach to loan processing reflects a broader trend in financial services toward automating and streamlining customer-facing operations. Virtual try-ons, powered by virtual reality (VR) technology, represent a novel way for customers to engage with products. This technology allows consumers to visualize how products would look or fit without physically trying them, offering a unique shopping experience that combines convenience with personalization (Javornik, 2016). Retailers adopting virtual try-on technologies are at the forefront of blending digital and physical shopping experiences.

The option for customers to buy online and pick up in-store (BOPIS) marries the convenience of online shopping with the immediacy of in-store pickup. This hybrid model addresses consumer preferences for quick, convenient shopping experiences while driving foot traffic to physical stores (Rigby, 2014). BOPIS represents a strategic response to the evolving retail landscape, demonstrating how businesses can leverage digital tools to enhance customer service and operational flexibility.

IT modernization, including the transition to cloud environments and the implementation of advanced solutions, is foundational to digital transformation. Modernizing such infrastructure not only supports remote readiness and operational agility but also facilitates the reskilling of employees to thrive in a digital-first environment (Ross, Beath, & Mocker, 2019). Companies undergoing IT modernization are better positioned to adapt to market changes and embrace innovation. Lastly, organizational change driven by digitization underscores the holistic nature of digital transformation. Embracing digital technologies requires a cultural shift within organizations, where digitization becomes a catalyst for innovation and growth (Kane et al., 2015). Companies that successfully navigate this transformational process recognize the value of integrating digital strategies into their core operations, fostering an environment conducive to continuous improvement and competitive advantage.

Moving from the examination of digital transformation within industry to its impact on educational systems, it becomes evident that the adoption of digital technologies in education has historically lagged behind that of the corporate sector. This delay in embracing digital innovations within educational institutions can be traced back to the gradual shift from traditional teaching aids, such as overhead projectors, to more contemporary digital tools like PowerPoint presentations. The advent of Google in 1998 and Wikipedia in 2001 marked a significant milestone in the accessibility of information, laying the groundwork for a digital revolution that would eventually permeate the educational sector. However, the path to integrating these and subsequent innovations into educational practices has been measured and incremental.

Educational institutions are increasingly leveraging digital avenues such as social media, websites, and email marketing to enhance student recruitment, retention, and the measurement of institutional success (Selwyn, 2016). These tools not only facilitate direct communication with prospective and current students but also enable the collection of data to inform strategic decision-making and improve educational offerings. The integration of AI in education represents a significant leap forward, offering the potential to personalize learning experiences, automate administrative tasks, and improve educational outcomes (Luckin & Holmes, 2016). AI-driven technologies can adapt to individual learning styles and needs, providing personalized feedback and support that enhances student engagement and facilitates mastery of subject matter.

Gamification, the incorporation of game elements into educational processes, is another innovative strategy that has been shown to increase student motivation, engagement, and knowledge retention (Dicheva et al., 2015). By making learning more interactive and enjoyable, gamification can help overcome traditional barriers to student engagement and foster a deeper connection to the material being taught. Similarly, virtual and augmented reality

(VR and AR) technologies are transforming educational environments by creating immersive learning experiences that enhance students' understanding of complex concepts (Freina & Ott, 2015). These technologies provide hands-on, experiential learning opportunities that can be particularly effective in fields such as science, history, and medicine, where visualization and interaction with abstract concepts are crucial.

Improved accessibility through digital platforms is a cornerstone of digital transformation in education. Online learning environments, e-textbooks, and digital libraries make educational resources available to a wider audience, ensuring that students with diverse needs and from various geographical locations can access high-quality education (Martin & Bolliger, 2018).

Personalized learning approaches, facilitated by digital technologies, tailor educational content and experiences to individual student preferences and needs (Xie et al., 2019). This customization supports differentiated instruction and allows students to progress at their own pace, thereby enhancing learning outcomes and ensuring that each student can achieve their full potential.

In fact, before the rise of GAI, artificial intelligence was already making significant strides across various academic disciplines, heralding a transformative era in higher education. This integration showcased the potential of AI to tailor personalized learning experiences, optimize learning outcomes, and expand access to diverse student populations. For example, AI applications in education, such as image classification systems and software like Deep Lens, alongside NLP tools, were commonplace in academia. Faculty and students regularly interacted with AI through everyday tools like Grammarly and virtual assistants, such as Siri and Alexa, indicating the pervasive influence of AI in academic life.

Furthermore, as institutional studies demonstrate, such as that carried out by Hutson et al. (2022), demonstrate, these technologies were already being actively utilized across various academic disciplines to enhance learning, teaching, and research, albeit not always knowingly. In the realm of education and human services, AI, particularly through VR and simulations, significantly impacted teaching methodologies and student learning outcomes. For example, VR simulations like TLE TeachLivE and Mursion provided immersive environments for teacher preparation and special education training, effectively supporting preservice teachers in developing essential skills such as classroom management and engagement strategies for students with autism spectrum disorder (Ade-Ojo et al., 2022; Fraser et al., 2020). Access to such tools still required considerable hardware acquisitions and applications were all pre-made and not bespoke.

In humanities and language arts, AI facilitated groundbreaking research and learning through the Digital Humanities (DH), where quantum computing and AI algorithms were applied to analyze vast amounts of literary and historical data. This integration enabled more nuanced and expansive studies in humanities disciplines, significantly benefiting language learning as well. AI-powered tools and intelligent tutoring systems were used to tailor language learning experiences to individual progress, demonstrating the potential to support traditional teaching methods rather than replace them (Ćalušić, 2021). Specialized knowledge and training were, however, required in order to effectively use these corpora.

The same can be said of the visual arts. The intersection of AI with art and design witnessed transformative changes, particularly through Generative Adversarial Networks (GANs) and AI enhancements in graphic design applications. Tools like Adobe's Sensei AI engine brought efficiencies to graphic design processes, enabling creatives to focus more on the artistic aspects of their work. AI facilitated novel artistic expressions and practical applications, such as creating photo-realistic images and enhancing VR experiences (Gabriele et al., 2017)). Access to GANs, it should be noted, was limited to specific research institutions and computer science departments with little crossover initially to art fields (Chakraborty et al., 2024).

Access to these technologies that were not merely "under the hood" of other applications was largely confined to physical science programs. In STEM fields, for instance, the role of AI was more pronounced, with significant applications in teaching and learning. AI and machine learning were embedded in educational platforms and resources to provide interactive, personalized learning experiences in subjects such as mathematics and computer science. Federal agencies and organizations, such as NASA, offered AI and machine learning resources and projects to engage students in practical, real-world applications, further demonstrating AI's potential to revolutionize STEM education (Gong et al., 2018; Zhang & Aslan, 2021).

Despite the broad usage of AI already prevalent across all disciplines pre-generative AI, there remains a lag in the rate of deliberate adoption today. The initial reluctance or slow adoption rate in education can be attributed to various factors, including institutional inertia, the need for comprehensive training for educators, and concerns regarding the efficacy and reliability of new technologies. Despite these challenges, the eventual realization of the potential of digital technologies to enhance teaching and learning has led to gradual, yet impactful, transformations within educational systems. The introduction of LMS, such as Canvas and Blackboard, to manage course materials and streamline grading processes represents significant steps forward in the digital evolution of education.

This transition underscores a broader trend of digital convergence, where educational practices begin to mirror the technological advancements and digital integration seen in the corporate world. The delayed, but steady, incorporation of digital technologies in education reflects a cautious approach to transforming pedagogical methods and curriculum delivery.

However, it also highlights the resilience and adaptability of the sector in adopting digital innovations that have proven to be instrumental in industries outside of education. In order to investigate this most recently, a study was conducted to ascertain just this. In an effort to better integrate artificial intelligence (AI) into educational settings, a comprehensive study was conducted, encompassing both institutional readiness and faculty engagement with AI in the classroom. The institution-wide study conducted in Spring 2024 at a mid-sized, private educational institution, boasting over 7,000 full-time students, provides pivotal insights into the perceptions of AI among faculty, staff, administration, and students (Hutson & Rains, 2024). The findings from our institutional study resonate with broader trends observed in recent research, including a notable Pew study, which illuminates the rapidly increasing adoption of AI across various segments of the population (Abulibdeh, Zaidan, & Abulibdeh, 2024; Alhumaid et al., 2023; Filgueiras, 2023; Rodway & Schepman, 2023).

This study reveals a significant correlation between educational attainment and AI usage frequency; notably, individuals with postgraduate degrees are the most likely to engage with AI technologies on a daily basis. Specifically, nearly one-third of postgraduates in the United States report using AI several times a day or "almost constantly." Age demographics also significantly influence AI adoption rates. A striking 57% of individuals aged 18–29 report using AI at least a few times a week, a figure that notably diminishes to 36% among those aged 65 and over. This age-related trend underscores the digital divide, reflecting younger generations' propensity to integrate AI into their daily routines more readily. Furthermore, the overall adoption of AI among Americans since the public introduction of ChatGPT in November 2022 has been remarkably swift. Across a wide range of demographics, half of the American population now reports using AI multiple times per week, suggesting a widespread and rapid embrace of these technologies. This broad adoption indicates a significant shift in the public's interaction with AI, highlighting its growing influence on daily life and routines. These insights align with the patterns observed in our study, emphasizing the increasing permeation of AI across educational settings and underscoring the necessity for institutions to adapt to this evolving landscape (Tyson & Kennedy, 2024).

Likewise, the institutional study here reveals a general optimism among both students and faculty/staff regarding the potential of AI within their domains. This optimism, however, is not without its reservations. Ethical considerations, the fear of dependency on AI, and concerns that it might undermine human skills and efforts are prominent. Notably, students display a significant awareness of and engagement with generative AI technologies, pointing toward a shift in how the younger generation perceives and interacts more with it. As well, echoing a broader societal discourse, both groups express apprehensions about the ethical and societal ramifications of

AI. Data privacy, job displacement, and the potential for misuse of AI technologies emerge as key concerns. This reflection of wider debates underscores the need for ethical guidelines and robust discussions around the deployment of AI in sensitive contexts.

The engagement with AI technologies is notably high among students, who utilize these tools for academic purposes, personal projects, and entertainment. This contrasts with faculty and staff, who, while also engaging with the tools, predominantly focus on productivity and administrative tasks. As with the variety of uses among the younger generations, the study also highlights the recognition of the group of the diverse applications of the new generative features of AI, from text generation and code creation to the production of original images and art, showcasing an awareness of the transformative potential offered by the technology. As such, a pronounced demand for AI literacy and ethical training emerges from the study, indicating a consensus on the importance of understanding capabilities and limitations. Both students and faculty/staff express a keen interest in learning more about generative AI technologies through courses or workshops.

The call for institutional support in preparing for integration is clear. Training, policy development, and the establishment of ethical guidelines are deemed crucial by both students and faculty/staff. This includes measures to combat plagiarism, enhance AI literacy, and align AI use with educational integrity. Furthermore, there is a widespread belief, especially among students, that AI will significantly influence future careers and fields of study. This anticipation highlights the imperative for educational institutions to prepare their communities for a future where AI plays a central role in the workforce. A full discussion of the study and the data shall follow, highlighting the nuanced perceptions of AI within an educational context. This includes a collective enthusiasm for possibilities while recognizing the need for careful consideration of its ethical, societal, and educational implications.

Along with the full, institutional study was a full-day teacher training workshop which was a key component of this study, offering faculty members a platform to explore and discuss the implications of AI in education (Morris & Hutson, 2024). The feedback from faculty participants provides invaluable insights into the current attitudes and preparedness toward AI across academic environments. Faculty responses highlighted a mix of enthusiasm and caution regarding the integration of AI tools into educational practices. One participant expressed a desire to enhance their pedagogical techniques by incorporating AI, stating, "I continue to reinforce my existing knowledge of good teaching practices but also adopt new ideas such as using AI and learning what students see as impactful." This sentiment was echoed by another educator who found practical value in AI for streamlining tasks like creating slide presentations and conducting initial proofreading, which can significantly reduce the time faculty need to spend on these activities.

However, the training also revealed a spectrum of familiarity and comfort with AI among faculty. While some attendees appreciated the introductory nature of the sessions, others sought more advanced content. A participant noted, "With using AI, in some instances fully embracing it can be beneficial," suggesting a readiness to integrate AI more deeply into their teaching strategies. Conversely, another attendee expressed disappointment in the foundational level of the sessions: "I honestly did not learn anything new, which is unfortunate… I would have appreciated a more in-depth workshop introducing new tools and strategies for implementation."

The varied feedback underscores the need for differentiated training sessions that cater to varying levels of AI expertise among faculty. Such tailored approaches could help foster more effective integration of AI into curricula and ensure that all faculty members are equipped to use these technologies ethically and effectively. Moreover, the workshop highlighted the potential for AI to enhance pedagogical practices and address specific educational challenges, such as supporting students with disabilities or streamlining administrative tasks. The data gathered from the teacher training day suggests a growing recognition of the benefits of AI in education, paired with a critical need for more structured, varied, and advanced training. Institutions must consider these factors as they formulate AI integration strategies and policies, ensuring that all faculty members are supported in their efforts to adapt to this transformative technology. Such initiatives will not only enhance the quality of education but also prepare students more effectively for a future where AI is ubiquitous in the workplace and beyond.

2.4 Leveraging Data Science for Strategic Insights

The integration of data science into strategic planning and operational management has marked a pivotal advancement in both the industrial and educational sectors, fundamentally altering the landscape of decision-making processes. This transformation is underpinned by the digital revolution, which has facilitated the collection, analysis, and interpretation of vast datasets. Digital transformation has not only democratized access to data but has also introduced sophisticated tools and methodologies for extracting valuable insights from this data. This capability is crucial for navigating the complexities of the global environment, characterized by rapid technological advancements and shifting market dynamics.

In the corporate world, the importance of data, particularly big data, cannot be overstated. Data science enables businesses to transform raw data into actionable insights, driving growth and competitive advantage. According to McAfee et al. (2012), companies that adopt data-driven decision-making enjoy significant productivity gains over their less data-oriented counterparts. Clean data, which refers to accurately processed and error-free data, is critical in this context as it ensures the reliability of analytics outcomes. Davenport (2014) emphasizes the strategic value of big data in industry, highlighting its role in optimizing operations, personalizing customer experiences, and innovating product development.

The advantages of leveraging data science in industry are multifaceted. It allows for more precise market segmentation, improved customer relationship management, and the identification of new revenue opportunities (Bughin et al., 2010). Moreover, predictive analytics can anticipate market shifts and consumer behavior, enabling proactive rather than reactive strategies.

Similarly, in the education sector, the application of data science holds significant promise for enhancing teaching and learning experiences. Daniel (2015) discusses the potential of learning analytics, a subset of data science, to tailor educational content to individual learner needs, thus improving learning outcomes. Clean and well-structured data is crucial in educational settings to ensure the accuracy of assessments, the effectiveness of personalized learning paths, and the integrity of academic research. Big data in education can inform curriculum development, identify at-risk students, and optimize resource allocation (Picciano, 2012). By analyzing data from digital learning tools and online platforms, educators can gain insights into student engagement, comprehension levels, and learning behaviors, facilitating more informed pedagogical decisions.

The significance of data across both industrial and educational landscapes is fundamentally anchored in its ability to facilitate comprehensive insights into present conditions and to furnish predictive foresight essential for strategic foresight. Nevertheless, the intricacies involved in managing, analyzing, and securing colossal volumes of data present formidable challenges. The focus on clean data—a concept denoting data that is precise, coherent, and devoid of inaccuracies—underscores the imperative for stringent data governance protocols that safeguard data quality and integrity.

Within this context, the advent of generative AI introduces a paradigm shift, revolutionizing the capabilities to query, organize, and interpret data with unprecedented efficiency and sophistication. Generative AI, through advanced algorithms and machine learning techniques, is redefining the boundaries of data analysis, offering the potential to generate new data, insights, and content based on existing datasets. This transformative capability not only enhances the depth and breadth of analysis but also accelerates the process of deriving actionable insights from vast data reservoirs. In industry, generative AI enables organizations to simulate and model complex scenarios, facilitating better-informed decision-making processes. Companies can now anticipate market trends, customer behaviors, and potential disruptions with greater precision, crafting strategies that are both proactive and adaptive. Moreover, generative AI's ability to synthesize and generate new content, such as reports, summaries, and visualizations, allows businesses to communicate complex data in accessible and meaningful ways, fostering a data-driven culture within the organization.

Similarly, in the realm of education, generative AI is transforming the way educational content is developed, personalized, and delivered. Educators can leverage these AI capabilities to tailor learning experiences to individual student needs, optimizing learning outcomes. Furthermore, generative AI can automate administrative tasks such as grading and feedback, freeing educators to focus on more strategic pedagogical activities. Additionally, the ability of generative AI to organize and present data in novel formats enhances research capabilities, enabling scholars to uncover new insights and contribute to knowledge creation in ways that were previously unimaginable. However, the integration of generative AI into data analysis and management processes also necessitates careful consideration of ethical and security implications. The automation and sophistication of data handling by generative AI systems require robust oversight to prevent biases, ensure data privacy, and maintain the integrity of generated insights.

Consequently, the development and implementation of generative AI technologies must be accompanied by comprehensive governance frameworks that address these concerns, ensuring that the revolutionary capabilities of generative AI are harnessed responsibly and effectively. Thus, the emergence of generative AI as a powerful tool for data analysis and management marks a significant milestone in the digital transformation journey of both industry and education. By enabling the querying, organizing, and outputting of data with unparalleled efficiency and depth, generative AI not only addresses the challenges associated with big data but also unlocks new horizons for innovation, personalized experiences, and strategic planning. As such, the advent of generative AI represents a critical advancement, underscoring the ongoing evolution of data's role in shaping the future of industry and education.

References

Abulibdeh, A., Zaidan, E., & Abulibdeh, R. (2024). Navigating the confluence of artificial intelligence and education for sustainable development in the era of industry 4.0: Challenges, opportunities, and ethical dimensions. *Journal of Cleaner Production*, *437*(15), 140527.

Ade-Ojo, G. O., Markowski, M., Essex, R., Stiell, M., & Jameson, J. (2022). A systematic scoping review and textual narrative synthesis of physical and mixed-reality simulation in pre-service teacher training. *Journal of Computer Assisted Learning*, *38*(3), 861–874.

Alhumaid, K., Naqbi, S., Elsori, D., & Mansoori, M. (2023). The adoption of artificial intelligence applications in education. *International Journal of Data and Network Science*, *7*(1), 457–466.

Bates, A. W. (2015). *Teaching in a digital age: Guidelines for designing teaching and learning*. BCcampus.

Berners-Lee, T., Cailliau, R., Luotonen, A., Nielsen, H. F., & Secret, A. (1994). The world-wide web. *Communications of the ACM*, *37*(8), 76–82.
Bharadwaj, A., El Sawy, O. A., Pavlou, P. A., & Venkatraman, N. (2013). Digital business strategy: Toward a next generation of insights. *MIS Quarterly*, *37*(2), 471–482.
Brin, S., & Page, L. (1998). The anatomy of a large-scale hypertextual Web search engine. *Computer Networks and ISDN Systems*, *30*(1–7), 107–117.
Bughin, J., Chui, M., & Manyika, J. (2010). Clouds, big data, and smart assets: Ten tech-enabled business trends to watch. *McKinsey Quarterly*, *56*(1), 75–86.
Ćalušić, M. (2021). *Artificial intelligence and language acquisition* [Master's thesis, University of Split]. Digitalni Akademski Arhivi i Repozitoriji.
Campbell-Kelly, M., & Aspray, W. (2004). *Computer: A history of the information machine*. Westview Press.
Ceruzzi, P. E. (2003). *A history of modern computing*. MIT Press.
Chakraborty, T., Naik, S. M., Panja, M., & Manvitha, B. (2024). Ten years of generative adversarial nets (GANs): A survey of the state-of-the-art. *Machine Learning: Science and Technology*, *5*(1), 011001.
Daniel, B. K. (2015). Big Data and analytics in higher education: Opportunities and challenges. *British Journal of Educational Technology*, *46*(5), 904–920.
Davenport, T. H. (2013). Analytics 3.0. *Harvard Business Review*, *91*(12), 64–72.
Davenport, T. (2014). *Big data at work: dispelling the myths, uncovering the opportunities*. Harvard Business Review Press.
Dicheva, D., Dichev, C., Agre, G., & Angelova, G. (2015). Gamification in education: A systematic mapping study. *Journal of Educational Technology & Society*, *18*(3), 75–88.
Fernandez-Vidal, J., Perotti, F. A., Gonzalez, R., & Gasco, J. (2022). Managing digital transformation: The view from the top. *Journal of Business Research*, *152*, 29–41.
Filgueiras, F. (2023). Artificial intelligence and education governance. *Education, Citizenship and Social Justice*, https://doi.org/10.1177/17461979231160674.
Fraser, D. W., Marder, T. J., deBettencourt, L. U., Myers, L. A., Kalymon, K. M., & Harrell, R. M. (2020). Using a mixed-reality environment to train special educators working with students with autism spectrum disorder to implement discrete trial teaching. *Focus on Autism and Other Developmental Disabilities*, *35*(1), 3–14.
Freina, L., & Ott, M. (2015, April). A literature review on immersive virtual reality in education: State of the art and perspectives. In *The international scientific conference elearning and software for education* (Vol. 1, No. 133, pp. 10–1007). Bucharest, Romania.
Gabriele, L., Marocco, D., Bertacchini, F., Pantano, P., & Bilotta, E. (2017). An educational robotics lab to investigate cognitive strategies and to foster learning in an arts and humanities course degree. *International Journal of Online Engineering*, *13*(4).
Gong, X., Wu, Y., Ye, Z., & Liu, X. (2018). Artificial intelligence course design: iSTREAM-based visual cognitive smart vehicles. In *2018 IEEE intelligent vehicles symposium (IV)* (pp. 1731–1735). IEEE.
Human-Centered AI (HAI). (2024). *2024 AI index report*. Stanford University. Retrieved: https://aiindex.stanford.edu/report/
Hutson, J. & Rains, T. (2024). *AI institutional adoption study [data set]*. Lindenwood University.
Hutson, J., Jeevanjee, T., VanderGraaf, V., Lively, J., Weber, J., Weir, G., Arnone, K., Carnes, G., Leary, M., Plate, D., Vosevich, K., Edele, S. (2022 December). Artificial intelligence and the disruption of higher education: Strategies for integrations across disciplines. *Creative Education*, *13*(12), 1–28.

Javornik, A. (2016). 'It's an illusion, but it looks real!' Consumer affective, cognitive and behavioural responses to augmented reality applications. *Journal of Marketing Management*, *32*(9–10), 987–1011.

Kane, G. C., Palmer, D., Phillips, A. N., Kiron, D., & Buckley, N. (2015). Strategy, not technology, drives digital transformation. *MIT Sloan Management Review*. Retrieved July 31, 2024: https://sloanreview.mit.edu/projects/strategy-drives-digital-transformation/

Kane, G. C., Palmer, D., Phillips, A. N., Kiron, D., & Buckley, N. (2020). Accelerating digital innovation inside and out. *MIT Sloan Management Review*. Retrieved July 31, 2024: https://sloanreview.mit.edu/projects/accelerating-digital-innovation-inside-and-out/

Kaplan, A. M., & Haenlein, M. (2010). Users of the world, unite! The challenges and opportunities of social media. *Business Horizons*, *53*(1), 59–68.

Leiner, B. M., Cerf, V. G., Clark, D. D., Kahn, R. E., Kleinrock, L., Lynch, D. C., … & Wolff, S. (2009). A brief history of the Internet. *Computer Communication Review*, *39*(5), 22–31.

Lemon, K. N., & Verhoef, P. C. (2016). Understanding customer experience throughout the customer journey. *Journal of Marketing*, *80*(6), 69–96.

Luckin, R., & Holmes, W. (2016). *Intelligence unleashed: An argument for AI in education*. Pearson.

Manyika, J., Chui, M., Brown, B., Bughin, J., Dobbs, R., Roxburgh, C., & Byers, A. H. (2011). *Big data: The next frontier for innovation, competition, and productivity*. McKinsey Global Institute.

Martin, F., & Bolliger, D. U. (2018). Engagement matters: Student perceptions on the importance of engagement strategies in the online learning environment. *Online Learning*, *22*(1), 205–222.

McAfee, A., Brynjolfsson, E., Davenport, T. H., Patil, D. J., & Barton, D. (2012). Big data: the management revolution. *Harvard business review*, *90*(10), 60–68.

Morris, E. & Hutson, J. (2024). *Teacher appreciation day study [data set]*. Lindenwood University.

Picciano, A. G. (2012). The evolution of big data and learning analytics in American higher education. *Journal of Asynchronous Learning Networks*, *16*(3), 9–20.

Puschmann, T. (2017). Fintech. *Business & Information Systems Engineering*, *59*, 69–76.

Rigby, D. (2014). Online shopping isn't as profitable as you think. *Harvard Business Review*. Retrieved July 31, 2024: https://hbr.org/2014/08/online-shopping-isnt-as-profitable-as-you-think

Riordan, M., & Hoddeson, L. (1997). *Crystal fire: The invention of the transistor and the birth of the information age*. W. W. Norton & Company.

Rodway, P., & Schepman, A. (2023). The impact of adopting AI educational technologies on projected course satisfaction in university students. *Computers and Education: Artificial Intelligence*, *5*, 100150.

Ross, J. W., Beath, C. M., & Mocker, M. (2019). *Designed for digital: How to architect your business for sustained success*. MIT Press.

Selwyn, N. (2016). *Digital technology and the contemporary university: Degrees of digitization*. Routledge.

Team Kissflow (2024). What Are the Steps to Digital Transformation? Retrieved: https://kissflow.com/digital-transformation/steps-to-digital-transformation/#:~:text=1%201.%20Assess%20the%20current%20digital%20state%20of,track%20them%20…%207%207.%20Measure%20the%20progress

Tyson, A. & Kennedy, B. (March 26, 2024). *Many Americans think generative AI programs should credit the sources they rely on. Pew Research Center*. Retrieved: https://www.pewresearch.org/short-reads/2024/03/26/many-americans-think-generative-ai-programs-should-credit-the-sources-they-rely-on/#:~:text=Adults%20with%20higher%20levels%20of%20education%20are%20more,with%20AI%20at%20least%20several%20times%20a%20week

Westerman, G., Bonnet, D., & McAfee, A. (2014). *Leading digital: Turning technology into business transformation*. Harvard Business Review Press.

Wright, L. T., Robin, R., Stone, M., & Aravopoulou, D. E. (2019). Adoption of big data technology for innovation in B2B marketing. *Journal of Business-to-Business Marketing*, *26*(3–4), 281–293.

Xie, H., Chu, H. C., Hwang, G. J., & Wang, C. C. (2019). Trends and development in technology-enhanced adaptive/personalized learning: A systematic review of journal publications from 2007 to 2017. *Computers & Education*, *140*, 103599.

Zhang, K., & Aslan, A. B. (2021). AI technologies for education: Recent research & future directions. *Computers and Education: Artificial Intelligence*, *2*, 100025.

3 Generative Transformation in the Age of Industry 4.0

3.1 Fundamentals of Generative AI

Generative artificial intelligence (GAI) stands at the edge of the digital revolution, presenting both industry and education with unprecedented opportunities to reshape their landscapes through the power of AI-driven creativity and innovation. Unlike conventional AI systems designed primarily for decision-making or predictive analytics based on existing data, GAI pushes the boundary further by producing entirely new content, whether it be text, images, or sounds, that did not previously exist (Feuerriegel et al., 2024; Goodfellow et al., 2014). This capability to generate novel outputs is what sets GAI apart from traditional AI, marking a significant leap in the evolution of these technologies (Khosrowi, Finn, & Clark, 2023).

The distinction between generative AI and traditional AI is fundamentally rooted in their operational frameworks and objectives. Traditional AI systems operate on a deductive approach, analyzing data within set parameters to provide answers, make predictions, or automate tasks (Alzubaidi et al., 2023). In contrast, generative AI employs more complex algorithms, such as generative adversarial networks (GANs) and transformers, to understand and replicate the underlying patterns and structures of the data it is trained on, thereby enabling the creation of new, original outputs that resemble the training data (Goodfellow et al., 2014; Vaswani et al., 2017). This novel capability of GAI opens up a whole host of applications, from designing realistic virtual environments for training simulations to automating creative processes in content creation (Xu et al., 2023).

The latest generative developments in AI operate through a sophisticated blend of technologies and methodologies rooted in machine learning (ML) and deep learning (DL). These subsets of AI facilitate the ability of generative models to learn from vast datasets and generate new data that mimics the original input. ML provides the foundational framework, enabling systems to learn and make decisions from data without being explicitly programmed. DL, a more advanced subset of ML, utilizes neural networks

DOI: 10.4324/9781003512813-3

with many layers (hence "deep") to analyze data patterns with a complexity and abstraction level that mimics human cognitive processes (Alwahedi et al., 2024; LeCun, Bengio, & Hinton, 2015).

Notably, the model training process is central to how GAI functions. It begins with data collection, where diverse and extensive datasets are gathered to train the model. The architecture of the model, which is essentially its design that specifies how data flows and is processed, plays a critical role in determining the model's effectiveness (Roumeliotis & Tselikas, 2023). Training techniques such as supervised, unsupervised, and reinforcement learning dictate how the model learns from the data (Table 3.1). In supervised learning, the model learns from labeled data, making it ideal for tasks where the output is known. Unsupervised learning, on the other hand, deals with unlabeled data, enabling the model to identify patterns and relationships within the data itself (Watson, 2023). Reinforcement learning involves learning to make decisions through trial and error, receiving feedback in the form of rewards or penalties (Goodfellow, Bengio, & Courville, 2016; Shuford, 2024).

Along with methods for training models, other key concepts in GAI include neural networks, GANs, and transformers (Table 3.2). Neural networks, inspired by the structure of the human brain, consist of neurons

Table 3.1 Comparative Overview of Machine Learning Training Techniques

Learning type	*Definition*	*Applications*	*Key characteristics*	*Challenges*
Supervised learning	Learning from labeled datasets to predict outcomes for new data.	Classification, regression tasks.	Model learns mapping from inputs to outputs; relies on labeled data.	Requires comprehensive, high-quality labeled data; risk of overfitting.
Unsupervised learning	Finding patterns or structures in data without labels.	Data clustering, dimensionality reduction.	Identifies similarities among data points or reduces complexity without explicit outcomes.	Interpreting results can be challenging due to lack of labels.
Reinforcement learning	Learning to make decisions by receiving feedback in the form of rewards or penalties.	Game playing, robotics, autonomous systems.	Involves trial and error; agent learns policy to maximize long-term rewards.	Balancing exploration of new actions with exploitation of known rewards; complex environment modeling.

Table 3.2 Overview of Key AI Architectures: Neural Networks, GANs, and Transformers

AI concept	*Description*	*How it works*	*Applications*
Neural networks (NNs)	A series of algorithms modeled after the human brain, designed to recognize patterns and interpret sensory data through machine perception, labeling, and decision-making.	Data is processed through layers of artificial neurons where each layer learns to transform its input data into a slightly more abstract and composite representation.	Image and speech recognition, medical diagnosis, financial forecasting, and many more.
Generative adversarial networks (GANs)	A class of machine learning frameworks where two neural networks contest with each other in a game (generative vs. discriminative) to capture and replicate data distributions.	The generative network generates candidates while the discriminative network evaluates them. Over time, the generator improves its ability to produce realistic data, and the discriminator becomes better at detecting fakes.	Creating realistic images, videos, and voice generation. Enhancing and generating art, photo realistic images, and deepfake content.
Transformers	An architecture for transforming one sequence into another one with the help of two parts (Encoder and Decoder) but does not require sequential data to be processed in order. Uses self-attention mechanisms.	It processes input data all at once, identifying the relevance of each part of the data to other parts and encoding this information in a way that allows for highly effective parallel processing and deep understanding of context.	Natural language processing tasks such as text summarization, translation, and generation. The backbone of models like BERT and GPT for understanding and generating human-like text.

arranged in layers that process and transmit signals. GANs, introduced by Goodfellow et al. (2014), involve two neural networks—the generator and the discriminator—working in tandem to produce highly realistic data. The generator creates data, while the discriminator evaluates its authenticity; through this process, the generator improves its ability to produce increasingly accurate data. Transformers, another critical innovation, have revolutionized natural language processing (NLP) by enabling models to handle sequential data more effectively, thanks to their self-attention mechanisms (Patwardhan, Marrone, & Sansone, 2023; Vaswani et al., 2017).

Perhaps the most widely known example has become nearly synonymous in popular culture with GAI, and that is ChatGPT, or "Chat Generative Pre-Trained Transformer." Developed by OpenAI, the conversational AI model leverages the transformer architecture, a breakthrough in NLP technology to generate text that mimics human conversation (Watters & Lemanski, 2023). Unlike traditional models that process words sequentially, transformers use a self-attention mechanism to process all words in a sentence simultaneously, allowing the model to dynamically focus on different parts of the sentence for a deeper understanding of context and relationships between words (Prasad, Sharmila, & Badrinarayanan, 2023). This architecture enables ChatGPT to predict the next word in a sequence with remarkable accuracy, drawing on a vast dataset of text from various sources to learn linguistic patterns, syntax, and semantics. Positional encoding adds awareness of the order of words, further enhancing the ability of the model to produce coherent and contextually relevant responses (Minaee et al., 2024). As a result, ChatGPT has shown exceptional performance in tasks ranging from answering questions and generating creative content to more complex applications like translation and summarization, illustrating the transformative potential of transformer-based models in advancing AI's natural language capabilities (Devi, Manjula, & Pattewar, 2023).

As the fastest adopted technology in history, gaining one million adopters in one month (February 2023), ChatGPT is most well-known for text generation, but the latest generation of tools are much more versatile, and multimodal (Zhou et al., 2023). In fact, a multitude of models and application programming interfaces (APIs) are continuously being developed, each designed to excel in specific applications ranging from text and image generation to music composition and synthetic data production (Lwakatare, Crnkovic, & Bosch, 2020; Steidl, Felderer, & Ramler, 2023). Eden AI compiles annual lists based on type and use cases, such as the 2024 list here: https://www.edenai.co/post/a-comprehensive-view-of-all-ai-apis These APIs can serve as crucial conduits in the tech ecosystem, enabling disparate software applications to interact seamlessly.

Within this broad category, specialized APIs leverage ML and NLP to facilitate a variety of advanced functions. Computer vision APIs, for example, empower applications to interpret visual data, identifying objects, individuals, and expressions, which opens up avenues for innovative image recognition systems and video analytics platforms. Similarly, speech recognition APIs transform spoken language into actionable data, underpinning the development of voice-activated devices, transcription services, and multilingual support features. Translation APIs, employing sophisticated NLP techniques, automatically convert text across languages, enabling real-time communication and content accessibility on a global scale. Text APIs delve deeper into written language, offering tools for sentiment analysis, entity recognition, and content generation, thus enriching text-based applications with deeper insights and automation. Document parsing APIs blend OCR and NLP to meticulously extract and process data from various documents, streamlining operations in content management and data analysis sectors. Finally, generative APIs represent the frontier of content creation, generating novel text, images, or other media based on specific input datasets, fueling a new wave of personalized and dynamic content generation (Magooda et al., 2023).

Together, these APIs underscore the transformative impact of AI across diverse sectors, from enhancing user interfaces and breaking language barriers to automating complex content creation and data processing tasks. These models underscore the versatility and transformative potential of GAI across various sectors. There are so many, in fact, that it is difficult to keep track of them. As such, Ithaka S+R has developed a Generative AI Product Tracker (https://sr.ithaka.org/our-work/generative-ai-product-tracker/) that compiles both the models and research databases. These include generative text, text-to-image, text-to-video, and synthetic models (Table 3.3).

Generative text models, spearheaded by advancements like OpenAI's GPT series (https://chat.openai.com/), have significantly transformed the field of NLP and DL. These models leverage sophisticated DL methodologies and are trained on vast datasets, enabling them to produce text that remarkably resembles human writing. A prime example of their potential is GPT-4 Turbo, which showcases the profound capabilities of these models by generating coherent, contextually appropriate text across a wide array of

Table 3.3 Overview of Generative AI Models: Text, Image, and Audio Applications

Model type	*Examples*	*Primary function/use case*
Generative text models	GPT-4 Turbo, Google's Gemini, Anthropic's Claude, Meta's Llama	Generating human-like text for diverse applications such as chatbots, article drafting, story creation, and code generation.
Image generation models	DALL-E, Midjourney, Stable Diffusion, Adobe's Firefly	Creating detailed, novel images from textual prompts for use in art, design, and digital marketing.
Music and audio generation models	AudioCraft (Meta AI), MusicGen, MuseNet	Producing music and sound effects based on text descriptions or auditory inputs, enhancing creative processes in music production and sound design.

applications. Whether creating realistic dialogue for chatbots and virtual assistants, drafting detailed articles, weaving captivating stories, or even developing functional code, the adaptability and efficiency of GPT-4 Turbo have markedly propelled the automation of content creation.

The domain of generative text models is not limited to GPT-4 Turbo but includes several significant contributions from major technology firms, each offering unique benefits to the advancement of generative AI in text creation. Among these are Google's Gemini, Anthropic's Claude (https://claude.ai/chats), and Meta's Llama (https://llama.meta.com/), each marking a milestone in the evolution of text generation technologies. Google Gemini stands out with its robust capacity to comprehend and generate language, capitalizing on Google's extensive data repositories. Its adeptness at interpreting and responding to complex queries showcases its potential to refine search algorithms and deliver nuanced user responses. Anthropic's Claude differentiates itself by emphasizing ethical AI development and safety protocols. Aimed at producing text that is not only contextually coherent but also ethically sound, Claude seeks to mitigate the risks of generating misleading or harmful content, prioritizing responsible AI utilization. Finally, Meta's Llama, distinguished by its open-source availability, offers the research and developer community widespread access to cutting-edge generative text model technology. This approach to democratizing powerful AI tools encourages a collective effort in pushing the boundaries of NLP technology, promoting innovation and collaboration within the field.

Image generation models represent a pivotal advancement in the intersection of AI and creative expression, showcasing extraordinary abilities in producing detailed, novel images from textual prompts (Hutson et al., 2023). Among these, DALL-E (https://openai.com/dall-e-2/) by OpenAI stands as a prime example, utilizing a variant of the GPT architecture to adeptly comprehend and transform intricate text descriptions into striking visual creations. This model's application extends significantly across creative industries, unlocking novel pathways for the generation of conceptual art, innovative graphic design, and enriched visual content tailored for digital marketing initiatives. However, DALL-E is just one of dozens of available generative tools for visual imagery.

Expanding beyond DALL-E, the landscape of image generation models is further enriched by contributions such as Midjourney (https://www.midjourney.com/), Stable Diffusion (https://stability.ai/news/stable-diffusion-3), and Adobe's Firefly (https://www.adobe.com/products/firefly.html), each bringing distinct capabilities to the forefront of generative art and design. Midjourney introduces an intuitive, research-driven approach to image creation, focusing on producing highly artistic and stylistically varied imagery. Its unique algorithm allows for the exploration of creative concepts with remarkable depth and nuance, though requires using the social media

Discord platform to access. Stable Diffusion, on the other hand, emphasizes accessibility and customization, enabling users to craft detailed images with fine control over the generation process. This model stands out for its flexibility and the ease with which it can be adapted to specific creative needs, making high-quality image generation more attainable for a broader audience.

At the same time, the swift adoption of AI-driven tools by the general public has prompted a considerable backlash from traditionally trained artists and designers, who have expressed concerns over copyright infringement and raised questions about the legitimacy of AI-generated art as a distinct genre (Ansari, 2022;). In response to these legal concerns, companies are finding solutions through agreements with organizations with large datasets. For instance, Adobe's Firefly integrates seamlessly into the professional creative workflow using Adobe Stock images, openly licensed content, and out-of-copyright content, making creations commercially safe. It is designed to generate high-fidelity, customizable images that adhere to the standards of the company for quality and utility. Firefly caters specifically to the needs of professional graphic designers and digital artists, providing a powerful tool for enhancing productivity and creative expression within the Adobe ecosystem (Haze, 2023). Together, these image-making models represent new types of digital creativity, offering artists, designers, and marketers unprecedented tools to realize their visions in increasingly innovative and efficient ways.

Along with text and image, moreover, tools have also emerged in the realm of music and audio generation. These models not only showcase the abilities of generative AI but also offer new possibilities for artists, producers, and the entertainment industry at large. For instance, AudioCraft by Meta AI (https://ai.meta.com/resources/models-and-libraries/audiocraft/) is a comprehensive platform for generative audio needs, including music and sound effects, and encompasses models like MusicGen and AudioGen, which generate music and audio from text-based inputs, respectively. This platform signifies developments in interactive AI systems, facilitating an easy and natural co-creation process between humans and AI models. MusicGen specifically shines in its ability to produce music conditioned on textual or melodic inputs, showcasing the versatility of AI in interpreting and translating complex descriptions into rich, auditory experiences.

On the other hand, MusicGen (https://huggingface.co/docs/transformers/en/model_doc/musicgen), accessible via Hugging Face, represents a simplification in the design of generative models for audio. As an auto-regressive Transformer model, it efficiently models audio sequences, capturing the intricacies of music through a unique token interleaving pattern. This approach enables the generation of high-quality audio by learning discrete audio tokens from raw waveforms, demonstrating the model's capability to bridge textual or auditory prompts with compelling musical outputs.

The opposite is true of MuseNet by OpenAI (https://openai.com/research/musenet) is a notable example of the AI's ability to generate complex musical compositions spanning various styles and instruments. Capable of producing four-minute pieces that blend genres ranging from classical to pop, MuseNet leverages unsupervised learning to identify patterns of harmony, rhythm, and style across a vast dataset of MIDI files. This model showcases the potential of generative AI to create new music that transcends traditional boundaries, offering tools for both musicians and non-musicians to explore novel musical landscapes.

These models, each with their unique focus, collectively advance the field of AI-driven music and audio generation. Whether through creating music and sound effects from textual descriptions, simplifying the music generation process, or blending diverse musical styles and instruments, they offer glimpses into a future where AI plays a central role in the creative processes of the music industry. The implications of these advancements extend beyond just new tools for creators, suggesting new ways of interacting with and experiencing music and sound, powered by the ever-evolving capabilities of artificial intelligence (Liu, 2023).

Synthetic data generation models have profoundly impacted a wide array of industries by addressing data scarcity, privacy concerns, and biases in ML training datasets (Joshi et al., 2024). In the realm of manufacturing, synthetic data is being utilized to create realistic artificial datasets for consumer product groups, facilitating scenario testing for supply chains and enhancing automation, particularly in robotics, to adapt to varying conditions like lighting and environments (Buggineni, 2023). Healthcare and life sciences have also greatly benefited, with generative neural networks enabling the recreation of complex genomic sequences. This advancement allows for safer sharing of patient health data while maintaining privacy, thereby accelerating collaborative research without compromising patient confidentiality (Chafai et al., 2023). Automotive and robotics industries leverage synthetic data to train self-driving car software and robots in simulated environments, significantly improving safety and crash prevention technologies through more diverse training data (Birchler et al., 2023).

Furthermore, advancements in synthetic data generation have been led by methods such as agent-based modeling and generative models, including LLMs (Niu, Zhang, & Zhao, 2024). These techniques have facilitated the generation of synthetic text, images, and tabular data that closely mimic real-world data, thereby enhancing the development and efficiency of AI models across various applications (Hassani & Silva, 2023). For example, Amazon's Alexa AI team utilizes synthetic data to train its natural language understanding systems for new languages without sufficient customer interaction data, showcasing the versatility of synthetic datasets in overcoming the challenges of data scarcity (Antonius et al., 2023). Similarly, Waymo and other automotive companies generate synthetic driving datasets to train autonomous vehicle systems, offering an efficient solution for including complex and varied scenarios in training data without the need for extensive real-world observation (Talwar et al., 2020).

3.2 Future Trends: The Trajectory of Generative AI

The future of AI-driven multimodal platforms like ChatGPT-4 Turbo, Google Gemini Advanced, and Microsoft Co-Pilot signifies a leap toward more integrated, secure, and versatile digital environments. These platforms are not just enhancing user experiences across various applications but are also emphasizing the importance of data privacy and security through innovative measures. Microsoft Co-Pilot, for example, showcases the integration of OpenAI's GPT-4 Turbo, offering users an advanced level of AI capabilities across Microsoft 365 applications such as Word, Excel, PowerPoint, Outlook, and OneNote. This integration promises to supercharge productivity and creativity for both personal and organizational use, ensuring a seamless AI experience across devices. The introduction of Copilot Pro and its expansion to businesses of all sizes underline Microsoft's commitment to making AI more accessible while prioritizing security, privacy, and compliance. The enterprise-grade security features highlight the proactive measures being taken to address concerns over proprietary data potentially being leaked through public models.

Furthermore, Microsoft's strategy includes semantic overlays as part of their Copilot offerings, a sophisticated approach aimed at enhancing understanding and generating more relevant responses by leveraging vast amounts of data from Bing image search and web search. This multimodal approach with search grounding demonstrates an innovative step toward maintaining data integrity and user trust by improving the AI's comprehension capabilities without compromising privacy. As we move forward, the emphasis on building AI models that are not only powerful and versatile but also secure and privacy-conscious will be crucial in addressing the evolving landscape of digital privacy and security. The advancements seen in these multimodal examples pave the way for a future where AI can assist in a range of tasks while ensuring that users' data remains protected.

At the same time, the adoption of generative AI models represents a pivotal shift in how institutions approach data analysis, content creation, and operational efficiency. Initially, leveraging existing models like OpenAI's GPT series has been a transformative first step for many organizations, enabling them to harness advanced AI capabilities without the need for extensive ML expertise. These models have been instrumental in generating human-like text, creating realistic images, and producing complex musical compositions, marking the dawn of a generative transformation across various sectors.

However, the future trajectory points toward institutions not just adopting but creating their own custom models tailored to specific tasks and needs. Microsoft Azure AI Studio emerges as a key platform in this evolution, offering a unified environment for building, deploying, and managing generative AI applications and custom copilots. Azure AI Studio provides access to a comprehensive model catalog, including state-of-the-art models from OpenAI, Meta, NVIDIA, and Microsoft Research, along with hundreds of open-source models (Wan & Chen, 2023). This enables organizations to ground their models with their own data, enhancing the relevance and effectiveness of AI applications.

Moreover, Azure AI Studio simplifies the entire development lifecycle, from prompt engineering and model integration to deployment and monitoring, facilitating the creation of multimodal applications that leverage language, vision, and speech. With built-in tools for evaluating AI applications for quality and safety and a focus on responsible AI, Azure AI Studio ensures that custom AI solutions adhere to the highest standards of security and compliance (Gao et al., 2023). In essence, as institutions progress from utilizing pre-built generative models to crafting their bespoke versions, platforms like Azure AI Studio are set to play a crucial role. They not only democratize access to advanced AI capabilities but also empower organizations to innovate with AI solutions that are deeply integrated with their unique operational contexts, setting the stage for a more personalized and efficient use of AI technology in the enterprise domain.

But available models alone will not allow organizations to take advantage of this significant milestone in technological evolution. Other milestones GAI is compared to include historical innovations like the steam engine and electricity, which drastically transformed societal operations. This comparison suggests that GAI is poised to fundamentally alter how businesses generate value, how work is conducted, and how daily life is experienced. Amidst this transformative potential, the urgency for businesses to move away from legacy systems and embrace new methodologies is highlighted, emphasizing a departure from the "burning platform" mentality toward a culture of innovation (Mattila, Yrjölä, & Hautamäki, 2021). The "burning platform" mentality refers to a crisis-driven approach to organizational change, where the perceived threat of not changing outweighs the risks associated with implementing new strategies or technologies. It stems from a dramatic incident on an offshore oil platform, symbolizing a critical point where staying in the current state is more dangerous than making a leap into the unknown. However, as GAI has exposed, leading through fear may inhibit innovation and risk-taking, advocating instead for creating a supportive environment that encourages experimentation and learning from failure.

As such, the successful integration of GAI into organizational practices hinges on the ability to foster a culture where innovation is not just encouraged but celebrated, even when it leads to failure. This approach, termed the

"Prototyping Effect," advocates for a model of incremental changes and learning from a wide array of ideas, championing a safe environment for experimentation (West & Dedrick, 1996). Such an environment is crucial for the adoption of GAI, as it allows teams to navigate the complexities of implementing new technologies without the fear of failure. Furthermore, the role of strategic leadership in navigating the AI landscape cannot be overstated. Leaders have been tasked with embedding AI into the very fabric of organizational culture, ensuring a broad understanding of its capabilities and ethical implications across all levels of staff (Roy et al., 2023). This broad understanding across technical and non-technical employees alike is crucial for leveraging AI to solve fundamental business problems and for creating a positive organizational culture around AI technology. Ethical considerations and societal impacts also form a significant theme in the discourse on GAI. The technology's potential to augment human efforts, rather than replace jobs, presents an optimistic future where AI assists in automating tedious tasks, thereby enhancing human efficiency. However, this optimistic future is contingent upon ethical AI development and application, stressing the importance of diversity within AI development teams to ensure the technology is empathetic and understanding of human emotions.

The urgency for businesses to adopt AI technologies has never been more critical, with the pace of adoption moving at an unprecedented speed, surpassing even the rapid advancements predicted by Moore's Law. According to research by Ho et al. (2024), the efficiency of algorithms for pre-training language models has seen compute requirements halve roughly every eight months—a rate significantly faster than the hardware improvements traditionally anticipated by Moore's Law. This acceleration in algorithmic progress, highlighted through a comprehensive analysis of over 200 language model evaluations from 2012 to 2023, underscores the critical window for companies to become early adopters of AI. Those who seize this opportunity are poised to gain significant market advantages, achieving greater efficiency and lower operational costs.

The essence of successfully integrating Generative AI into business practices hinges on a multifaceted strategy. This strategy not only involves adopting a culture of innovation and strategic leadership but also prioritizes ethical considerations and a proactive approach to technology adoption. Companies are advised to aim for quick wins in AI projects, building momentum for more extensive initiatives. The rapid advancements in algorithmic progress, as detailed by Ho et al. (2024), serve as a compelling call to action. Organizations that engage with these technologies are not merely updating their operational tools; they are actively participating in a broader societal transformation, driven by the rapid evolution of AI (Davenport & Mittal, 2023). This transformative period represents a pivotal point in technological history, where the acceleration of algorithmic advancements demands prompt and thoughtful engagement from the business community.

3.3 Readiness and Resilience: Tools for Assessment

Implementing generative tools and platforms within an organization presents both a significant opportunity and a formidable challenge. Insights gleaned from numerous interactions with companies and professional groups for this study underscore the complexity of this journey. A key takeaway is the critical role of leadership in spearheading AI initiatives and fostering an organizational culture conducive to innovation (Delhi et al., 2024). However, leadership alone is not enough; the involvement of associates in validating business use cases is crucial (Basole, Park, & Seuss, 2024). Legal and IT departments also play pivotal roles in ensuring the responsible and secure use of GenAI, though some organizations are still in the preliminary stages of policy development and security enhancement (Humayun et al., 2024). As well, there is a growing trend toward the creation of AI advisory boards.

There are few (if any) organizations that do not currently believe AI is a priority for themselves and their industries, but what strategy to take is unclear. The urgency can be seen in the strategic shift in the allocation of resources for GAI initiatives, with some companies planning budgets for 2024, despite the lack of funding in 2023 (Hjaltalin & Sigurdarson, 2024; Mohite et al., 2024). This foresight contrasts with the surprising revelation that a significant portion of company associates and professional group members and key decision makers have not yet engaged with these technologies themselves (Heath, 2024). This gap suggests an untapped potential for education and hands-on experience in industry, underscoring the importance of professional groups in raising awareness about the potential benefits.

Such potential, however, has been hampered by the rapid advancement of AI technologies and the proliferation of tools with integrated GAI capabilities contribute to a "massive swirl of noise." Where should decision makers put their efforts and give their attention? There are so many use cases and proliferation of API that determining a strategy is daunting, to say the least. The first step then is to step back and look at the situation holistically, take inventory of capabilities and capacities, review the institution's mission and vision, and consider where industry is moving. Whether in industry or education, this entails considering the evolution of careers, essential skills, and likely potential futures.

Pre-pandemic and generative AI, Lesgold (2019) had called for a radical rethinking of educational curricula and the evolution of education systems in response to the technological disruptions that defined the era. The observation that education has remained largely unchanged for 75 years, adhering to an official curriculum focused on punctuality, obedience, and task completion, mirrors the requirements of a bygone industrial age, Lesgold argues.

This traditional model, premised on front-loading students with skills and knowledge for lifelong careers, is increasingly at odds with the dynamic nature of work in the age of AI (Poquet & De Laat, 2021). Instead, a new educational paradigm emphasizes the assembly of just-in-time teams capable of tackling emergent problems through collaboration, quick learning, and adaptation. This approach, supported by research from Weise (2020) and Detweiler (2021), underscores the importance of durable skills such as socioemotional abilities, civic participation, critical evaluation of information, and financial literacy, alongside a foundational knowledge in reading, mathematics, and science.

Furthermore, the historical pattern of disruptions leading to short-term economic upheaval but eventual higher standards of living and new job creation provides a compelling reason for this educational shift (Arthi & Parman, 2021). As cognitive work has become more valued over physical labor due to automation, the need for skills that cannot be easily replicated by machines has become paramount. The advent of AI and computing technologies further accelerates this trend, transforming traditional roles and creating a demand for new kinds of intelligent job aids (Ciccarelli, Papetti, & Germani, 2023). As Lesgold argues,

> Anyone with a job for which there are standard education and training paths (such as job-specific community college programs) can expect that the more secure and lucrative that job seems, the more likely that it will be taken over eventually by smart machines (2019, p. 17).

Therefore, the future of various professions and industries will require adaptability, collaboration, and continual learning as the cornerstones of societal and professional success. This ongoing evolution anticipates a range of potential futures, from the displacement of jobs leading to government-supported guaranteed incomes to the necessity for individuals to invent new roles in a landscape where job security is redefined by technological advancements (Table 3.4).

The rapid development of AI technologies offers both opportunities and challenges. For Generation Alpha (also called Gen AI) and subsequent generations, the ability to continually adapt to an unpredictable world becomes crucial (O'Farrell & Weaver, 2024). Jobs that require strong interpersonal skills, the application of mathematics to business problems, and roles in human health and environmental sciences are predicted to thrive amidst the rise of smart machines. These insights underscore the importance of preparing students not just in technical skills but in the "four Cs"—*critical thinking, communication, collaboration*, and *creativity*—augmented by the ability to quickly retool for different jobs, associate well with others, and navigate life's disruptions (Thornhill-Miller et al., 2023). Lesgold warns of the

Table 3.4 Navigating the Future: Adapting to an AI-Driven World (Lesgold, 2019)

Potential futures	*Areas to thrive in the age of smart machines*	*Educational imperatives*
1 **Machines displace middle and some upper-class jobs,** leading to government-provided guaranteed income during times of disruption.	**People with strong interpersonal skills** (e.g., CEOs, school psychologists, social work teachers, supervisors of trades).	**Prepare students with the four Cs**: critical thinking, communication, collaboration, and creativity.
2 **Machines displace most current jobs**, but humans invent new jobs to preserve the notion of employment. Finances become less predictable without standard work life, necessitating self-regulated finances.	**Jobs relying on applying math to business problems** (e.g., economics).	**Teach skills and dispositions** for quick retooling for different jobs.
3 **For Generation Alpha and the next generation**, the future becomes unpredictable, requiring continual adaptation to a changing world.	**Human health-related jobs** (e.g., allergists, immunologists, microbiologists). **Jobs that manage the physical world** (e.g., engineers, environmental scientists).	**Foster the ability to associate** well with others and to be hired for personal services. Equip students to handle life with periodic disruptions of routine and income.

automation potential for jobs with standard education and training paths, suggesting that the more formulaic a job, the easier it is to automate. This realization prompts a need for educational systems (and industry training programs) to evolve beyond traditional curricula, incorporating lessons that foster durable skills for an AI-driven future.

Once an organization has momentum and is looking forward to generative transformation, developing a framework and identifying tools to assess in decision-making is key (Table 3.5). This approach should start with a robust SWOT (Strengths, Weaknesses, Opportunities, and Threats) analysis, which serves as a foundational framework to evaluate internal capabilities against external opportunities and threats. Such an analysis not only sheds

Table 3.5 Comprehensive Approach to Assessing Technological Adoptions

Assessment tool	*Purpose and application*
SWOT analysis	To evaluate internal capabilities and external opportunities and threats, identifying areas of strength and potential for strategic positioning in the face of technological advancements.
Capability maturity models (CMMs)	To gauge the current operational readiness and maturity level of processes and systems related to IT infrastructure and data management, guiding steps to elevate capabilities.
Gap analysis	To pinpoint specific areas requiring enhancements to bridge the gap between the current and desired states of technology adoption.
Resource inventory applications	To provide an overview of available technological assets, human resources, and financial reserves, aiding in effective resource leveraging and investment planning.
Stakeholder analysis	To map out the needs, expectations, and potential resistances of different groups impacted by technological adoption, ensuring inclusive and responsive strategy development.
Benchmarking software	To compare institutional performance against industry standards or peers, identifying competitive advantages and areas needing improvement.
Financial analysis tools	To evaluate the potential return on investment and financial viability of new technology integrations, informing strategic financial planning.

light on existing strengths and areas for improvement but also pinpoints where the institution can strategically position itself in the face of technological advancements. Following this, employing Capability Maturity Models (CMMs) offers insights into the current operational readiness and the maturity level of processes and systems related to IT infrastructure and data management. Understanding where an institution stands in terms of maturity helps identify necessary steps to elevate capabilities to adequately support new technological integrations.

The EDUCAUSE Higher Education Generative AI Readiness Assessment (2024) provides an invaluable tool for educational institutions to gauge their preparedness for implementing AI strategies and technologies. This comprehensive assessment guides through a variety of pivotal areas, including strategy and governance, ethical use, application, and overall institutional resilience. Among the key takeaways, the assessment underscores the necessity of strategic alignment and engagement across all institutional levels—from executive leadership to technology and academic leaders, and importantly, students, faculty, and staff. The inclusion of various stakeholders in the development of AI strategies is crucial for fostering a holistic approach to AI integration, ensuring that initiatives are well-rounded and considerate of the entire institutional ecosystem. Furthermore, the assessment stresses the importance of having a robust IT governance framework that supports strategic investment decisions and accommodates the fast-evolving nature of AI technology, highlighting the need for agility, flexibility, and comprehensive stakeholder involvement in governance processes.

Additionally, the readiness assessment highlights critical aspects of AI implementation, such as the ethical use of AI, capacity for change, and the development of AI literacy across the institution. It brings to light the significant need for educational institutions to develop clear criteria and processes for evaluating and approving AI use cases, ensuring they align with the institution's strategic priorities and ethical standards. The assessment also emphasizes the importance of preparing the institutional leadership to swiftly adapt to technological advancements and drive changes across various domains, including pedagogy, operations, and workforce development. By documenting and evaluating the current state of AI readiness and fostering discussions around potential enhancements, institutions can better prepare themselves to integrate AI effectively, addressing both the opportunities and challenges it presents.

A gap analysis further complements this evaluation by pinpointing the specific areas—be it in skills, systems, or processes—where enhancements are needed to bridge the gap between the current and desired states of technology adoption. This analysis is critical for setting actionable strategies for technology integration. Equally important is the utilization of resource inventory applications, which provide a comprehensive overview of available technological assets, human resources, and financial reserves. Such tools are indispensable for planning, as they help in leveraging existing resources effectively and determining areas requiring additional investment.

In parallel, stakeholder analysis is vital for mapping out the needs, expectations, and potential resistances across different groups impacted by the technological adoption. This analysis ensures that the strategy for introducing new technologies is inclusive, addressing the concerns and leveraging the insights of all stakeholders involved. Benchmarking against industry standards or peers through dedicated software enables institutions to identify their competitive edge as well as areas lagging behind, guiding targeted improvements. Additionally, financial analysis tools are crucial for evaluating the potential return on investment (ROI), providing a clear picture of the financial viability and impact of adopting new technologies.

In synthesizing insights from these varied tools and analyses, institutions are better equipped to make informed decisions about technology adoption. This not only aligns with their strategic objectives but also positions them advantageously in an increasingly competitive and technologically driven landscape. The essence of this process is not merely in adopting new technologies but in fostering a culture of continuous learning, adaptation, and innovation that resonates with the broader goals of the institution.

Therefore, the concept of digital transformation is not merely a continuation but a profound evolution, necessitating new marketing strategies, adoption practices, and organizational agility. The advent of tools allowing for rapid deployment and scalability challenges traditional approaches, emphasizing the need for quicker, more flexible decision-making processes. The shift toward dynamic subscription models and the reliance on smaller, potentially transient tech companies for innovative solutions highlight the need for agility not only in technology adoption but also in administrative and operational practices.

3.4 Economic Aspects: Investments and Returns

The economic landscape of GAI adoption presents a compelling narrative of shifting paradigms in assessing investments and returns. Traditionally, the quantification of GAI's ROI has been anchored in its ability to drive productivity gains and enhance process efficiencies. Metrics such as workload reduction, workflow optimization, and time saved on tasks have been the primary indicators for evaluating the worthiness of integrating GAI solutions within organizational frameworks. These metrics serve as tangible benchmarks for organizations to predict the immediate value brought by GAI technologies (Gusain et al., 2023; Horodyski, 2023; Nawaz et al., 2024; Rathore, 2023; Shaik, 2023).

The statistics associated with time savings, speed, and efficiencies of AI across industries reveal significant impacts on productivity and operational processes. For instance, in the realm of software engineering, the deployment of generative AI has the potential to enhance productivity by reducing the time spent on tasks like generating initial code drafts and code correction. A specific study found that software developers using tools like GitHub Copilot completed tasks 56% faster than those not using such AI assistance (Dakhel et al., 2023). In broader industry applications, generative AI is making strides in research and development (R&D), offering productivity gains potentially accounting for 10–15% of overall R&D costs (Babina et al., 2024). This is particularly notable in the life sciences and chemical industries, where AI is accelerating the development of new drugs and materials through generative design (Gutierrez et al., 2023; Hajkowicz et al., 2023; Lu et al., 2023). Moreover, the application in sales and customer service illustrates its capacity to enhance efficiency and customer interactions. Despite a skills gap that may hinder adoption, those who have utilized generative AI report it has helped increase sales by improving customer interaction speed. In customer service, the technology is applied to automate and personalize communications, significantly enhancing service delivery and customer satisfaction (Cao et al., 2024; Wang et al., 2023).

These findings underscore the transformative potential of GAI in driving efficiencies and accelerating tasks across various sectors, however, recent research has broadened the scope of considerations. The value proposition, in fact, extends beyond mere efficiency and productivity. The innovative insights unlocked by GAI, attributed to its capability to process and analyze vast datasets, emerge as critical factors in the decision-making process regarding the adoption of GAI tools and platforms. This expanded view encourages organizations to consider not only the direct impact on operational metrics but also the strategic advantages of harnessing GAI for deeper, data-driven insights (Apell & Eriksson, 2023).

As a catalyst for innovation, the technology aids in decision-making processes, and creativity, fundamentally altering various the operational landscapes of industries. This technology not only aids in the generation of new ideas by making connections between seemingly unrelated concepts but also changes the way creative work is approached. Text and image generators like GPT-3 and DALL-E, for instance, have already transformed content creation processes by providing initial drafts for a wide range of outputs, from text to imagery, thus expediting and diversifying creative output for rapid prototyping (Bilgram & Laarmann, 2023; Kadaruddin, 2023). But new multimodal capabilities have further accelerated the ability to harness innovation within creative verticals, moving from code generation to imagery to writing copy back to data analytics (Pierre et al., 2023). Moreover, the innovation process itself has been redefined. Businesses now leverage it to not just enhance product designs and accelerate research but also to streamline business processes and improve customer services, ultimately driving market innovation (Poland, Sharad, & Wigen-Toccalino, 2024). Its role extends beyond mere task automation to generating strategic insights, enabling companies to rapidly iterate on ideas and explore various future scenarios, thereby enhancing both productivity and creative output (Doron et al., 2023).

The timeline for adoption and the corresponding investments in professional development are also influenced by this broader perspective. As organizations deliberate on integrating GAI into their ecosystems, the potential for transformative insights and the capacity for data-driven innovation become pivotal considerations. This shift underscores the importance of not only equipping teams with the necessary tools but also investing in their ability to leverage the tools for competitive advantage. As such, the economic aspects of adoption are evolving from a narrow focus on operational efficiencies to a more holistic view that includes the strategic value of insights and innovation. As such, organizations are encouraged to recalibrate their investment strategies, considering both the immediate and long-term benefits of GAI, encompassing productivity gains, process enhancements, and the unlocking of innovative potential through advanced data analysis.

The economic aspects of implementing the implementation plan within an organization encompass a series of critical steps, beginning with a comprehensive needs assessment (previously discussed). This initial phase is vital for identifying specific organizational gaps and opportunities where GAI can offer significant advantages. It involves a detailed evaluation of current operational inefficiencies, potential areas for innovation, and alignment with long-term strategic goals. By understanding these needs, organizations can better navigate the vast landscape of GAI technologies and pinpoint solutions that offer the most value.

Following the needs assessment, the next crucial step is conducting a market analysis of available solutions. This process entails a thorough examination of the current GAI technology landscape, comparing different tools and platforms based on their capabilities, costs, implementation complexity, and alignment with the identified needs. Market analysis also includes assessing vendor reputation, technology maturity, scalability options, and the potential for integration with existing systems. This stage is critical for making informed decisions about which GAI solutions to pursue, ensuring that investments are both strategic and conducive to achieving desired outcomes.

Investment in GAI technology should be viewed not just as a financial commitment but as an investment in future capabilities and competitive edge. The returns from GAI adoption can be manifold, including enhanced operational efficiencies, accelerated product development cycles, improved customer experiences, and the creation of new revenue streams. However, realizing these returns requires careful planning, including the allocation of resources for professional development and the establishment of metrics to track performance improvements and ROI. The decision-making process must also consider the broader economic implications of GAI adoption, such as its impact on workforce dynamics and the potential for generating intellectual property (IP). Organizations should be prepared for an iterative process of implementation, learning, and adaptation as they integrate GAI technologies into their operations.

Given the complexity of choosing the right solutions for higher education and industry, a market analysis highlights various offerings, showcasing how companies like Microsoft, OpenAI, Anthropic, Google, Cohere, and potential open-source options hosted on AWS are shaping the landscape.

Microsoft's Higher Education Solutions focus on student engagement, operational transformation, and ensuring a secure, connected campus. Offering targeted solutions for various educational stakeholders, Microsoft emphasizes AI and ML with tools designed to support reading fluency, enhance teaching with AI training, and streamline administrative tasks with generative AI capabilities like Copilot in Bing.

OpenAI distinguishes itself with versatile tools like ChatGPT and collaborations, such as with Khan Academy, to integrate GPT-4 into educational tools. OpenAI's solutions aim to personalize learning experiences and enhance student support, demonstrating significant potential in improving efficiency and facilitating dynamic learning environments.

Anthropic focuses on AI safety and reliability, creating systems like Claude, a conversational assistant. Although specifics for higher education are less detailed, Anthropic's commitment to safe and steerable AI systems suggests potential applications in student support and administrative automation, prioritizing secure and responsible AI deployment.

Google's Gemini, developed by DeepMind, represents a significant advancement with its multimodal capabilities, understanding a range of information types. Optimized in versions tailored for different tasks, Gemini demonstrates Google's investment in creating highly capable AI models for varied applications, including education.

Cohere, with its recent funding boost, focuses on providing AI models for enterprises through an API, allowing flexibility in cloud provider choice to enhance data privacy. Specializing in text generation and offering scalability and customization, Cohere's models hold promise for enterprise-level educational applications.

AWS and Open-Source Options like Meta's Llama 2 and Mistral's models offer foundational AI capabilities through services like Amazon's Bedrock. These services provide access to a variety of foundation models, enabling customization and integration for specific educational needs, from chatbots to content creation.

The market analysis underscores the importance of a strategic approach to adopting GAI technologies within various institutions. For such a critical undertaking, a broad spectrum of stakeholders should be involved in the decision-making process. This includes not just IT professionals, such as the CIO and CTO, and educational technology specialists but also faculty members, administrators, students for education, and potentially external partners for industry who understand the nuances of the landscape and the evolving AI ecosystem. These diverse perspectives can ensure that the selected solutions align with the institution's goals, operational needs, and long-term vision.

In evaluating the myriad of AI options, decision-makers must consider several key factors. For education, these include the potential impact on student learning experiences and outcomes, the ability to streamline administrative processes, and the ways in which AI can facilitate more personalized and engaging educational pathways. Furthermore, considerations around data privacy, security, and ethical use of AI are paramount. The chosen AI solutions should not only advance educational and operational efficiency but also adhere to the highest standards of data stewardship and ethical practice. Moreover, the adoption of these technologies necessitates an assessment of the current technological infrastructure and readiness of the institution to integrate and scale these solutions. This includes evaluating existing digital platforms, network capabilities, and the need for professional development among faculty and staff to effectively leverage AI tools in their work.

The process of integrating GAI is not merely about deploying new technologies but about fostering a culture of innovation, continuous learning, and adaptation. As institutions navigate this path, they must remain agile and open to evolving their strategies in response to new insights and developments in the AI field. The goal is to enhance the educational ecosystem in a way that prepares students for the future, enriches the teaching and learning experience, and optimizes institutional operations. In all, the adoption of GAI represents a significant opportunity to transform institutional practices and outcomes. By involving a wide range of stakeholders in a thoughtful market analysis and considering the broad implications of AI adoption, institutions can position themselves to make informed, strategic decisions that propel them forward in an increasingly AI-driven world.

References

Alwahedi, F., Aldhaheri, A., Ferrag, M. A., Battah, A., & Tihanyi, N. (2024). Machine learning techniques for IoT security: Current research and future vision with generative AI and large language models. *Internet of Things and Cyber-Physical Systems*, *4*, 167–185.

Alzubaidi, L., Bai, J., Al-Sabaawi, A., Santamaría, J., Albahri, A. S., Al-dabbagh, B. S. N., … & Gu, Y. (2023). A survey on deep learning tools dealing with data scarcity: Definitions, challenges, solutions, tips, and applications. *Journal of Big Data*, *10*(1), 46.

Ansari, T. (2022). How AI transformed the art world in 2022. *Analytics India Magazine (AIM)*. https://analyticsindiamag.com/how-ai-transformed-the-art-world-in-2022/ Accessed 30 October.

Antonius, F., Alapati, P. R., Ritonga, M., Patra, I., El-Ebiary, Y. A. B., Orosoo, M., & Rengarajan, M. (2023). Incorporating natural language processing into virtual assistants: An intelligent assessment strategy for enhancing language comprehension. *International Journal of Advanced Computer Science and Applications*, *14*(10). http://dx.doi.org/10.14569/IJACSA.2023.0141079

Apell, P., & Eriksson, H. (2023). Artificial intelligence (AI) healthcare technology innovations: The current state and challenges from a life science industry perspective. *Technology Analysis & Strategic Management*, *35*(2), 179–193.

Arthi, V., & Parman, J. (2021). Disease, downturns, and wellbeing: Economic history and the long-run impacts of COVID-19. *Explorations in Economic History*, *79*, 101381.

Babina, T., Fedyk, A., He, A., & Hodson, J. (2024). Artificial intelligence, firm growth, and product innovation. *Journal of Financial Economics*, *151*, 103745.

Basole, R. C., Park, H., & Seuss, C. D. (2024). Complex business ecosystem intelligence using AI-powered visual analytics. *Decision Support Systems*, *178*, 114133.

Bilgram, V., & Laarmann, F. (2023). Accelerating innovation with generative AI: AI-augmented digital prototyping and innovation methods. *IEEE Engineering Management Review*, *51*(2), 18–25.

Birchler, C., Khatiri, S., Bosshard, B., Gambi, A., & Panichella, S. (2023). Machine learning-based test selection for simulation-based testing of self-driving cars software. *Empirical Software Engineering*, *28*(3), 71.

Buggineni, V. (2023). *Utilizing synthetic data generation techniques to improve the availability of data in discrete manufacturing for AI applications: A review and framework*. (Dissertation) University of Georgia.

Cao, L., Sarkar, S., Ramesh, B., Mohan, K., & Park, E. H. (2024). Shift of ambidexterity modes: An empirical investigation of the impact of artificial intelligence in customer service. *International Journal of Information Management*, *76*, 102773.

Chafai, N., Bonizzi, L., Botti, S., & Badaoui, B. (2023). Emerging applications of machine learning in genomic medicine and healthcare. *Critical Reviews in Clinical Laboratory Sciences*, *61*(2), 140–163

Ciccarelli, M., Papetti, A., & Germani, M. (2023). Exploring how new industrial paradigms affect the workforce: A literature review of Operator 4.0 *Journal of Manufacturing Systems*, *70*, 464–483.

Dakhel, A. M., Majdinasab, V., Nikanjam, A., Khomh, F., Desmarais, M. C., & Jiang, Z. M. J. (2023). Github copilot ai pair programmer: Asset or liability?. *Journal of Systems and Software*, *203*, 111734.

Davenport, T. H., & Mittal, N. (2023). *All-in on AI: How smart companies win big with artificial intelligence*. Harvard Business Press.

Delhi, A., Sana, E., Bisty, A. A., & Husain, A. (2024). Innovation in business management exploring the path to competitive excellence. *APTISI Transactions on Management*, *8*(1), 58–65.

Detweiler, R. A. (2021). *The evidence liberal arts needs: Lives of consequence, inquiry, and accomplishment*. MIT Press.

Devi, K. V., Manjula, V., & Pattewar, T. (2023). *ChatGPT: Comprehensive study on generative AI tool*. Academic Guru Publishing House.

Doron, G., Genway, S., Roberts, M., & Jasti, S. (2023). New Horizons: Pioneering Pharmaceutical R&D with Generative AI from lab to the clinic--an industry perspective. *arXiv preprint arXiv:2312.12482*.

EDUCAUSE (2024). *Higher education generative AI readiness assessment (EDUCAUSE)*. AI Advisory Boards. Retrieved: https://aiadvisoryboards.wordpress.com/2024/04/09/higher-education-generative-ai-readiness-assessment-educause/

O'Farrell, J., & Weaver, C. (2024). Technology and transformation: Redefining higher education for generations Z and alpha. *Available at SSRN 4833043*.

Feuerriegel, S., Hartmann, J., Janiesch, C., & Zschech, P. (2024). Generative AI. *Business & Information Systems Engineering*, *66*(1), 111–126.

Gao, Y., Li, R., Caskey, J., Dligach, D., Miller, T., Churpek, M. M., & Afshar, M. (2023). Leveraging a medical knowledge graph into large language models for diagnosis prediction. *arXiv preprint arXiv:2308.14321*.

Goodfellow, I., Pouget-Abadie, J., Mirza, M., Xu, B., Warde-Farley, D., Ozair, S., ... & Bengio, Y. (2014). Generative adversarial nets. *Advances in Neural Information Processing Systems*, 27.

Goodfellow, I., Bengio, Y., & Courville, A. (2016). *Deep learning*. MIT Press.

Gusain, A., Singh, T., Pandey, S., Pachourui, V., Singh, R., & Kumar, A. (2023, March). E-recruitment using artificial intelligence as preventive measures. In *2023 International conference on sustainable computing and data communication systems (ICSCDS)* (pp. 516–522). IEEE.

Gutierrez, D. P., Folkmann, L. M., Tribukait, H., & Roch, L. M. (2023). How to accelerate R&D and optimize experiment planning with machine learning and data science. *Chimia*, *77*(1/2), 7–16.

Hajkowicz, S., Sanderson, C., Karimi, S., Bratanova, A., & Naughtin, C. (2023). Artificial intelligence adoption in the physical sciences, natural sciences, life sciences, social sciences and the arts and humanities: A bibliometric analysis of research publications from 1960–2021. *Technology in Society*, *74*, 102260.

Hassani, H., & Silva, E. S. (2023). The role of ChatGPT in data science: How AI-assisted conversational interfaces are revolutionizing the field. *Big Data and Cognitive Computing*, *7*(2), 62.

Haze, K. (2023). Empowering educational creativity with adobe express. *The School Librarian*, *71*(3), 24–24.

Heath, R. (January 15, 2024). Executives say they're not ready for AI. *Axios AI+*. Retrieved: https://www.axios.com/2024/01/15/executives-say-theyre-not-ready-for-ai

Hjaltalin, I. T., & Sigurdarson, H. T. (2024). The strategic use of AI in the public sector: A public values analysis of national AI strategies. *Government Information Quarterly*, *41*(1), 101914.

Ho, A. Besiroglu, T., Erdil, E. Owen, D., Rahman, R., Guo, Z., Atkinson, D., Thompson, N. & Sevilla, J. (2024). Algorithmic progress in language models. *arXiv:2403.05812*.

Horodyski, P. (2023). Recruiter's perception of artificial intelligence (AI)-based tools in recruitment. *Computers in Human Behavior Reports*, *10*, 100298.

Humayun, M., Tariq, N., Alfayad, M., Zakwan, M., Alwakid, G., & Assiri, M. (2024). Securing the internet of things in artificial intelligence era: A comprehensive survey. *IEEE Access*. (99), 1. https://doi.org/10.1109/ACCESS.2024.3365634

Hutson, J., Lively, J., Robertson, B., Cotroneo, P., & Lang, M. (2023). *Creative convergence: The AI renaissance in art and design*. Springer Nature.

Joshi, I., Grimmer, M., Rathgeb, C., Busch, C., Bremond, F., & Dantcheva, A. (2024). Synthetic data in human analysis: A survey. *IEEE Transactions on Pattern Analysis and Machine Intelligence*, *46*(7), 4957–4976.

Kadaruddin, K. (2023). Empowering education through generative AI: Innovative instructional strategies for tomorrow's learners. *International Journal of Business, Law, and Education*, *4*(2), 618–625.

Khosrowi, D., Finn, F., & Clark, E. (2023, August). Diffusing the creator: Attributing credit for generative AI outputs. In *Proceedings of the 2023 AAAI/ACM conference on AI, ethics, and society* (pp. 890–900). Montreal, Canada.

LeCun, Y., Bengio, Y., & Hinton, G. (2015). Deep learning. *Nature*, *521*(7553), 436–444.

Lesgold, A. M. (2019). *Learning for the age of artificial intelligence: Eight education competences*. Routledge.

Liu, W. (2023). Literature survey of multi-track music generation model based on generative confrontation network in intelligent composition. *The Journal of Supercomputing*, *79*(6), 6560–6582.

Lu, M., Yin, J., Zhu, Q., Lin, G., Mou, M., Liu, F., … & Zhu, F. (2023). Artificial intelligence in pharmaceutical sciences. *Engineering*, *27*, 37–69.

Lwakatare, L. E., Crnkovic, I., & Bosch, J. (2020, September). DevOps for AI–Challenges in Development of AI-enabled Applications. In *2020 international conference on software, telecommunications and computer networks (SoftCOM)* (pp. 1–6). IEEE.

Magooda, A., Helyar, A., Jackson, K., Sullivan, D., Atalla, C., Sheng, E., … & Chen, M. (2023). A framework for automated measurement of responsible AI harms in generative AI applications. *arXiv preprint arXiv:2310.17750*.

Mattila, M., Yrjölä, M., & Hautamäki, P. (2021). Digital transformation of business-to-business sales: What needs to be unlearned?. *Journal of Personal Selling & Sales Management*, *41*(2), 113–129.

Minaee, S., Mikolov, T., Nikzad, N., Chenaghlu, M., Socher, R., Amatriain, X., & Gao, J. (2024). Large language models: A survey. *arXiv preprint arXiv:2402.06196*.

Mohite, R., Kanthe, R., Kale, K. S., Bhavsar, D. N., Murthy, D. N., & Murthy, R. D. (2024). Integrating artificial intelligence into project management for efficient resource allocation. *International Journal of Intelligent Systems and Applications in Engineering*, *12*(4s), 420–431.

Nawaz, N., Arunachalam, H., Pathi, B. K., & Gajenderan, V. (2024). The adoption of artificial intelligence in human resources management practices. *International Journal of Information Management Data Insights*, *4*(1), 100208.

Niu, T., Zhang, W., & Zhao, R. (2024). Solution-oriented agent-based models generation with verifier-assisted iterative in-context learning. *arXiv preprint arXiv:2402.02388*.

Patwardhan, N., Marrone, S., & Sansone, C. (2023). Transformers in the real world: A survey on nlp applications. *Information*, *14*(4), 242.

Pierre, K., Gupta, M., Raviprasad, A., Sadat Razavi, S. M., Patel, A., Peters, K., … & Forghani, R. (2023). Medical imaging and multimodal artificial intelligence models for streamlining and enhancing cancer care: Opportunities and challenges. *Expert Review of Anticancer Therapy*, *23*(12), 1265–1279.

Poland, S., Sharad, S., & Wigen-Toccalino, G. (2024). Powering innovation: The comprehensive impact of generative AI. *Climate and Energy*, *40*(7), 1–11.

Poquet, O., & De Laat, M. (2021). Developing capabilities: Lifelong learning in the age of AI. *British Journal of Educational Technology*, *52*(4), 1695–1708.

Prasad, S. G., Sharmila, V. C., & Badrinarayanan, M. K. (2023, May). Role of artificial intelligence based chat generative pre-trained transformer (ChatGPT) in cyber security. In *2023 2nd international conference on applied artificial intelligence and computing (ICAAIC)* (pp. 107–114). IEEE.

Rathore, B. (2023). Future of AI & generation alpha: ChatGPT beyond boundaries. *Eduzone: International Peer Reviewed/Refereed Multidisciplinary Journal*, *12*(1), 63–68.

Roumeliotis, K. I., & Tselikas, N. D. (2023). Chatgpt and open-AI models: A preliminary review. *Future Internet*, *15*(6), 192.

Roy, A., Newman, A., Round, H., & Bhattacharya, S. (2023). Ethical culture in organizations: A review and agenda for future research. *Business Ethics Quarterly*, *34*(1), 97–138, https://doi.org/10.1017/beq.2022.44.

Shaik, M. (2023). Impact of artificial intelligence on marketing. *East Asian Journal of Multidisciplinary Research*, *2*(3), 993–1004.

Shuford, J. (2024). Deep reinforcement learning unleashing the power of AI in decision-making. *Journal of Artificial Intelligence General Science (JAIGS)* ISSN: 3006-4023, *1*(1). https://doi.org/10.60087/jaigs.v1i1.36

Steidl, M., Felderer, M., & Ramler, R. (2023). The pipeline for the continuous development of artificial intelligence models—Current state of research and practice. *Journal of Systems and Software*, *199*, 111615.

Talwar, D., Guruswamy, S., Ravipati, N., & Eirinaki, M. (2020, August). Evaluating validity of synthetic data in perception tasks for autonomous vehicles. In *2020 IEEE International Conference On Artificial Intelligence Testing* (AITest) (pp. 73–80). IEEE.

Thornhill-Miller, B., Camarda, A., Mercier, M., Burkhardt, J. M., Morisseau, T., Bourgeois-Bougrine, S., … & Lubart, T. (2023). Creativity, critical thinking, communication, and collaboration: Assessment, certification, and promotion of 21st century skills for the future of work and education. *Journal of Intelligence*, *11*(3), 54.

Vaswani, A., Shazeer, N., Parmar, N., Uszkoreit, J., Jones, L., Gomez, A. N., … & Polosukhin, I. (2017). Attention is all you need. *Advances in Neural Information Processing Systems, 30.*

Wan, T., & Chen, Z. (2023). Exploring Generative AI assisted feedback writing for students' written responses to a physics conceptual question with prompt engineering and few-shot learning. *arXiv preprint arXiv:2311.06180.*

Wang, L., Huang, N., Hong, Y., Liu, L., Guo, X., & Chen, G. (2023). Voice-based AI in call center customer service: A natural field experiment. *Production and Operations Management*, *32*(4), 1002–1018.

Watson, D. S. (2023). On the philosophy of unsupervised learning. *Philosophy and Technology*, *36*(2), 28.

Watters, C., & Lemanski, M. K. (2023). Universal skepticism of ChatGPT: A review of early literature on chat generative pre-trained transformer. *Frontiers in Big Data*, *6*. https://doi.org/10.3389/fdata.2023.1224976

Weise, M. R. (2020). *Long life learning: Preparing for jobs that don't even exist yet.* John Wiley & Sons.

West, J., & Dedrick, J. (1996). *Competing through standards: DOS/V and Japan's PC market.* Center for Research on Information Technology and Organizations.

Xu, M., Niyato, D., Chen, J., Zhang, H., Kang, J., Xiong, Z., … & Han, Z. (2023). Generative AI-empowered simulation for autonomous driving in vehicular mixed reality metaverses. *IEEE Journal of Selected Topics in Signal Processing*, *17*(5), 1064–1079.

Zhou, J., Ke, P., Qiu, X., Huang, M., & Zhang, J. (2023). ChatGPT: Potential, prospects, and limitations. *Frontiers of Information Technology & Electronic Engineering*, 1–6.

4 Vision and Administration

4.1 Leadership in AI Strategy Implementation

The integration of AI technologies confronts educational institutions and industries with significant challenges, not least of which stem from their structural and cultural intricacies. Large institutions often grapple with the agility required for embracing rapid innovation, a predicament exacerbated by the inherent complexity of their operational and organizational frameworks (Holbeche, 2023). In education especially, the semi-autonomous nature of many colleges, where departments and classrooms operate independently, further complicates cohesive change, even in the presence of innovative individuals (Maassen, Gornitzka, & Fumasoli, 2017). Moreover, the educational mandate to challenge societal norms can, paradoxically, create resistance to adopting new technologies perceived as mainstream. Rosenberg summed it up in his recent *Whatever It Is, I'm Against It* (2023), citing the structural and cultural barriers that have led to declining enrollment and accompanying financial strains (Jabbari et al., 2023).

In the discussion surrounding AI strategy implementation within higher education, a poignant analysis by former college presidents including Brian Mitchell and, again, Brian Rosenberg offers a critical perspective on the systemic challenges that educational institutions face (Rosowsky, 2023). Their insights, shared through various publications and interviews, underscore a common theme of frustration with the slow pace of transformative change within colleges and universities, a sentiment echoed across both private liberal arts colleges and public research universities. Mitchell, for example, emphasizes the urgent need for educational leaders to "wake up to the new realities they now face," advocating for more proactive governance models that transcend traditional periodic board meetings. He warns that faculty and administrators must adapt to a pace of change that is likely faster than they are accustomed to, a point that resonates with Rosenberg's critique of shared governance as an impediment to rapid and significant reform.

Rosenberg, in his writings, argues that shared governance structures often dilute the potential for substantial change, as the consensus-driven approach

DOI: 10.4324/9781003512813-4

tends to favor the least objectionable outcomes rather than bold, transformational shifts. This perspective is particularly relevant as educational leaders grapple with integrating AI into their strategic frameworks, where innovation and flexibility are paramount. Both leaders highlight the broader challenges of adapting to external pressures such as economic strains, political polarization, and evolving educational and employer expectations, which are compounded by entrenched institutional processes and cultures resistant to change. As AI continues to influence various sectors significantly, the insights from these educational leaders illuminate the critical need for higher education institutions to rethink their governance models and embrace a more dynamic approach to leadership that can effectively respond to the rapid developments in AI technology.

Therefore, effective leadership in this context transcends mere administrative oversight, necessitating a strategic vision that aligns AI integration with the core mission and values of each institution. This should first involve the establishment of a dedicated AI Task Force, encompassing a cross-section of the community—faculty, staff, and students in education or technical experts, operational and strategic leaders, and stakeholders in industry—to catalyze innovation and ensure comprehensive engagement with AI initiatives (Papyshev & Yarime, 2023). Such a working group can serve as a conduit for breaking down institutional silos, fostering a culture of collaborative innovation and shared learning. Moreover, leveraging existing frameworks and initiatives, such as collaborations with Career Services, can bridge the gap between academic preparation and workforce demands, aligning AI strategies with practical applications and market needs (Rosenberg, 2023). Comprehensive training programs for employees on the use of AI are pivotal, ensuring that the community is equipped to harness the potential of AI while navigating the balance between autonomy and organizational coherence (Kelley, 2022).

Addressing the challenges of AI integration requires more than strategic vision; it demands an inclusive approach that respects the diverse perspectives and expertise within the institution (Table 4.1) (Shams, Zowghi, & Bano, 2023). Through fostering a culture of innovation, promoting cross-disciplinary collaboration, and aligning technological adoption with strategic objectives, leaders can guide their institutions toward realizing the transformative potential. This journey toward embracing AI not only enhances educational outcomes and operational efficiencies but also positions institutions at the forefront of technological advancement, ensuring their relevance and competitiveness in an increasingly digitized world. The journey toward successful implementation begins with leadership defining clear, strategic objectives that align with the broader goals of an organization. Leaders must then identify where GAI can streamline operations and augment work processes, enhancing organizational value (Kulkov et al., 2023). But they cannot do this alone.

Table 4.1 Leadership Recommendations for AI Integration

Area of focus	*Recommendation*	*Key considerations*
Strategic vision and AI alignment	Establish a dedicated AI Task Force including faculty, staff, and students or technical experts, operational and strategic leaders, and stakeholders to ensure alignment with institutional missions and market needs.	Encourage collaboration across departments to break down silos and foster a culture of innovation.
Navigating organizational complexity	Assess and streamline work processes across the organization for GAI integration, focusing on enhancing employee and customer experiences and modernizing applications.	Identify specific areas where GAI can add value without overextending resources.
Leveraging unstructured data	Utilize GAI's capacity to process unstructured data for gaining insights and aiding in decision-making, such as through analyzing patent texts for innovation trends.	Prioritize data interpretation and application of insights for strategic advantage.
Fostering an augmented workforce	Promote training programs for employees on AI use to balance autonomy with organizational coherence and maximize the potential of the augmented workforce.	Ensure the workforce is equipped to harness AI's capabilities while aligning with organizational goals.
Addressing skill discrepancies	Bridge the gap between CEO optimism and C-suite realism regarding organizational readiness for GAI, focusing on realistic capability assessment and strategic skill development.	Tackle the impending shift in value from technical proficiency to capabilities that AI cannot replicate.

From a top-down perspective, the integration of AI and ML into the corporate decision-making process is prompting a fundamental reassessment of the roles and responsibilities of board members and senior executives. This reevaluation is underscored by an emerging crisis of engagement within corporate boardrooms, where disengagement among directors is not only prevalent but growing (Bote, Wang, & Genet, 2023). A significant study conducted by PwC and The Conference Board highlights the extent of this crisis: nearly half (48%) of over 700 corporate directors surveyed expressed a desire to replace at least one of their fellow board members, citing a reluctance among nearly 20% of peers to challenge management decisions. Compounding this, a subsequent survey involving over 600 C-suite leaders found a startling disconnect in the perception of board performance; only 29% of these executives deemed their boards' performance as "good or excellent." Moreover, a mere 21% believed that boards dedicate sufficient time to their responsibilities, with two-thirds of respondents indicating that boards often fail to engage in critical inquiry or ask probing questions. This level of complacency is particularly alarming considering the substantial compensation awarded to board members, with S&P 500 directors receiving an average annual total compensation exceeding $300,000 last year (Barsky, 2023).

The widespread availability of new AI tools presents a unique opportunity to address these challenges by augmenting or even redefining co-governance structures within organizations. For instance, leveraging tools like ChatGPT can enhance board preparedness and engagement. A simple exercise, where ChatGPT was asked to generate questions a board member of a public company should inquire about, produced a comprehensive ten-point agenda covering crucial aspects such as strategy, risk management, financial health, and market opportunities in less than a minute and at no cost. This exercise starkly contrasts the current state of affairs, where some board members remain silent throughout their tenure, content with their compensation and the status quo. This growing reliance on AI for enhancing board engagement and decision-making is set against a backdrop of notable board failures, which underscore the urgent need for reform. The Lehman Brothers collapse and the scrutiny faced by Southwest Airlines for its board's age, experience, and perceived indifference, particularly in the absence of a technology committee, highlight the consequences of inadequate governance and the potential benefits of integrating AI into these processes (Joshi, 2023).

While decision-making and the role of the board in it is certainly evolving, the role of institutional leadership cannot be overstated. The commitment of leadership to navigating the complexities of integration is paramount for achieving transformative growth and innovation. Recent insights from industry experts underscore the unique capacity of GAI to process unstructured data, which comprises a significant portion of new enterprise data (Hendrick & Struggles, 2024). This capability presents an unparalleled opportunity to unlock insights buried in communications platforms and project management tools, aiding in more accurate forecasting and strategic decision-making. For instance, processing patent texts through these platforms has yielded more precise insights into innovation trends, underscoring the transformative potential of GAI in providing competitive intelligence and identifying market opportunities. Effective leadership in strategy implementation goes beyond leveraging technology for operational efficiency. It involves fostering an augmented workforce where employees, empowered by these tools, can perform their roles with increased efficiency and versatility.

The challenge for leaders lies in selecting use cases that deliver tangible value without overextending organizational resources. Focusing on areas where GAI can address immediate challenges—such as enhancing employee experiences, customer service, and application modernization—can clear pathways for transformation (Lokesh & Harish, 2023).

In order to support decision makers in this time of change, there have been a number of guides that have been created. IBM, for instance, has created a useful resource with *The CEO's guide to Generative AI* (2024). In the era of GAI, the role of leadership, especially for CEOs and organizational leaders, is underscored by a unique blend of strategic vision and the nuanced understanding that underscores the fact that "Leadership can't be automated." The promise of technology to revolutionize industries by fostering innovation and growth highlights the critical role of leadership in driving this transformation. For leaders, the journey begins with establishing precise goals aligned with the strategic vision of the organization and delineating concrete steps for integration. At the same time, navigating deployment requires leaders to strategically assess and identify how it can streamline and enhance operations across the organization, such as by enriching employee and customer experiences or by modernizing legacy systems (Aldoseri, Al-Khalifa, & Hamouda, 2024; Rane, 2023). The unique human ability to derive meaningful insights from data complements the capabilities of GAI, paving the way for an augmented workforce where employees, supported by AI tools, achieve greater efficiency and versatility. This collaborative synergy between human ingenuity and AI's power is essential for realizing the full potential of GAI in any enterprise (Xu et al., 2024). This last point is crucial as focus has been placed on maximizing output and leveraging the efficiencies promised by the technology. The question has become: Will AI lead to broad job displacement? As will be argued, upskilling the workforce should be central to an adoption strategy instead of looking to make human capital cuts and downsizing, which have, historically, not led to long-term gains (Alnahedh & Alrashdan, 2021; De Meuse & Dai, 2013; Pekovic, Wagner, & Vogt, 2022).

At the same time, the optimism of CEOs regarding their organizational readiness for adoption contrasts sharply with the perspectives of their C-suite colleagues—a discrepancy that can significantly hinder the strategic shifts necessary for organizational advancement. While a substantial 74% of CEOs believe their teams are well-equipped with GAI skills, only a mere 29% of C-suite executives share this confidence (IBM, 2024). Such disconnects not only delay vital strategic initiatives but also underscore a critical need for a realistic assessment of organizational capabilities in the face of the emerging role of the latest evolution in AI. This is compounded by the fact that the impact of GAI will be indiscriminate, affecting roles across all levels of an organization. By 2025, it is projected that 77% of entry-level positions will undergo significant changes due to these tools, with more than a quarter of senior executive roles also experiencing shifts (Tarulli & Sokol, 2024).

This pervasive influence challenges longstanding perceptions regarding the value of certain skills and raises the question of what capabilities will distinguish the most successful organizations in a landscape increasingly defined by technical proficiency provided by AI and not human workers (Chuang, 2024).

Further limitations to scaling have been identified, despite the promise of efficiency leaps and productivity gains. As Flemin (2023) has noted, the anticipated 40% improvement in productivity, as suggested by research, has not fully materialized due to several barriers. Firstly, the deployment of AI in businesses is often fragmented, focusing on automating discrete tasks such as email management without a cohesive strategy to enhance overall productivity. This piecemeal approach can lead to an increase in email volume, paradoxically resulting in more work with no substantive improvement in productivity. The challenge lies not just in enhancing individual tasks but in leveraging AI to reimagine and streamline end-to-end business processes.

As such, the strategy requires a different approach from previous digital transformations like mobile or cloud-based technologies. These earlier efforts, starting in the early 2000s, required IT and training and upskilling a workforce in a particular technology, while slowly phasing out older versions (Andal-Ancion, Cartwright, & Yip, 2003; Lanzolla & Anderson, 2008; Mahra, 2005). On the other hand, the new demand for generative transformation demands a strategic pivot, moving the conversation around AI from the technical confines of the server room to the strategic echelons of the boardroom as it is more process change management (Reddy, 2024). It is imperative for leadership to champion AI not merely as a tool for task automation but as a fundamental driver of strategic transformation. Such a paradigm shift ensures that AI initiatives are seamlessly aligned with overarching business objectives, fostering an environment where innovation transcends organizational silos (units or academic departments) to enhance the entirety of business processes—from customer/student service to product development (Young, 2023).

The paradigm shift requires a holistic perspective, recognizing GAI as an essential element of strategic planning rather than merely a set of isolated technological tools (Table 4.2). According to recent research by Purnawati (2024), the integration of technology in market segmentation reveals immense potential for optimizing marketing strategies and enhancing customer engagement, emphasizing the strategic value of AI in driving business objectives. Gupta and Bansal (2023) further underscore the competitive advantage companies can gain by incorporating AI into their marketing strategies, highlighting the importance of personalized experiences and resource optimization facilitated by AI.. But in order to benefit from this potential, the strategic focus on value creation through targeted AI applications necessitates identifying and pursuing use cases where AI can address the most critical organizational challenges, thereby ensuring that transformation efforts have a meaningful impact.

Table 4.2 Strategic Recommendations for GAI Integration

Strategic area	*Recommendations*
Strategic vision and leadership	Leadership must steer AI transformation from a strategic viewpoint, moving discussions from the server room to the boardroom to ensure alignment with broader business objectives.
Holistic integration	AI strategy should transcend deploying isolated applications for specific tasks, aiming instead to reimagine entire business processes to enhance customer service, product development, and operational efficiency.
Focused use cases and value creation	Identifying use cases where AI can deliver substantial value is essential, with efforts focused on solving critical organizational challenges and areas with the highest impact.
Cultivating an AI-savvy workforce	Upskilling the workforce is crucial as AI redefines roles, with the goal of augmenting human capabilities and enabling more strategic work aligned with sustainable growth.
Security and ethical considerations	AI integration must carefully consider limitations and potential risks, emphasizing security, responsible AI use, and data privacy.
Leadership involvement	Involving top decision-makers ensures AI strategy aligns with the organization's strategic goals, championing AI as a strategic enabler.
Focused use case selection	A focused strategy on use cases where GAI can have a significant impact helps allocate resources to the most promising areas for innovation and efficiency.
Risk management	Adopting a consistent, enterprise-wide approach to GAI integration is vital for managing risks and upholding ethical standards.
Iterative rollout and performance incentives	Encouraging a culture of risk-taking and rapid learning through iterative GAI project rollouts and performance-based incentives can enhance GAI readiness and adoption.
Cross-functional accountability	Joint responsibility among leaders from business, IT, and HR for GAI adoption outcomes fosters collaboration and emphasizes GAI's strategic importance.
Empowering teams	Empowering teams to explore GAI applications, particularly starting with HR, can model broader engagement with AI technologies, enhancing efficiency and decision-making.

The use case approach aligns with insights identified by Trad (2024) on the risks associated with siloed AI integration and the benefits of adopting a polymathic enterprise architecture-based learning strategy to enhance enterprise-wide AI adoption and innovation. Thus, effective leadership ensures that AI initiatives are not only in harmony with business objectives but also contribute to sustainable growth and competitive advantage. Again, this necessitates a shift from viewing AI as a mere technological upgrade to recognizing its potential as a strategic enabler across the organization, a sentiment echoed in recent studies which call for a more integrated, strategic approach to AI adoption (Tanase, 2024). The limitations of "grass roots" promotion and integration have been witnessed across organizations for this study (Hutson & Rains, 2024a). Oftentimes, an individual champions the integration of the tools in their own unit or department. If successful in getting buy-in from their team, resources may be allocated to training, software or hardware. However, these efforts often are confined to one or even a few scattered units across the organization and fail to reach the broader institution. For instance, some educational institutions will have dedicated AI investment and training only in one department, such as Engineering or Health Care. Given the hierarchical and siloed nature of the organization, the initiatives rarely extend beyond the limited scope of a handful of individuals.

In order to see broad adoption, leadership and HR need to be involved. Empowering teams to explore and implement applications, particularly within HR, is pivotal for catalyzing broader engagement with AI technologies across organizations and makes clear to employees that the use of the tools is not only acceptable, but incentivized. This strategic move not only streamlines efficiency and decision-making processes but also emphasizes the significance of the adoption in enhancing operational agility and strategic acumen within every sector of an enterprise. While specific research directly linking GAI applications in HR to organizational growth is still emerging, insights from related fields indicate the transformative potential across various domains, including healthcare, where the creativity and flexibility of GAI have been highlighted for optimizing operations and resource allocation (Coucke, 2024). Through such adoption, HR departments can serve as trailblazers within organizations, demonstrating how AI can transcend traditional operational boundaries to foster a culture of innovation and strategic growth. The application of which can encompass a wide range of functions, from talent acquisition and employee engagement to workforce analytics and personalized learning and development pathways, showcasing the versatile impact of GAI on enhancing human capital management (Alam, Dhar, & Munira, 2020; Hmoud, 2021). Moreover, the successful deployment in HR can establish a resilient, future-ready foundation for organizations, driving value creation and competitive differentiation in the digital age (Panda, Pasumarti, & Hiremath, 2023).

Adoption of the workflow and processes afforded by GAI among leadership and HR makes the initiative clearly visible to all employees. At the same time, proper use should also be modeled as successful integration is intrinsically linked to effective risk management strategies that address the unique challenges and opportunities presented. Establishing a consistent, enterprise-wide approach to risk management is pivotal, as underscored by recent research that highlights the significance of adopting comprehensive frameworks to mitigate the risks associated with AI technologies. For instance, Susanto et al. (2023) emphasize the importance of qualitative insights from healthcare professionals in resource-constrained settings, suggesting that adopting AI for cardiovascular risk prediction necessitates a careful evaluation of how it is used, including its inherent risks. The recommendations were echoed by Wirtz, Weyerer, and Kehl (2022) and Prasad Agrawal (2023) in business and educational contexts. This does not mean that innovation should be stifled in the process of establishing these strategies.

The promotion of a culture of innovation, balanced with stringent ethical standards and data protection measures, is crucial in navigating the complexities of adoption. This balance ensures that while organizations pursue innovative AI-driven solutions, they also uphold ethical considerations and protect sensitive data. Furthermore, the adoption of performance-based incentives and the encouragement of an iterative rollout of projects are instrumental in enhancing organizational readiness for GAI adoption, as highlighted by De Haro (2024), who proposes a biosecurity risk management approach tailored to the unique features of AI applications in synthetic biology. To encourage adoption, along with incentivizing, it is essential to ensure that the use of these technologies extends beyond the confines of individual departments or units, fostering a cross-departmental integration (Whitlock & Strickland, 2022). Fostering cross-functional accountability is in fact essential for ensuring that the integration aligns with organizational goals and addresses the multifaceted risks associated with adoption. It also avoids the limitations of "grass roots" approaches where the initiative does not extend beyond a unit. Therefore, empowering teams across the organization, starting notably with HR, to explore and implement these applications can serve as a model for broader engagement with AI technologies. This not only enhances efficiency and decision-making but also underscores the strategic importance of adoption across all facets of the enterprise. Through such a comprehensive and strategic approach, organizations are poised to leverage GAI as a catalyst for growth, driving value creation, and establishing a resilient, future-ready enterprise in the digital age.

4.2 Synchronizing AI with Organizational Goals

Unlike previous digital transformation technologies like mobile or cloud, the latest generative iteration is not merely a new tool to teach employees and phase out an older version; they become part of the very process and workflow of business in general. As such, aligning AI with organizational goals is pivotal for ensuring the successful integration of these technologies within a broader institutional mission and vision (Table 4.3). This alignment

Table 4.3 Strategies for Aligning AI with Organizational Objectives

Organizational goal	*Recommendations for AI alignment*
Enhance operational efficiency	Deploy AI tools to automate routine tasks and optimize business processes, allowing staff to focus on higher-value activities. Evaluate AI-driven analytics to identify areas for improvement and implement predictive maintenance in operations.
Improve customer satisfaction	Utilize AI-powered chatbots and virtual assistants to provide 24/7 customer support, ensuring timely and personalized responses. Implement AI to analyze customer feedback and behavior, enabling tailored product recommendations and services.
Drive innovation	Foster a culture of innovation by using AI to explore new business models and product development opportunities. Encourage cross-functional teams to leverage AI for creative problem-solving and to identify untapped market potentials.
Enhance decision-making	Integrate AI with data analytics to provide comprehensive insights and predictive analyses, supporting more informed decision-making across all levels of the organization. Ensure AI systems are transparent and their recommendations are interpretable by decision-makers.
Foster employee development and training	Implement AI-driven personalized learning platforms to support employee skill development, adapting to individual learning paces and styles. Use AI to identify skill gaps within the organization and tailor training programs accordingly.
Strengthen security and risk management	Utilize AI for advanced threat detection and response in cybersecurity efforts. Implement AI-based tools for real-time risk assessment and management, ensuring proactive identification and mitigation of potential risks.
Commit to ethical standards and social responsibility	Ensure AI deployment aligns with ethical guidelines and promotes social responsibility, including fairness, transparency, and accountability in AI algorithms. Engage stakeholders in discussions on the ethical use of AI and its societal impacts, fostering trust and adherence to organizational values.
Promote sustainability	Leverage AI for optimizing resource use and reducing waste, contributing to the organization's sustainability goals. Use AI-driven data analysis to assess and improve the environmental impact of operations and products.

is essential to prevent unnecessary friction or redundancies and to avert the potential for initiative failure. More importantly, alignment ensures consistent messaging to help process and workflow evolution. The latest research emphasizes the necessity of integrating AI into organizational strategies to bolster digital transformation efforts effectively. As seen in previous studies, such as the one by Akram, Sultan, and Deveci (2024), the digitization of the global economy presents a framework for evaluating digital transformation initiatives, emphasizing the need for such efforts to be synchronized with organizational goals. The approach is crucial for ensuring that AI and digital transformation initiatives are not pursued in isolation but are instead deeply integrated into the strategic planning processes of the organization, thereby supporting its overarching objectives.

Best practices for digital transformation underscore the importance of a transdisciplinary approach, focusing on balancing external market strategies with internal organizational tactics. Trappey et al. (2024) highlight the significance of managing uncertainty through transdisciplinary engineering methods, which include the synchronization of digital transformation efforts with organizational goals. Such methods ensure that the deployment of generative AI models is in perfect harmony with strategic objectives, thereby enhancing efficiency and innovation. To facilitate this synchronization, organizations must adopt a holistic view of digital transformation, considering not only the technological aspects but also the human, ethical, and strategic dimensions. This entails fostering a culture that values continuous learning, ethical use of technology, and a strategic focus on leveraging AI to enhance decision-making processes, operational efficiency, and innovation. Examples of successful AI integration within organizational strategies include the development of AI-driven platforms for innovation and entrepreneurship in educational settings (Fang, 2023), and the application of AI in human resource management to align recruiting with strategic goals (Das et al., 2023).

An example of such an alignment in education can be found in the state-wide initiative in Virginia undertaken in the spring of 2024. The plan encompasses the entire educational system in the state, a move reflecting a broader commitment to preparing students and workers for a future increasingly shaped by these technologies. The *Guidelines for AI Integration throughout Education in the Commonwealth of Virginia* document serves as a case study in aligning educational goals with AI integration, offering insights into best practices for digital transformation that supports institutional missions and visions without creating unnecessary friction or redundancies (Commonwealth of Virginia, 2024). The guidelines underscore the transformative potential of AI in education, emphasizing the need for a balanced approach that recognizes capabilities to enhance learning and operational efficiency while acknowledging the indispensability of human judgment, wisdom, and interpersonal skills in educational contexts (Markauskaite et al., 2022). The principle of augmenting rather than replacing human capabilities is central to the strategic approach and should be at the forefront of any communications on organizational strategy to allay concerns over job loss (Hassani et al., 2020).

Building on the foundation laid by the ethical guidelines for AI integration, it is imperative for educational institutions to ensure that the deployment of AI technologies aligns with their overarching mission and vision. This alignment is crucial in fostering an institutional framework that not only embraces technological advancements but also promotes the educational values and objectives fundamental to developing well-rounded, ethically grounded citizens. To effectively integrate AI into the educational fabric, it is essential that all initiatives are designed to complement and enhance institutional learning outcomes and graduate attributes. This approach ensures that AI tools are not merely ancillary technologies but are integral to the curriculum, enriching the educational experience and offering students hands-on, practical exposure to advanced technologies. By embedding AI into all units and outcomes, educational institutions can provide a cohesive learning journey that equips students with critical skills and competencies relevant to the digital age. Moreover, adopting a "train the trainer" model amplifies the impact of AI integration. This model empowers educators by providing them with the necessary tools and knowledge to incorporate AI into their teaching practices effectively. Educators become conduits of change, facilitating the transition to an AI-enhanced learning environment. This not only improves the educators' proficiency with new technologies but also ensures that the educational delivery is consistent with the institution's goals of fostering an environment conducive to the ethical use of AI (Khan & Seto, 2023).

Leadership and administration should be very involved in learning these tools to speak intelligibly about them and then to have their various units trained (Fountaine, McCarthy, & Saleh, 2019). Starting with employees to support customers—or in this case, teachers to support students—is necessary for appropriate oversight and expertise in the use of the tools within specific domains (Sofia et al., 2023). These trainings involve facilitating opportunities for educators to directly engage with AI tools, thereby enabling them to discover potential applications and address ethical considerations proactively. Moreover, professional development initiatives and collaborative exploration are highlighted as essential strategies for empowering employees to effectively integrate them into their daily practices. The focus on educator empowerment and professional growth is seen as critical for ensuring that AI technologies are used responsibly and effectively to enhance instructional quality and student learning outcomes (Sun et al., 2023). Furthermore, the guidelines emphasize the importance of partnership and collaboration among state education agencies, educational institutions, and technology experts. This collaborative approach aims to create a supportive ecosystem for integration that includes advisory resources, policy development, stakeholder training, and continuous monitoring and adaptation to the ever-changing landscape of these technologies.

Such a comprehensive and collaborative approach seen in the Virginia case can help ensure that integration is effectively aligned with educational goals and institutional missions, fostering an environment of continuous innovation and improvement. At the same time, institutions across various sectors are increasingly looking for adoption plans due to the spectrum of ethical, legal, and operational challenges that must be navigated. Drawing on the example here, several universal recommendations emerge, applicable to organizations seeking to align their institutional goals with AI adoption. For instance, clearly defining objectives is paramount for any organization planning for generative integration. Institutions should articulate specific goals that such technologies are expected to achieve, ensuring these are in harmony with the broader mission and vision (Mohamed, Stankosky, & Murray, 2006). These goals are unique for each entity but should bring the integration goal in alignment with the institutional goal. An example would be a healthcare facility that aims to leverage AI for predictive analytics in patient care, seeking to enhance treatment outcomes and patient experiences while maintaining privacy and ethical standards (Ibrahim & Saber, 2023). Given that the goals of a healthcare facility also include supporting patient health while maintaining the same standards, there is a synergy between the two.

Additionally, the establishment of a robust ethical framework is essential for the responsible adoption of any technology, though the application may vary across industries. But regardless of industry, such a framework will respect data privacy, maintain transparency, and uphold the fundamental rights of involved parties. The ethical foundation is critical in guiding the deployment and operation of systems and in building trust among users and stakeholders (Huda, 2019). The healthcare sector can be used as an example again in a scenario with the implementation of AI for patient diagnosis and treatment planning. Guidelines that need be developed must address issues such as the accuracy of diagnostics, the confidentiality of patient data, and the need for transparent communication regarding the role of AI in patient care decisions (Chintala, 2023). In the educational domain, the tools may be used for personalized learning platforms and automated grading systems, which can significantly enhance the learning experience (Maghsudi et al., 2021). However, they also raise concerns regarding data privacy, the potential for bias in grading, and the transparency of AI-driven recommendations (Vashishth et al., 2024). An ethical framework in this context must guarantee that the tools are used to support and enrich the educational process without compromising academic integrity or student privacy.

Along with healthcare and education, the retail industry increasingly employs AI for customer behavior analysis and personalized marketing and faces its own set of ethical challenges (Gkikas & Theodoridis, 2022). Here, the ethical framework should address consent for data collection, the avoidance of invasive advertising practices, and the assurance that personalized recommendations do not discriminate or exploit vulnerable consumer groups (Allhoff & Henschke, 2018). Likewise in the realm of public services and governance, where AI can be utilized for everything from resource allocation to social welfare decisions, the ethical framework becomes particularly complex. It must ensure that applications do not reinforce existing inequalities or biases, that there is accountability for decisions made with AI assistance, and that privacy and rights are rigorously protected (Kuziemski & Misuraca, 2020).

Having established the foundational importance of ethical considerations for adoption, it is important to pivot toward a comprehensive risk assessment, a process that enables organizations to identify and address the myriad challenges associated with data privacy, cybersecurity, and compliance. The process enables the identification of potential vulnerabilities and the development of strategies to mitigate these risks, ensuring the safe and responsible use of AI technologies (Goel, Kumar, & Haddow, 2020). In the healthcare industry, the same considerations carry over, including patient diagnoses and treatments potentially compromising the confidentiality of patient records and the accuracy of AI-generated diagnoses. Risk assessments in this context must evaluate the potential for data breaches, the reliability of AI diagnostic tools, and compliance with health information privacy regulations (Albahri et al., 2023). Similarly, the financial services sector uses AI applications in fraud detection, credit scoring, and algorithmic trading necessitates a detailed examination of risks related to financial data security, algorithmic bias, and regulatory adherence (Giudici, 2018). Developing encryption standards, auditing AI algorithms for bias, and establishing compliance monitoring systems are critical measures for mitigating these risks (Shah, 2021). For public sector organizations utilizing AI in public safety, resource allocation, and civic engagement platforms, risk assessments must address concerns about citizen privacy, the potential for surveillance, and the ethical implications of algorithmic decision-making. Strategies to mitigate these risks include the adoption of privacy-preserving technologies, the establishment of ethical oversight committees, and adherence to principles of transparency and accountability in tool deployments (Mehr, Ash, & Fellow, 2017; Wirtz, Weyerer, & Geyer, 2019).

After conducting a thorough risk assessment to identify potential vulnerabilities, the subsequent step involves prioritizing professional development to empower stakeholders with the essential expertise required for the proficient and secure application of AI technologies. Investing in professional development cannot be overlooked as it empowers employees to understand

and utilize these tools effectively, and in turn help their colleagues and customers understand potential use cases for different contexts (Kitcharoen, Howimanporn, & Chookaew, 2024). Workforce training initiatives should be tailored to the specific needs of the organization and its workforce, encompassing a range of activities from workshops and seminars to hands-on training and collaborative projects. In healthcare, such training might involve medical staff learning the use of diagnostic tools and patient management systems. Hospitals and clinics can host seminars led by industry experts to discuss the latest advancements in healthcare, coupled with hands-on training sessions that allow medical professionals to interact directly with AI applications, simulating real-life patient scenarios to improve diagnostic accuracy and patient care (Sapci & Sapci, 2020).

The same hands-on approach to training can be tailored to industry-specific needs across various sectors. For the financial services and manufacturing industries, workshops and training sessions can focus on ethical AI usage, risk management, predictive maintenance, and quality control (Dwivedi et al., 2021). Financial institutions could benefit from training in analyzing complex data sets for fraud detection, while manufacturing companies might explore the integration of AI with IoT devices for equipment monitoring (Jagatheesaperumal et al., 2021). Both sectors could also engage IT staff in hackathons to devise solutions that enhance operational efficiency and customer service. Educational institutions and the retail industry can center such efforts on leveraging AI to improve service delivery—whether enhancing educational outcomes or customer experiences (Grewal, Motyka, & Levy, 2018). Educators and administrative staff might engage in seminars discussing ethical considerations and collaborative projects to incorporate the tools into curricula, administrative processes, or retail strategies. Similarly, retail companies could focus on employing technology for market research, inventory management, and the personalization of marketing strategies, including the use of chatbots for customer interaction (Stoilova, 2021).

Just as professional development can strengthen connections across an organization, fostering collaboration and partnerships can also prove central in a successful adoption plan across sectors. The approach is strategic and not only broadens access to expertise and resources but also cultivates innovation through the synergy of diverse knowledge bases. In healthcare, partnerships between hospitals and technology firms can drive advancements in patient care through the development of the aforementioned diagnostic and treatment planning tools (Chen & Decary, 2020). Collaborating with academic researchers specializing in medical AI can further enhance the efficacy of contacts, incorporating cutting-edge research into practical applications that improve patient outcomes and operational efficiency (Topol, 2019). In a similar manner, the financial services industry can form mutually advantageous relationships with fintech startups and data analytics companies to harness AI in fraud detection and risk assessment (Onsori et al., 2023;

Riemer et al., 2017). These collaborations can yield sophisticated models that enhance the accuracy and speed of financial operations, benefiting from the agility of startups and the innovative algorithms developed by data scientists. The same benefits can be realised by educational institutions that partner with edtech companies and developers to create personalized learning platforms and automated administrative tools (Kim et al., 2023).

The establishment of collaboration and partnerships can lead to new innovative directions, the momentum of which can be supported through continuous monitoring and adaptation. Such conscientiousness can help ensure that integrations are not only informed by collective expertise but also remain dynamic and responsive to evolving organizational needs and external challenges. One such example would be digital media platforms and music streaming services utilizing AI to personalize content and recommendations, necessitating ongoing analysis of user engagement and feedback to refine algorithms and enhance user experience (Amudharasan, 2023). Manufacturing companies employing predictive maintenance tools must adjust their models based on actual equipment performance data, optimizing operational efficiency and reducing downtime (Molęda et al., 2023). Similarly, the financial sector relies on constant monitoring of systems used in fraud detection and customer service to identify and correct potential biases or inaccuracies, ensuring secure and efficient customer transactions (Hassan, Aziz, & Andriansyah, 2023). These approaches underscore an iterative, responsive strategy across industries, where adaptation and feedback loops are essential for aligning AI and other technological initiatives with changing landscapes and stakeholder needs, thereby sustaining their relevance and efficacy over time.

As well, in the dynamic landscape of educational transformation facilitated by AI, establishing collaborative workshops with industry partners such as IBM can significantly enhance the strategic integration of AI within institutional goals. These workshops are essential for syncing AI initiatives with organizational objectives, leveraging both internal and external expertise to optimize outcomes. For instance, a two-day workshop involving a diverse group from an educational institution—including members from student affairs, advising, fiscal affairs, and the provost's office alongside IT and AI leadership—can be instrumental in harnessing AI for enhanced operational efficiency and academic success.

The first day of the workshop could be dedicated to a Design Thinking session facilitated by an external AI engineer from IBM, focusing on user experience and technical integration. This session would serve to cluster big ideas into actionable plans, incorporating insights from both internal stakeholders and IBM's Client Engineering team. The collaboration aims to co-create solutions that define and deliver value through a series of targeted sprints, transitioning smoothly to allow the organization to take ownership post-workshop. This process starts with identifying high-value use cases through stakeholder voting, which could include AI-driven solutions like AI tutoring for courses and academic advising, ensuring that these initiatives align well with the institution's strategic goals and return on investment.

The second day could delve deeper into administrative use cases, addressing specific needs such as enrollment management and student engagement. This part of the workshop might involve analyzing existing processes to identify pain points and opportunities for AI integration, supported by data discovery sessions that highlight necessary resources and databases. Here, the partnership with IBM could provide not only technical expertise but also access to advanced AI tools and methodologies for predictive analytics and market analysis. By engaging in such comprehensive, co-creative experiences, institutions can effectively align their AI strategies with broader organizational goals, ensuring that the adoption of AI contributes positively to both immediate needs and long-term strategic objectives.

4.3 Risk and Reward: Navigating the AI Landscape

After considering how to align AI adoption with institutional goals, and looking at potential platforms or solutions to adopt, risk management becomes necessary in confronting the dual forces of risk and reward (Nishant et al., 2023). Therefore, the procurement of AI systems, particularly within high-stakes domains such as employment, health, education, housing, finance, public assistance, and more, necessitates a nuanced understanding of the many risks involved in each. It is within this context that the Risk Management Framework for Procuring AI Systems (RMF PAIS 1.0), outlined by Miller and Waters (2024), can prove a useful instrument, guiding organizations through the complex terrain of AI integration. The framework underscores the imperative of establishing a risk appetite at the inception of AI procurement processes. *Risk appetite* is the level of risk that an organization is willing to accept or retain in pursuit of its objectives before action is deemed necessary to reduce it (Schuett, 2023); the step enables organizations to shape the trajectory of procurement in alignment with organizational values and objectives. To assist the framework outlines a clear methodology for establishing a risk appetite aligned with organizational goals by using a risk appetite scorecard and matrix to quantitatively assess and visually represent system risks, thus guiding procurement decisions and vendor negotiations based on defined risk tolerance levels. At the heart of this framework is the principle that AI systems, while offering substantial potential for operational efficiency and decision-making enhancement, must operate within the bounds of the procuring risk tolerance of an organization (Hong & Xiao, 2024). This principle is particularly critical in the context of high-risk systems, which have the potential to significantly impact human lives like healthcare fields. The framework thus provides a structured methodology for navigating the AI landscape, balancing the pursuit of technological advancement with the imperative of safeguarding human rights.

Moreover, the RMF establishes a crucial distinction between the roles of AI system buyers and developers, emphasizing the nuanced responsibilities that fall upon the former. The delineation underscores the importance of procuring systems that not only align with organizational goals but also adhere to stringent ethical standards and comply with legal mandates, especially pertinent now with the recent European AI act (Helberger & Diakopoulos, 2023). The approach recognizes the diversity of stakeholders in the AI ecosystem, including end-users, developers, legislators, policy makers, and society at large, all of whom are integral to the ethical deployment and management of AI technologies. Highlighting the significant role of buyers, the framework emphasizes their responsibility to procure and apply systems ethically and thoughtfully, ensuring these technologies not only improve efficiency but also positively impact human lives, according to Miller and Waters (2024).

In order to ensure such a goal, organizations should support and promote AI literacy across their employees, and especially their procurement staff, ensuring they possess a comprehensive grasp of both the technical and managerial dimensions of the systems for informed decision-making. Additionally, in the context of the rapidly changing regulations surrounding AI, acquiring a solid understanding of legal and policy issues is crucial for maintaining compliance with such initiatives. The framework also identifies organizational readiness as a critical foundation for effective adoption, which includes having clear AI policies, defined roles and responsibilities, an evaluation of data maturity, and a broad understanding of AI literacy levels within the organization (Akbarighatar, Pappas, & Vassilakopoulou, 2023). The initiation of any AI procurement process, therefore, begins with a thorough analysis of the underlying business need, ensuring that the pursuit of solutions is rooted in legitimate operational requirements. In evaluating the underlying business need, the framework emphasizes the critical roles of consensus, communication, and a cohesive approach in deciding on a system, guiding organizations to articulate a risk appetite statement that fosters shared understanding and strategic alignment between technological goals and risk tolerance. This ensures a responsible and informed process, aiming to identify solutions that not only meet organizational objectives but also adhere to ethical and human-centered principles.

Moving into the risk assessment and control stages, there are many frameworks, such as the RMF, that mandate a thorough evaluation of systems and vendors, going beyond technical capabilities to examine governance practices and potential risks (Miller & Waters, 2024). MIT has also developed a framework for assessing risk for organizations, especially considering potential bias (Stackpole, 2024). Notable instances where medical algorithms have disadvantaged certain populations, AI-enabled recruiting tools have exhibited bias, and facial recognition technologies have led to wrongful arrests underscore the critical need for proactive AI governance (Abràmoff et al., 2023). Furthermore, the phenomenon of "hallucination" in generative

AI, where the technology generates unfounded or inaccurate information, adds another layer of complexity to the governance challenge (Salvagno, Taccone, & Gerli, 2023).

Considering these challenges in adoption, Dominique Shelton Leipzig, a partner at Mayer Brown and leader of the firm's global data innovation practice, emphasizes the importance of early and continuous AI governance to safeguard against these risks. Speaking at the EmTech MIT conference, Shelton Leipzig highlighted that while the promise of AI is immense, realizing its full potential requires diligent oversight from the initial stages of development through to constant evaluation and tending in its application (Stackpole, 2024). The approach is vital not only for protecting the brand but also for fostering trust among customers, employees, and business partners (Douglas, 2024). Shelton Leipzig advocates for a structured framework to categorize the risk level associated with specific AI use cases, drawing on a red light, yellow light, and green light model inspired by proposed legislation and governance practices across 78 countries (Table 4.4). This model serves as a starting point for organizations navigating the complexities of AI

Table 4.4 AI Risk Spectrum with Red, Yellow, and Green Light Framework

Risk category	*AI use cases*	*Considerations*
Red light	• Surveillance undermining democratic values • Continuous public space monitoring	Prohibited due to high potential for harm. These applications are often restricted by legal frameworks to protect privacy and democratic freedoms.
Green light	• Chatbots • Customer service enhancements • Product recommendations • Entertainment and video games	Considered low risk. These applications have been employed safely over the years and generally do not pose significant ethical or safety concerns.
Yellow light	• AI in HR (Human Resources) • Family planning and care • Surveillance in non-public contexts • Applications affecting democracy • Manufacturing • Financial applications (e.g., evaluating creditworthiness, managing investment portfolios, underwriting financial instruments)	High risk, requiring rigorous oversight. These applications necessitate thorough governance measures to mitigate potential biases, ethical issues, and ensure safety and compliance.

implementation and governance. To navigate high-risk or yellow-light AI applications effectively, companies should adhere to best practices drawn from the European Union Artificial Intelligence Act and insights from the White House's Blueprint for an AI Bill of Rights (Park, 2023). These include ensuring the use of high-quality, accurate data, embracing continuous testing for algorithmic bias and accuracy, enabling human oversight to correct deviations, and creating fail-safes to halt applications when deviations cannot be corrected. The approach seeks to ensure that systems are deployed responsibly, safeguarding against biases, ensuring data privacy and security, and maintaining compliance with evolving regulations. By adopting these precautions, organizations can harness the transformative power of these tools while mitigating the risks associated with their use, thereby establishing a foundation of trust and safety in their initiatives.

As organizations move to the implementation of risk controls, considerations should differentiate foundational organizational governance controls and those specific to the selection process of certain AI solutions. Organizational controls underscore the importance of a solid foundation of AI literacy, responsible AI policies, and a clear understanding of legal and policy landscapes. Such controls can be instrumental in establishing a culture primed for the successful management of AI-related risks. For AI-specific procurement, organizations should embed risk controls directly into contractual agreements with vendors, which span from standard AI clauses addressing common concerns across AI systems to vendor-specific clauses tailored to the unique risks identified during the assessment phase. At the same time, dynamic clauses should be included that can adapt to the evolving nature of these technologies and the regulatory environment, ensuring ongoing alignment with the risk appetite of the organization. This includes provisions for addressing breaches in risk tolerance, establishing "circuit breaker" mechanisms for rapid response to unanticipated issues, and outlining specific measures for managing and rectifying such breaches (Miller & Waters, 2024).

Therefore, creating a responsible institutional adoption plan for generative AI necessitates a comprehensive assessment of risks and the formulation of strategic solutions, particularly from an IT perspective, focusing on data privacy and cybersecurity (Table 4.5). The proliferation of applications, such as Bing Chat/Co-Pilot, within tools like Microsoft 365, Turnitin, and LMS, brings to the fore critical considerations for safeguarding sensitive institutional data and ensuring compliance with privacy laws and cybersecurity protocols. The integration of generative technologies into the institutional fabric introduces a wide array of risks that necessitate careful consideration and strategic management. Among the primary concerns is the issue of data privacy and access. There is a very real danger that applications could inadvertently gain access to and reveal sensitive data, effectively circumventing the

Table 4.5 Strategic Framework for Navigating Risks and Maximizing Rewards in AI Integration

Key takeaways	*Recommendations*
Risk assessment	
Data privacy and access	Implement detailed privacy controls and access management at user and group levels.
Cybersecurity threats	Invest in advanced cybersecurity measures, including anomaly detection, encryption, and regular security audits.
Compliance and legal risks	Develop a comprehensive policy framework that aligns with privacy laws and regulatory requirements.
User responsibility and accountability	Educate users on responsible AI use, emphasizing privacy settings and data encryption.
Scale of impact	Consider the extensive use of AI and its potential widespread impact in risk management strategies.
Potential solutions	
Privacy settings and access controls	Ensure AI tools adhere to the principle of least privilege for data access and activation.
Cybersecurity measures	Deploy state-of-the-art cybersecurity solutions to protect against unauthorized AI access.
Policy and compliance framework	Align AI use with existing privacy laws and prepare for regulatory evolutions through comprehensive policy development.
Education and training	Institute programs to foster a security culture among all stakeholders regarding AI use.
Process reengineering	Reassess and redesign organizational processes for AI compatibility, prioritizing data security and privacy.
Responsibility and accountability	Assign managerial responsibilities for overseeing privacy and data protection practices.
Acknowledgment of understanding	Use tools to confirm users' understanding of privacy practices and acceptance of liabilities.
Monitoring and auditing	Continuously monitor and audit data access permissions and adjust as necessary.
Legal counsel consultation	Regularly consult with legal experts to navigate AI integration implications and ensure compliance.
Feedback loop	Establish a feedback mechanism for ongoing evaluation and improvement of AI tools and privacy controls.

existing restrictions set at the user or group level (Wylde et al., 2023). The situation occurred at one institution within this study whereby when Microsoft Co-Pilot went live, and the appropriate permissions were not preset, that everyone in the organization could see everyone else's files when searching. Such examples underscore the need for robust privacy controls and meticulous access management to prevent unintended data exposure. Furthermore, the enhanced capabilities of GAI in conducting comprehensive data analysis and retrieval significantly elevate the risk of cybersecurity threats. The variety of potential threats ranges from unauthorized data breaches to the leakage of confidential information, highlighting the critical need for advanced cybersecurity measures to protect against such vulnerabilities.

Another critical area of concern centers on compliance and legal risks associated with the deployment of GAI. Given the ability of these tools to parse through a vast array of communication forms, there arise substantial legal challenges related to consent and data ownership. Ensuring that the adoption of generative AI is in strict alignment with existing privacy laws and regulations is imperative to avoid legal entanglements and uphold ethical standards. The aspect of user responsibility and accountability also presents a considerable challenge. The reliance on individual users to appropriately manage privacy settings and understand the implications of encryption levels can lead to inconsistencies in implementation, potentially leaving gaps in the security framework, especially considering the varying levels of technological proficiency across employees. The variability in user competency and diligence underscores the importance of comprehensive education and training programs to ensure a uniformly high level of privacy and data protection across the institution (Johnson & Easttom, 2020).

Addressing the challenges presented by the integration of GAI into organizational frameworks necessitates a comprehensive and multifaceted strategy. At the core of this strategy is the implementation of robust privacy settings and meticulous access control measures. With the establishment of granular privacy controls and access management at both the user and group levels, organizations can adhere to the principle of least privilege, ensuring that tool activation and data access are strictly regulated to prevent unauthorized exposure. Investments in advanced cybersecurity measures form another critical component of this strategy. The deployment of state-of-the-art cybersecurity solutions, including anomaly detection systems, robust encryption techniques, and regular security audits, is essential for protecting against unauthorized access and mitigating the risk of data breaches facilitated by AI systems.

Furthermore, the development of a comprehensive policy and compliance framework is indispensable for navigating the legal and ethical landscape of integration. This framework should cover the use of tools, ensuring alignment with existing privacy laws and adequately preparing for future regulatory changes. It also necessitates thorough reviews of service agreements and terms of use to safeguard organizational interests and compliance. Education and training for all stakeholders on the responsible use of AI, with an emphasis on privacy settings and data encryption, is imperative for cultivating a culture of security and awareness. Such educational initiatives equip users with the knowledge and skills required to navigate the complexities of AI integration responsibly.

Reassessing and potentially redesigning organizational processes to ensure AI compatibility, with a strong focus on data security and privacy, is also strongly recommended. This process reengineering aims to align existing workflows and practices with the demands of a secure AI-operational environment. Assigning clear managerial responsibilities for the oversight of privacy and data protection practices is necessary to ensure consistent and uniform compliance across the organization. This involves designating specific individuals or teams to monitor adherence to established privacy standards and data protection measures. Utilizing tools like Workday surveys or Microsoft Forms to gauge user understanding of privacy practices and secure their acknowledgment of associated responsibilities can significantly enhance accountability and compliance.

A culture of continuous improvement should be cultivated. Continuous monitoring and auditing of data access permissions, with timely adjustments to reflect changes in roles or responsibilities, are vital for maintaining data integrity and security. Regular consultations with legal experts to understand the implications of AI integrations and ensure compliance with current and future legislation are paramount for navigating the complex legal terrain of AI adoption. And, lastly, establishing a feedback loop for the continual assessment of AI tool effectiveness and privacy controls enables iterative improvements based on real-world use and stakeholder feedback. This proactive approach ensures that AI tools and policies remain effective, secure, and compliant with evolving standards and expectations.

4.4 Case Studies from the Field

In the evolving landscape of generative AI, qualitative insights gleaned from those at the forefront of its application in both industry and education are invaluable for understanding the practical challenges and opportunities that AI presents. This section delves into a series of anonymized case studies, drawing from in-depth interviews with a diverse group of professionals who are actively engaging with generative AI technologies within their institutions (Hutson & Rains, 2024b). Each case study highlights the experiences, perceptions, and strategic approaches of individuals from different types of institutions—ranging from higher education to various industries—and their roles within these organizations. By exploring these narratives, we aim to uncover key takeaways that illustrate the real-world impact of AI, providing insights into how different sectors are navigating its integration and harnessing its potential to enhance operational efficiency and educational outcomes.

The first interview of a Deputy CIO at a large public doctoral-degree granting institution highlights a three-year journey of integrating digital and generative AI technologies within the campus community. In this role, the interviewee oversees key areas such as Student Information Systems (SIS), data services, and intelligence. The scope of work has expanded significantly due to the integration of advanced technologies, and their leadership in AI initiatives reflects a commitment to navigating the evolving digital landscape, marked by a progression from web development to mobile technologies, and now to AI.

Throughout their career, the interviewee has noted a pattern of skepticism followed by acceptance, similar to the adoption cycles of cloud and mobile technologies. This historical perspective is informative for understanding the unique challenges posed by AI, particularly in terms of accessibility and institutional readiness. The interviewee's strategy involves phased integration, aligning with the EDUCAUSE model for digital transformation, which was accelerated by the pandemic. This strategy is underpinned by ongoing learning and engagement across the campus, emphasizing the critical role of diversity, equity, and inclusion (DEI) principles in technology adoption.

As a leader in AI adoption, the interviewee underscores the importance of institutional culture and leadership in overcoming barriers. Their role as Co-Director of the Community of Practice (CoP) facilitates a campus-wide dialogue on AI, involving faculty, administrators, staff, and students in the conversation. This collaborative approach ensures that the AI adoption process is inclusive and reflective of the diverse needs of the campus community. The establishment of the CoP in January 2024 formalized previously informal discussions, thereby structuring the integration of AI into the institutional academic and administrative frameworks. These efforts underscored the desire to take advantage of the potential of these new tools, while minimizing risk. As they noted,

> And so part of that then is like, how do you make sure that we're using AI responsibly so we don't have unintended consequences so that we minimize the…harm that can be done through certain communities, but it's also taking full advantage of that very powerful technology within the policies and guidelines of the university.

Key lessons from the AI adoption process at this institution highlight the significance of engagement, community input, and communication strategies tailored to support an AI-friendly culture. The experiences of the interviewee, compared with other institutions like Arizona State University, University of Notre Dame, and Michigan University, emphasize a common need for community-driven approaches to technology adoption. The interviewee also addresses the technical and policy challenges associated with AI integration, advocating for practices that are responsible and equitable, aimed at minimizing potential harm while maximizing the benefits of AI within the university's operational and ethical boundaries. Their leadership navigates the complexities of AI adoption and sets a standard for integrating these technologies in ways that respect and enhance the institution's mission and values.

The next interviewee, a Business Systems Specialist in the Collaboration & Productivity Services at a large public research university in Ontario, Canada, provides an in-depth view into the transformative role of digital technologies in academic settings, particularly during and after the rapid shift induced by the pandemic. Reflecting on the last decade, their work has primarily centered around technology enablement, leading to significant changes in course design and the integration of technology in teaching, enhancing both learning outcomes and the overall educational experience. They highlight the shift from trying to get people to adopt technology to now managing the integration and governance of these tools in a fully online learning and working environment.

With a focus on the practical aspects of integrating AI and digital tools within the university's IT framework, the interviewee details their role in navigating the challenges posed by the rapid deployment of new technologies like Microsoft 365 and AI integrations. They emphasize the critical aspect of governance in technology adoption, questioning how change management, risk management, and risk assessment are approached within the institution. They note, "At the end of the day, it's the governance; how do you approach change management, manage risk, how do you even determine risk?"

The conversation also considered the specific challenges associated with GAI technologies in particular, such as the pace at which these technologies evolve and are rolled out. The interviewee discusses the complexities of creating an assessment framework for new technologies that are not "ready-made" and whose terms of use and integration into educational settings are continuously changing. This leads to a cautious approach, preferring a "no, but…" stance over a "yes, but…," emphasizing the need for robust governance and provisional guidelines in response to rapid technological changes.

Lastly, they discuss the broader implications of AI adoption for policy development, focusing on the necessity of revisiting and potentially revising foundational policies such as data and record management to align with the new realities of AI integration. They argue for a granular approach to AI policies, breaking down existing frameworks to address the specifics of generative AI, highlighting the absence of comprehensive AI policies due to the pervasive impact of these technologies across various domains of university operations. They stress,

> We do not have an AI policy but are more specific; we need to break things down to the building blocks of what this constitutes and addressing all of that, then see where the gaps are in terms of what it should be.

At a public research university in New York with over 25,000 students, the Director of the Innovation Lab also shared insights into the AI integration process within educational settings. The interviewee describes their role as an engagement specialist, working to educate the campus community about the potential applications of AI in teaching and learning. Despite being an early advocate for AI, it was not until January 2024 that the university began to form organizational committees to explore AI, indicating a delayed but growing interest among faculty and administrative bodies. The most significant impact noted involves the adoption of AI among faculty, particularly within STEM and medical disciplines. Concerns have been raised about the accuracy of AI-generated information, especially in sensitive areas like medical treatments. The hesitance of the faculty is attributed to longstanding traditional teaching methods and the challenge of integrating new technologies into established curricula. Additionally, there are apprehensions about the ability of the tools to maintain academic integrity and the quality of content it produces, compared to human expertise.

Administratively, there are concerns about information security and the adequacy of AI tools like co-pilot, which have not met the community's needs due to issues such as data retention and adaptability to individual user styles. The interviewee highlights the ongoing struggle to balance innovation with security and usability, reflecting a broader challenge faced by institutions attempting to navigate the rapid evolution of digital tools. Collectively, the approach of this institution to AI is characterized by a grassroots effort, lacking a cohesive institutional strategy but slowly gaining traction through collaborative efforts across departments. This incremental adoption underscores the complexities of integrating AI within large educational institutions, where varying degrees of enthusiasm and resistance must be managed to foster a conducive environment for technological advancement.

In an in-depth discussion with another large public research university in the United States, the Dean of Libraries provided comprehensive insights into how AI is transforming various facets of university life. The Dean emphasized the significant changes in learning pedagogy and student behavior, facilitated by the proactive efforts of the university's staff. He mentioned, "There's just a really wide range of things happening at our institution," highlighting the initiative taken by the Center for the Advancement of Teaching to offer instruction and shape policies regarding syllabus expectations for both students and faculty. From an administrative perspective, AI has been instrumental in enhancing the university's approach to understanding student demographics and performance metrics. The Dean stated, "Knowing a lot more about our own institutional internal character and the characteristics of our students…understanding the way all the potential analytics can be used" has proven to be a straightforward yet impactful application of AI, already integrated into the university's administrative practices.

The discussion also covered the adaptation of academic programs to include AI, particularly in the School of Art and the School of Media and Communication. These programs have seen a significant integration of AI into journalism and graphic design curricula, supported by librarians who are actively developing online learning modules on AI and its research applications. This effort is aimed at building digital literacy across the academic community. Regarding the challenges and future directions for AI at the university, the Dean highlighted the necessity of an adaptive, AI-ready culture that encourages curiosity and engagement among staff and faculty. This involves fostering a community that is technically literate and open to exploring new technologies, which is crucial for navigating the rapidly evolving AI landscape. The Dean pointed out the importance of managing this dynamic environment effectively, noting the diverse applications and integrations of AI across the university's departments and initiatives.

Turning to a smaller organization, at a private Jesuit university, the Manager of Instructional Technology describes their role in facilitating AI integration into the educational framework. This manager is heavily involved in faculty development and the management of learning management systems, despite the absence of a formal teaching center. The ongoing initiatives focus on using AI to create efficient educational artifacts and assessments and to train faculty across various disciplines. The manager notes, "We're really pushing AI as a partner in the classroom, trying to help faculty become comfortable and innovative with these tools." The university's approach to AI adoption is described as decentralized and organic, with significant reliance on grassroots efforts. Departments independently seek resources, leading to varied levels of AI integration across the institution. This fragmentation has led to challenges in forming a cohesive institutional strategy. As the manager points out, "Every department is kind of doing its own thing, which makes it difficult to have a unified approach or to scale our efforts effectively." Resource constraints are a major hurdle, as highlighted by the manager's efforts to support AI initiatives within the scope of limited budgets. The lack of a centralized strategy has led to opportunistic rather than strategic resource allocation, affecting the scope and depth of AI-related projects. The manager expresses frustration, stating, "It's always a challenge to secure the necessary resources, which means we have to be creative in how we support and deploy AI tools." The manager also reflects on the cultural aspects of AI adoption within the university. There is an evident divide between enthusiastic adopters and those resistant to integrating new technologies into their teaching practices. This cultural divide complicates the widespread adoption of AI and shapes the discourse around its use in educational settings. The manager candidly shares, "There's a mix of excitement and skepticism about AI. We're trying to navigate these attitudes by emphasizing the practical benefits and addressing the concerns head-on."

The final interview was with a mid-sized private liberal arts university and its Director of Employee Development. The discussion included the transformative role of generative expectations and specialized training sessions, which are crucial for integrating AI effectively within educational settings. They pointed out the work being done at their learning academy to tailor training that aligns with operational needs and strategic objectives of the institution, emphasizing that AI is intended to assist rather than replace human roles. The senior administrator expanded on the broader implications of AI, focusing on how it redefines job roles and responsibilities. They stressed the importance of strategic professional development that leverages AI to enhance productivity and decision-making processes. A significant part of the discussion addressed the anxieties around job security due to AI integration, with both parties agreeing on the importance of transparent communication about AI's role as a supportive tool rather than a replacement. The Director remarked, "AI has been around for a long time and it's been used in the background…it's not replacing any of us."

Further, the need for a cultural shift within the institution to fully embrace AI technologies was identified. The Director noted challenges in integrating AI into existing workflows and underscored the importance of offering targeted, role-specific training to help faculty and staff understand and use AI tools effectively. They explained the varying needs for support among staff, saying, "Some people will take a link that you send them and say, 'Alright, I've got it.' Others need to see it within their context, in their job, for them to actually gravitate to the tool."

The role of institutional policies in facilitating or hindering the adoption of AI tools also came under scrutiny. Policies, they argued, should enable rather than restrict the use of AI, with the senior administrator pointing out, "Folks will do what they're allowed to do by policy."

The interview yielded several key recommendations:

1 **Develop Clear and Supportive Policies**: Institutions should establish policies that actively support the use of AI and are adaptable to rapid technological advancements.
2 **Enhanced Communication and Training**: Continuous efforts in communication and training are essential. These should clearly demonstrate how AI tools can be beneficial within the institution's framework, ensuring that all staff members are supported and well-informed.
3 **Address Cultural Resistance**: Managing cultural resistance is crucial. Institutions should promote an understanding of the benefits of AI and incorporate AI training into existing professional development programs to foster acceptance.
4 **Personalized Training Approaches**: Training should be customized to meet the diverse needs of various roles within the institution, facilitating smoother transitions and greater acceptance of AI technologies.

This dialogue underscores the evolving trend toward integrating AI in higher education and highlights the need for a supportive ecosystem that aligns technological advancements with institutional goals and the professional growth of its members. Through the detailed interviews conducted with various stakeholders across educational institutions, it becomes evident that the integration of AI in educational environments is multifaceted, requiring thoughtful consideration of both the technological and human aspects. The interviews collectively underscore the transformative potential of AI, yet also highlight the essential need for clarity in role expectations, robust training programs, and supportive policy frameworks.

A common narrative among the interviewees is the critical importance of clarity in role definitions. As AI technologies evolve, so too do the roles and responsibilities of faculty and staff. Effective communication regarding these changing expectations is crucial. This clarity not only helps in aligning staff and faculty with institutional goals but also mitigates anxiety and resistance to change, fostering a more receptive environment for AI integration. Moreover, the necessity for comprehensive and ongoing training emerges as a pivotal factor. Interviewees across the board stressed that for AI to be effectively integrated into educational practices, both staff and faculty must be equipped with the knowledge and skills to utilize these tools. This training should not only address the technical aspects of AI but also its ethical implications and potential impacts on job roles and responsibilities.

Policy and governance also play a significant role in the successful adoption of AI. Institutions must develop and maintain policies that support the ethical use of AI while protecting the interests of all stakeholders. Clear policies not only provide a framework for responsible AI usage but also help in building trust among users by ensuring transparency and accountability. Thus, the integration of AI in education is not merely a technological upgrade but a comprehensive change management challenge that involves rethinking job roles, enhancing skill sets, and establishing supportive policies. Institutions that approach AI integration with a strategic, holistic perspective are likely to not only enhance their operational efficiencies but also enrich the educational experiences of their students.

References

Abràmoff, M. D., Tarver, M. E., Loyo-Berrios, N., Trujillo, S., Char, D., Obermeyer, Z., … & Maisel, W. H. (2023). Considerations for addressing bias in artificial intelligence for health equity. *npj Digital Medicine*, *6*(1), 170.

Akbarighatar, P., Pappas, I., & Vassilakopoulou, P. (2023). A sociotechnical perspective for responsible AI maturity models: Findings from a mixed-method literature review. *International Journal of Information Management Data Insights*, *3*(2), 100193.

Akram, M., Sultan, M., & Deveci, M. (2024). An integrated multi-polar fuzzy N-soft preference ranking organization method for enrichment of evaluations of the digitization of global economy. *Artificial Intelligence Review*, *57*(3), 1–44.

Alam, M. S., Dhar, S. S., & Munira, K. S. (2020). HR Professionals' intention to adopt and use of artificial intelligence in recruiting talents. *Business Perspective Review*, *2*(2), 15–30.

Albahri, A. S., Duhaim, A. M., Fadhel, M. A., Alnoor, A., Baqer, N. S., Alzubaidi, L., ... & Deveci, M. (2023). A systematic review of trustworthy and explainable artificial intelligence in healthcare: Assessment of quality, bias risk, and data fusion. *Information Fusion*, *96*, 156–191.

Aldoseri, A., Al-Khalifa, K. N., & Hamouda, A. M. (2024). Methodological approach to assessing the current state of organizations for AI-based digital transformation. *Applied System Innovation*, *7*(1), 14.

Allhoff, F., & Henschke, A. (2018). The internet of things: Foundational ethical issues. *Internet of Things*, *1*, 55–66.

Alnahedh, M., & Alrashdan, A. (2021). To downsize or not to downsize: When and how does corporate downsizing create long-term value?. *Management Research Review*, *44*(11), 1539–1564.

Amudharasan, A. (2023). The impact of recommendation algorithms: Analyzing the influence of data on marketing strategies in the media sector. *Open Journal of Business and Management*, *11*(06), 3373–3384.

Andal-Ancion, A., Cartwright, P. A., & Yip, G. S. (2003). The digital transformation of traditional business. *MIT Sloan Management Review*. Retrieved July 31, 2024: https://sloanreview.mit.edu/article/the-digital-transformation-of-traditional-business/

Barsky, N. (September 5, 2023). Is AI better than your board? 60 seconds can prove it. *Forbes*. Retrieved: https://www.forbes.com/sites/noahbarsky/2023/09/05/is-ai-better-than-your-board/?ss=ai&sh=7da0ab2c4595

Bote, R., Wang, T., & Genet, C. (2023). You say social agenda, I say my job: Navigating moral ambiguities by frontline workers in a social enterprise. *Journal of Business Ethics*, *192*, 225–241.

Chen, M., & Decary, M. (2020, January). Artificial intelligence in healthcare: An essential guide for health leaders. In *Healthcare management forum* (Vol. 33, No. 1, pp. 10–18). SAGE Publications.

Chintala, S. (2023). AI-driven personalised treatment plans: The future of precision medicine. *Machine Intelligence Research*, *17*(02), 9718–9728.

Chuang, S. (2024). Indispensable skills for human employees in the age of robots and AI. *European Journal of Training and Development*, *48*(1/2), 179–195.

Commonwealth of Virginia. (2024). *Guidelines for AI integration throughout education in the Commonwealth of Virginia*. Retrieved: https://www.education.virginia.gov/media/governorvirginiagov/secretary-of-education/pdf/AI-Education-Guidelines.pdf

Coucke, P. (2024). Generative artificial intelligence and large language models in healthcare. *Revue Médicale de Liège*, *79*(1), 54–59.

Das, S. R., Sarkar, P., Patil, S., Sharma, R., Aggarwal, S., & Lourens, M. (2023, December). Artificial intelligence in human resource management: Transforming business practices. In *2023 10th IEEE Uttar Pradesh section international conference on electrical, electronics and computer engineering (UPCON)* (Vol. 10, pp. 1699–1703). IEEE.

De Haro, L. P. (2024). Biosecurity risk assessment for the use of artificial intelligence in synthetic biology. *Applied Biosafety*, *29*(2). https://doi.org/10.1089/apb.2023.0031

De Meuse, K. P., & Dai, G. (2013). Organizational downsizing: Its effect on financial performance over time. *Journal of Managerial Issues*, *25*(4), 324–344.

Douglas, D. D. (2024). *Responsibilities of an executive leading AI projects: Navigating federal directives for safe and inclusive development*. https://doi.org/10.20944/preprints202402.0815.v1

Dwivedi, Y. K., Hughes, L., Ismagilova, E., Aarts, G., Coombs, C., Crick, T., … & Williams, M. D. (2021). Artificial intelligence (AI): Multidisciplinary perspectives on emerging challenges, opportunities, and agenda for research, practice and policy. *International Journal of Information Management*, *57*, 101994.

Fang, L. (2023, December). Research on the design of college innovation and entrepreneurship platform system based on artificial intelligence technology. In *2023 3rd international conference on mobile networks and wireless communications (ICMNWC)* (pp. 1–7). IEEE.

Flemin, R. (November 26, 2023). When 40% productivity improvement turns into 0%. Retrieved: https://www.linkedin.com/pulse/when-40-productivity-improvement-turns-0-ray-fleming-doajc/?trackingId=JAcfYoHyRrmvHDVxExmy1w%3D%3D

Fountaine, T., McCarthy, B., & Saleh, T. (2019). Building the AI-powered organization. *Harvard Business Review*, *97*(4), 62–73.

Giudici, P. (2018). Fintech risk management: A research challenge for artificial intelligence in finance. *Frontiers in Artificial Intelligence*, *1*, 1.

Gkikas, D. C., & Theodoridis, P. K. (2022). AI in consumer behavior. *Advances in artificial intelligence-based technologies: Selected papers in honour of professor Nikolaos G. Bourbakis*—Vol. 1, 147–176. Springer Cham.

Goel, R., Kumar, A., & Haddow, J. (2020). PRISM: A strategic decision framework for cybersecurity risk assessment. *Information & Computer Security*, *28*(4), 591–625.

Grewal, D., Motyka, S., & Levy, M. (2018). The evolution and future of retailing and retailing education. *Journal of Marketing Education*, *40*(1), 85–93.

Gupta, T & Bansal, S. (2023). Navigating the AI revolution: a new era in marketing. *International Journal of Science and Research (IJSR) 12*(12), 2065.

Hassan, M., Aziz, L. A. R., & Andriansyah, Y. (2023). The role artificial intelligence in modern banking: An exploration of AI-driven approaches for enhanced fraud prevention, risk management, and regulatory compliance. *Reviews of Contemporary Business Analytics*, *6*(1), 110–132.

Hassani, H., Silva, E. S., Unger, S., TajMazinani, M., & Mac Feely, S. (2020). Artificial intelligence (AI) or intelligence augmentation (IA): What is the future?. *Ai*, *1*(2), 8.

Helberger, N., & Diakopoulos, N. (2023). The European AI act and how it matters for research into AI in media and journalism. *Digital Journalism*, *11*(9), 1751–1760.

Hendrick & Struggles (2024). *Route to the top*. CEO & Board of Directors Practice. Hendrick & Struggles International, Inc.

Hmoud, B. (2021). The adoption of artificial intelligence in human resource management and the role of human resources. In *Forum Scientiae Oeconomia* (Vol. 9, No. 1, pp. 105–118). Wydawnictwo Naukowe Akademii WSB.

Holbeche, L. (2023). *The agile organization: How to build an engaged, innovative and resilient business*. Kogan Page Publishers.

Hong, Z., & Xiao, K. (2024). Digital economy structuring for sustainable development: The role of blockchain and artificial intelligence in improving supply chain and reducing negative environmental impacts. *Scientific Reports*, *14*(1), 3912.

Huda, M. (2019). Empowering application strategy in the technology adoption: Insights from professional and ethical engagement. *Journal of Science and Technology Policy Management*, *10*(1), 172–192.

Hutson, J. & Rains. T. (2024a). *AI institutional adoption study [data set]*. Lindenwood University.

Hutson, J. & Rains. T. (2024b). *Qualitative leadership interview study [data set]*. Lindenwood University.

IBM. (2024). *The CEO's guide to generative AI.* IBM Corporation. Retrieved: https://www.ibm.com/downloads/cas/BN9Y6QPN

Ibrahim, M. S., & Saber, S. (2023). Machine learning and predictive analytics: Advancing disease prevention in healthcare. *Journal of Contemporary Healthcare Analytics*, *7*(1), 53–71.

Jabbari, J., Despard, M., Kondratjeva, O., Gupta, B., & Grinstein-Weiss, M. (2023). Nothing to show for it: Financial distress and re-enrollment aspirations for those with non-degreed debt. *Research in Higher Education*, *64*(1), 1–32.

Jagatheesaperumal, S. K., Rahouti, M., Ahmad, K., Al-Fuqaha, A., & Guizani, M. (2021). The duo of artificial intelligence and big data for industry 4.0: Applications, techniques, challenges, and future research directions. *IEEE Internet of Things Journal*, *9*(15), 12861–12885.

Johnson, R., & Easttom, C. (2020). *Security policies and implementation issues*. Jones & Bartlett Learning.

Joshi, U. (2023). Bankruptcy and failure of Lehman Brothers: A study on modus operandi, prevention technique and a way forward. *Prevention technique and a way forward (January 23, 2023)*. http://dx.doi.org/10.2139/ssrn.4334913

Kelley, S. (2022). Employee perceptions of the effective adoption of AI principles. *Journal of Business Ethics*, *178*(4), 871–893.

Khan, W. U., & Seto, E. (2023). A "do no harm" novel safety checklist and research approach to determine whether to launch an artificial intelligence–based medical technology: Introducing the biological-psychological, economic, and social (BPES) framework. *Journal of Medical Internet Research*, *25*, e43386.

Kim, D., Borowiec, K., Yatsu, D. K., & Wortham, S. (2023). Voices from the industry: How edtech leaders responded to the COVID-19 pandemic *ECNU Review of Education*, *7*(2), 420–441. https://doi.org/10.1177/20965311241237239

Kitcharoen, P., Howimanporn, S., & Chookaew, S. (2024). Enhancing teachers' AI competencies through artificial intelligence of things professional development training. *International Journal of Interactive Mobile Technologies*, *18*(2), 4–15.

Kulkov, I., Kulkova, J., Rohrbeck, R., Menvielle, L., Kaartemo, V., & Makkonen, H. (2023). Artificial intelligence-driven sustainable development: Examining organizational, technical, and processing approaches to achieving global goals. *Sustainable Development*, *32*(3), 2253–2267.

Kuziemski, M., & Misuraca, G. (2020). AI governance in the public sector: Three tales from the frontiers of automated decision-making in democratic settings. *Telecommunications Policy*, *44*(6), 101976.

Lanzolla, G., & Anderson, J. (2008). Digital transformation. *Business Strategy Review*, *19*(2), 72–76.

Lokesh, G. R., & Harish, K. S. (2023). Synergizing an intelligent communication terminal: An evolution of a sophisticated HRM framework empowered by augmented analytics. *Remittances Review*, *8*(4), 1886–1899.

Maassen, P., Gornitzka, Å., & Fumasoli, T. (2017). University reform and institutional autonomy: A framework for analysing the living autonomy. *Higher Education Quarterly*, *71*(3), 239–250.

Maghsudi, S., Lan, A., Xu, J., & van Der Schaar, M. (2021). Personalized education in the artificial intelligence era: What to expect next. *IEEE Signal Processing Magazine*, *38*(3), 37–50.

Mahra, A. K. (2005). Management information technology: Managing the organisation in digital era. *International Journal of Advanced Science and Technology*, *4238*(29), 6.

Markauskaite, L., Marrone, R., Poquet, O., Knight, S., Martinez-Maldonado, R., Howard, S., … & Siemens, G. (2022). Rethinking the entwinement between artificial intelligence and human learning: What capabilities do learners need for a world with AI?. *Computers and Education: Artificial Intelligence*, *3*, 100056.

Mehr, H., Ash, H., & Fellow, D. (2017). Artificial intelligence for citizen services and government. *Ash Center for Democratic Governance and Innovation at the Harvard Kennedy School*, no. August, 1–12.

Miller, C. & Waters, G. (2024). *Risk management framework for procuring AI systems*. AI Procurement Lab.

Mohamed, M., Stankosky, M., & Murray, A. (2006). Knowledge management and information technology: Can they work in perfect harmony?. *Journal of Knowledge Management*, *10*(3), 103–116.

Molęda, M., Małysiak-Mrozek, B., Ding, W., Sunderam, V., & Mrozek, D. (2023). From corrective to predictive maintenance—A review of maintenance approaches for the power industry. *Sensors*, *23*(13), 5970.

Nishant, R., Nguyen, T., Teo, T. S., & Hsu, P. F. (2023). Role of substantive and rhetorical signals in the market reaction to announcements on AI adoption: A configurational study. *European Journal of Information Systems*, 1–43. https://doi.org/10.1080/0960085X.2023.2243892

Onsori, A., Khamseh, A., Torabi, T., & Yazdani, H. (2023). Enhancing cooperation: A futuristic ANFIS model for anticipating strategic alliances between fintech start-ups and the banking sector. *Fuzzy Optimization and Modeling Journal*, *4*(3), 16–33.

Panda, A., Pasumarti, S. S., & Hiremath, S. (2023). Adoption of artificial intelligence in HR practices: An empirical analysis. In *The adoption and effect of artificial intelligence on human resources management*, Part B (pp. 65–80). Emerald Publishing Limited.

Papyshev, G., & Yarime, M. (2023). The state's role in governing artificial intelligence: Development, control, and promotion through national strategies. *Policy Design and Practice*, *6*(1), 79–102.

Park, E. (2023). The AI bill of rights: A step in the right direction. *Orange County Lawyer Magazine*, *65*(2), 25–28.

Pekovic, S., Wagner, M., & Vogt, S. (2022). Differential effects of corporate social responsibility on downsizing: Evidence from the United States. *Corporate Social Responsibility and Environmental Management*, *29*(4), 1021–1033.

Prasad Agrawal, K. (2023). Towards adoption of generative AI in organizational settings. *Journal of Computer Information Systems*, 1–16. https://doi.org/10.1080/08874417.2023.2240744

Purnawati, E. (2024). The influence of digital technology on marketing strategy. *Management Studies and Business Journal (PRODUCTIVITY)*, *1*(3), 432–446.

Rane, N. (October 13, 2023). Enhancing customer loyalty through Artificial Intelligence (AI), Internet of Things (IoT), and Big Data technologies: Improving customer satisfaction, engagement, relationship, and experience. *Internet of things (IoT), and big data technologies: Improving customer satisfaction, engagement, relationship, and experience*. http://dx.doi.org/10.2139/ssrn.4616051

Reddy, S. (2024). Generative AI in healthcare: An implementation science informed translational path on application, integration and governance. *Implementation Science*, *19*(1), 1–15.

Riemer, K., Hafermalz, E., Roosen, A., Boussand, N., El Aoufi, H., Mo, D., & Kosheliev, A. (2017). *The Fintech Advantage: Harnessing digital technology, keeping the customer in focus*. http://hdl.handle.net/2123/16259

Rosenberg, B. (2023). *"Whatever it is, I'm against it": Resistance to change in higher education*. Harvard Education Press.

Rosowsky, D. (October 1, 2023). The enemy within: Former college presidents offer warnings. *Forbes*. Retrieved: https://www.forbes.com/sites/davidrosowsky/2023/10/01/the-enemy-within-former-college-presidents-offer-warnings/?sh=67d67e4d1929

Salvagno, M., Taccone, F. S., & Gerli, A. G. (2023). Artificial intelligence hallucinations. *Critical Care*, *27*(1), 180.

Sapci, A. H., & Sapci, H. A. (2020). Artificial intelligence education and tools for medical and health informatics students: Systematic review. *JMIR Medical Education*, *6*(1), e19285.

Schuett, J. (2023). Risk management in the artificial intelligence act. *European Journal of Risk Regulation*, 1–19. https://doi.org/10.1017/err.2023.1

Shah, V. (2021). Machine learning algorithms for cybersecurity: Detecting and preventing threats. *Revista Espanola de Documentacion Cientifica*, *15*(4), 42–66.

Shams, R. A., Zowghi, D., & Bano, M. (2023). AI and the quest for diversity and inclusion: A systematic literature review. *AI and Ethics*, *13*, 1–28.

Sofia, M., Fraboni, F., De Angelis, M., Puzzo, G., Giusino, D., & Pietrantoni, L. (2023). The impact of artificial intelligence on workers' skills: Upskilling and reskilling in organisations. *Informing Science: The International Journal of an Emerging Transdiscipline*, *26*, 39–68.

Stackpole, B. (January 3, 2024). *A framework for assessing AI risk*. MIT Management Sloan School. Retrieved: https://mitsloan.mit.edu/ideas-made-to-matter/a-framework-assessing-ai-risk

Stoilova, E. (2021). AI chatbots as a customer service and support tool. *ROBONOMICS: The Journal of the Automated Economy*, *2*, 21–21.

Sun, J., Ma, H., Zeng, Y., Han, D., & Jin, Y. (2023). Promoting the AI teaching competency of K-12 computer science teachers: A TPACK-based professional development approach. *Education and Information Technologies*, *28*(2), 1509–1533.

Susanto, A. P., Lyell, D., Akbar, S., Widyantoro, B., Berkovsky, S., & Magrabi, F. (2023) Applying Ai to Support Cardiovascular Risk Prediction in Resource-Constrained Settings: Qualitative Insights from Indonesian Doctors. *Available at SSRN 4771862*.

Tanase, G. C. (2024). The integration of emotional intelligence into AI marketing: Connecting brands with consumers. *Romanian Distribution Committee Magazine*, *15*(1), 29–37.

Tarulli, B., & Sokol, M. (2024). A call to action for rethinking workforce planning. *Strategic workforce planning: Best practices and emerging directions*, 371. Oxford Academic.

Topol, E. J. (2019). High-performance medicine: The convergence of human and artificial intelligence. *Nature Medicine*, *25*(1), 44–56.

Trad, A. T. (2024). Enterprise transformation projects: The polymathic enterprise architecture-based generic learning processes (PEAbGLP). In *Machine learning and data science techniques for effective government service delivery* (pp. 29–66). IGI Global.

Trappey, A. J., Li, F., Lee, C. H., Mo, J. P., Stjepandic, J., & Jiao, R. (2024). How to manage and balance uncertainty by transdisciplinary engineering methods focusing on digital transformations of complex systems. *Advanced Engineering Informatics*, *59*, 102330.

Vashishth, T. K., Sharma, V., Sharma, K. K., Kumar, B., Panwar, R., & Chaudhary, S. (2024). AI-driven learning analytics for personalized feedback and assessment in higher education. In *Using traditional design methods to enhance AI-driven decision making* (pp. 206–230). IGI Global.

Whitlock, C., & Strickland, F. (2022). Leading the Program. In *Winning the National Security AI Competition: A Practical Guide for Government and Industry Leaders* (pp. 47–77). Berkeley, CA: Apress.
Wirtz, B. W., Weyerer, J. C., & Geyer, C. (2019). Artificial intelligence and the public sector—applications and challenges. *International Journal of Public Administration, 42*(7), 596–615.
Wirtz, B. W., Weyerer, J. C., & Kehl, I. (2022). Governance of artificial intelligence: A risk and guideline-based integrative framework. *Government Information Quarterly, 39*(4), 101685.
Wylde, V., Prakash, E., Hewage, C., & Platts, J. (2023). Ethical challenges in the use of digital technologies: AI and big data. In *Digital transformation in policing: the promise, perils and solutions* (pp. 33–58). Springer International Publishing.
Xu, M., Du, H., Niyato, D., Kang, J., Xiong, Z., Mao, S., ... & Poor, H. V. (2024). Unleashing the power of edge-cloud generative AI in mobile networks: A survey of AIGC services. *IEEE Communications Surveys & Tutorials, 26*, 1127–1170.
Young, C. (July 14, 2023). Building a winning AI strategy for your business. *Harvard Business Review*. Retrieved: https://hbr.org/2023/07/build-a-winning-ai-strategy-for-your-business

5 Organizational Culture and Skill Development

5.1 Formulating AI Use Policies

As AI becomes increasingly embedded in academic and industry environments, the necessity for clear, actionable policies governing its use is becoming more urgent. Recent findings from Inside Higher Ed's annual survey of chief academic officers highlight a significant gap in preparedness across higher education institutions (Quinn, 2024). Notably, only one in five provosts reported that their colleges or universities have established policies regulating AI use in teaching and research. This lack of policy framework is concerning, given the rapid advancement of generative AI technologies and their potential for misuse, such as in the production of deceitfully authentic academic work. Gregor Thuswaldner, Provost at Whitworth University and President of the Association of Chief Academic Officers, reflects on the current landscape, acknowledging that while some institutions rely on existing plagiarism policies to govern AI use, this approach may not suffice given AI's unique challenges and capabilities. He emphasized the need for institutions to not ignore the sweeping changes AI is bringing, stating, "AI is here to stay, and we cannot put our heads in the sand. Our world will be completely dominated by AI and, at this point, we ain't seen nothing yet." This sentiment underscores the growing necessity for educational institutions to proactively address AI's implications through comprehensive policy-making.

The survey also revealed a disconnect in curriculum adaptation, with only about one in seven provosts indicating that their curricula have been revised to prepare students for AI-driven workplaces. This suggests a broader need for institutions to integrate AI literacy and ethical considerations into their educational frameworks. Provost George Justice of the University of Tulsa highlighted the varied responses within academic circles, ranging from outright bans on AI in coursework to proactive integration strategies aimed at maximizing AI's educational benefits. He advocates for a balanced approach, suggesting that "if AI can produce what universities are asking students to do, then we're probably asking the wrong question," thereby promoting an

DOI: 10.4324/9781003512813-5

educational focus on process over product. This perspective aligns with the need for AI use policies that not only prevent misuse but also enhance educational outcomes and prepare students for future challenges. These policies should not only address the potential risks associated with AI but also harness its capabilities to enrich learning and operational efficiency.

The development of such policies will require a concerted effort among institutional leaders, educators, and industry partners to ensure they are comprehensive, forward-thinking, and aligned with the overarching goals of educational excellence and integrity. When formulating policies on the utilization of AI in higher education institutions, several crucial considerations must be deliberated upon (Sticker, 2023). Firstly, a fundamental decision must be made regarding the permissibility of AI tools during examinations and tests. Institutions must weigh the merits of either implementing an outright ban on AI usage or permitting its deployment under specific conditions, which would necessitate meticulous delineation. Another pertinent consideration lies in the realm of student assignments and written work. A policy must be established to determine whether students should be mandated to explicitly indicate when AI tools have contributed to their assignments, and if so, the precise mechanisms for such disclosure. This transparency would foster academic integrity and accountability. As well, institutions must develop guidelines governing the etiquette surrounding the use of chatbots, such as Claude, Bing, and ChatGPT, in classroom settings. A policy should outline whether students are obligated to disclose their reliance on such chatbots when answering questions or preparing for class, thereby promoting transparency and fairness.

The use of AI by employees in their professional capacities must also be addressed. Guidelines should be established regarding the permissibility of AI-assisted development of instructional materials, case studies, and other educational resources by faculty members. If permitted, mechanisms must be implemented to ensure the quality and accuracy of AI-generated content.

These considerations merely scratch the surface of the multitude of issues that must be deliberated upon when formulating comprehensive AI policies for higher education institutions. As the prevalence of generative AI continues to accelerate, the establishment of clear and transparent guidelines becomes increasingly imperative. Such policies would not only foster academic integrity and accountability but also create a safe and ethical framework for the responsible integration of AI into the educational landscape.

One of the earliest to attempt to outline what an institutional AI policy should consider was WCET (2023). A survey in the spring of 2023 conducted by WCET revealed that at the time only 8% of respondents reported that their institution had developed and/or implemented at least one AI-related policy. This statistic underscores the urgent need for comprehensive policy frameworks to address the multifaceted implications of AI integration in higher education.

The survey further indicated that an overwhelming majority of institutions, 65%, either have or intend to develop AI policies, but have yet to do so. While initial policy discussions on campuses have primarily centered on academic integrity concerns, a holistic approach necessitates considerations that extend beyond this singular aspect. To aid institutions in identifying and addressing the myriad policy areas that demand attention, WCET has developed an AI Policy and Practice Framework. This framework categorizes institutional AI policy needs into three critical dimensions: Governance, Operations, and Pedagogy (Table 5.1).

Table 5.1 Dimensions of AI Implementation in Higher Education Institutions

Dimension	*Description*
Governance	The Governance dimension emphasizes the oversight and decision-making responsibilities of senior institutional leadership, including positions such as the Chancellor/President, Chief Academic Officer, Chief Information Officer, Vice Presidents, Deans, and Chairs of academic units. This dimension encompasses several crucial areas.
Data governance	Developing policies and processes to ensure effective and responsible management, security, and control of institutional data throughout its lifecycle, in alignment with business objectives.
Evaluation of AI use	Overseeing and evaluating the effectiveness of AI implementation across the institution, harnessing data and feedback for continuous improvement.
Promoting and monitoring faculty/staff AI usage	Encouraging appropriate AI utilization by campus personnel while monitoring ethical, effective, and appropriate use, including in research endeavors.
Inclusive, equitable access	Ensuring equitable access to AI technologies for all students, faculty, administrators, and staff, fostering an inclusive learning environment.
Intellectual property	Defining and protecting intellectual property, including research, course materials, and student-produced work, when created using AI, in accordance with relevant laws and regulations.
AI use and promotion, tenure, & reappointment practices	Considering the role of AI-assisted works in faculty promotion, tenure, and reappointment processes, while guarding against plagiarism.
Operations	The Operations dimension assists in the understanding and implementation of AI across the institution, involving key areas such as Academic Affairs, Information Technology, and Centers for Teaching & Learning Effectiveness/Excellence. This dimension encompasses:

(*Continued*)

Table 5.1 (Continued)

Dimension	*Description*
Professional development (training & support)	Offering comprehensive training and support on AI technologies to administrators, staff, faculty, and students, fostering confidence and capability in navigating the AI landscape.
Developing and maintaining AI infrastructure	Ensuring the development and maintenance of an institution's AI infrastructure, likely led by Information Technology in consultation with other units.
Review and recommend AI implementation	Engaging operational units in reviewing and recommending AI platforms and tools to enhance the efficiency and effectiveness of institutional operations, including student services, instruction, admissions, recruitment, staff workflows, and resource planning.
Pedagogy	The Pedagogy dimension emphasizes the practical implementation of AI to support instruction and learning in the classroom, with faculty as the initiators. This dimension includes:
Academic integrity	Developing policies and guidelines regarding the appropriate use and attribution of AI technologies in academic work, ranging from outright bans to permitted and encouraged use with proper acknowledgment.
Assessment practices	Reevaluating assessment methods to balance the benefits of AI with the need to maintain academic integrity.
Clear communication to students	Clearly articulating expectations for AI use in course syllabi and verbal communications.
Developing student AI competencies and skills/workforce preparation	Preparing students for the AI-infused workforce by equipping them with relevant skills, knowledge, and ethical considerations.
Understanding algorithmic bias	Raising awareness among students about the potential for discrimination and bias in AI systems due to human involvement in data inputs and development processes.
Regular & substantive interaction	Addressing the extent to which faculty can automate instruction through AI and leveraging AI while maintaining meaningful student-instructor interactions.
Learner accessibility	Ensuring that AI tools and interfaces are accessible to all students, including those with disabilities and learning challenges, and support the use of assistive technologies.

The Governance dimension of the AI Policy and Practice Framework underscores the pivotal role of senior institutional leadership in shaping the strategic direction and oversight of AI integration within higher education. This cohort, encompassing positions such as the Chancellor/President, Chief Academic Officer, Chief Information Officer, Vice Presidents, Deans, and Chairs of academic units, bears the responsibility of initiating and guiding the institution's AI agenda. Their decision-making authority enables them to set the tone for effective and innovative AI use across the campus, ensuring that all policies and practices foster an equitable and inclusive environment while supporting the overarching mission and goals of the institution. Key areas of focus within the Governance dimension include data governance, evaluating the impact of AI implementation, promoting and monitoring appropriate faculty and staff usage, ensuring inclusive and equitable access, addressing intellectual property considerations, and aligning AI practices with promotion, tenure, and reappointment processes.

The Operations dimension assists in the practical understanding and implementation of AI technologies across the institution. This dimension involves collaborative efforts from various operational units, such as Academic Affairs, Information Technology, and Centers for Teaching & Learning Effectiveness/Excellence. It encompasses crucial responsibilities, including providing comprehensive professional development, training, and support to all stakeholders engaged with AI, ranging from administrators and staff to faculty and students. This investment in capacity-building can alleviate concerns and foster confidence in navigating the complexities of the AI landscape. Additionally, the Operations dimension is responsible for developing and maintaining the institution's AI infrastructure, a task that will likely be led by Information Technology in consultation with other units to determine needs, evaluate costs, and assess the efficacy of available tools. Furthermore, operational units play a vital role in reviewing and recommending AI platforms and tools that can enhance the efficiency and effectiveness of various institutional processes, such as student services, instruction, admissions, recruitment, staff workflows, and resource planning.

The Pedagogy dimension emphasizes the practical implementation of AI to support instruction and learning within the classroom environment. Faculty members serve as the initiators of this dimension, working collaboratively with those in the Operations realm to actualize policies and planning from the Governance level, while consistently considering ethical dimensions. Instructors are ultimately responsible for designing and implementing curricula, activities, and assessments that leverage AI technologies in a manner that enhances students' learning experiences. Key areas of focus within the Pedagogy dimension include developing policies and guidelines to uphold academic integrity, reevaluating assessment practices to balance the benefits of AI with maintaining academic rigor, clearly communicating expectations for AI use to students, developing students' AI competencies and skills to prepare them for the workforce, raising awareness about algorithmic bias, addressing the extent to which AI can automate instruction while maintaining meaningful student-instructor interactions, and ensuring accessibility of AI tools for all learners, including those with disabilities.

Since 2023, numerous resources have become available to guide the development of communication strategies and policies for the use of GAI in educational settings. A comprehensive collection can be found here: https://padlet.com/cetl6/university-policies-on-generative-ai-m9n7wf05r7rdc6pe Many educational institutions offer these resources on their websites, providing diverse strategies ranging from adapting assignments to include GAI (NYU, 2024) to integrating AI tools into classroom activities and supporting educators in their use (TU, 2024). A synthesis of such recommended policies for student use of AI can be found in Table 5.2. A critical early step in this process involves establishing clear classroom expectations through a syllabus statement. Such a statement not only clarifies expectations for students but also serves as a vital document for upholding academic integrity should violations occur. Without a clearly defined AI use policy in the syllabus, faculty members may have limited recourse if students breach established rules.

While some may suggest a total prohibition of AI tools due to their integration into various word-processing platforms (Yu, 2023), a more balanced approach is often more practical. For example, guidelines can specify permissible uses of AI, such as assisting in tutoring, brainstorming, grammar editing, and outline creation, while explicitly prohibiting its use in composing the final draft of an assignment (Mollick & Mollick, 2023). This approach recognizes the ubiquity of AI tools and their potential to enhance educational experiences without compromising academic rigor. Regardless,

Table 5.2 University Policies on the Use of AI in Coursework

Policy category	*Examples*	*Key points*
No use allowed	Duke University (No AI-generated submissions in writing courses, considered plagiarism)—Duke Learning Innovation & Lifetime Education	AI-generated content is strictly prohibited and treated as academic dishonesty.
Some use allowed	Harvard T.H. Chan School of Public Health (Use allowed with explicit permission and must be cited, varies by course)—Office of Educational Programs	AI use is permitted under specific conditions set by instructors; requires full disclosure and appropriate citations.
All use allowed	Stanford University (Generative AI tools can be used freely for all coursework, following data privacy guidelines)—Teaching and Learning Hub	Unrestricted use of AI tools in coursework, subject to university's data privacy guidelines.

institutions tend to adopt one of three general policies regarding AI tool usage: Prohibition of AI Use, Conditional Use, and Unrestricted Use (Dempere et al., 2023; Kobeissi, 2023; Lund, 2023; Plata et al., 2023; Xiao et al., 2023). These policies reflect the varied approaches institutions take based on their specific educational philosophies and the technological literacy of their communities. Each policy type aims to balance the benefits of AI in education with the need to maintain integrity and critical engagement in students' academic work.

The educational landscape has witnessed divergent institutional approaches to the integration of AI tools within course activities and assignments. These disparate strategies are underpinned by distinct educational philosophies and technological integration methodologies (Chan, 2023). Certain institutions have adopted a conservative stance, prohibiting the employment of AI tools in any aspect of graded assignments or course activities. This prohibition emanates from concerns pertaining to academic integrity, encompassing apprehensions that AI might facilitate plagiarism or hinder the development of critical thinking and original writing proficiencies (Ghimire & Edwards, 2024). Through the attempted enforcement of a stringent ban, these institutions endeavor to ensure that all work submitted by students is authentically their own, thereby safeguarding academic standards. Conversely, other institutions permit the utilization of AI tools, albeit under stringent conditions. This conditional use policy mandates that all AI-generated content be properly cited, akin to traditional sources. Restrictions are frequently imposed on the types of assignments or stages of the coursework where AI can be employed, typically during brainstorming or drafting phases (Ibrahim et al., 2023). Within this framework, AI is perceived as a tool to augment the educational process rather than replace it, helping to strike a balance between the benefits of technological assistance and the necessity of maintaining rigorous academic standards and accountability (Crawford et al., 2023).

An alternate perspective is embraced by some educational institutions that permit unrestricted utilization of AI tools across all coursework, provided students properly cite any AI-generated content (Lau & Guo, 2023). This progressive policy acknowledges the potential of AI to significantly enhance learning and creative processes. Within this framework, AI is regarded as a valuable resource that can bolster a broad spectrum of educational activities, ranging from idea generation and research to drafting and revising documents. Such institutions perceive AI as a means to enrich the academic experience without compromising educational outcomes, placing trust in the capacity of these tools to effectively supplement traditional educational methods (Gimpel et al., 2023).

The policy also takes into account the current state of AI-detection software, particularly as exemplified by tools like Turnitin, which warrants judicious scrutiny. As of May 14, 2023, Turnitin reported that, among 38.5 million submissions analyzed for AI-generated content, approximately 9.6% contained over 20% of text likely produced by AI writing tools, while 3.5% exhibited between 80% and 100% AI-generated content (Chechitelli, 2023). These data underscore the increasing prevalence of AI assistance in academic writing. It is noteworthy that the AI writing detection model predominantly targets prose text, commonly found in long-form writing such as essays. Its efficacy diminishes when dealing with non-prose formats, including poetry, scripts, code, ordered or unordered lists, tables, or annotated bibliographies (Chaka, 2023). This limitation poses a significant challenge in environments where diverse forms of writing are prevalent. Moreover, the accuracy of these AI detection tools is a matter of ongoing concern. Misidentifications, both in flagging human-generated text as AI-produced and vice versa, necessitate additional layers of human analysis to verify conclusions drawn by different detectors (Rashidi et al., 2023). This raises questions about the reliability of relying solely on such tools to identify AI-generated content, particularly in high-stakes academic settings where the consequences of erroneous classifications could be severe.

Therefore, whether banning of embracing these tools, these divergent policies reflect varying degrees of openness and control in integrating AI into educational frameworks for students. The chosen approach is often contingent upon the overarching educational objectives of the institution, the specific needs of its student body, and the level of confidence in students' ability to utilize these tools responsibly. Nonetheless, irrespective of the policy adopted by an institution, they will be continually revisited and revised as the technology evolves and expectations of fluency in its use are heightened. But these so far have focused on student use, and not on that of employees.

Whether in industry or education, the evolving landscape of workplace technology finds organizations increasingly focusing on developing comprehensive policies for the responsible use of generative AI tools. As these tools can significantly enhance productivity and innovation, it is crucial for companies to establish clear guidelines that govern their use. According to the Future of Privacy Forum, organizations should ensure that their policies align with existing legal frameworks and internal data protection policies. This includes revising existing policies to accommodate the integration of AI technologies while ensuring that all employees are aware of their legal responsibilities when using these tools (Budhwar et al., 2023). Employee education and training play a pivotal role in the responsible deployment of generative AI in the workplace. Organizations are advised to provide thorough training programs that cover the ethical use, potential risks, and technical aspects of AI tools. This not only helps in mitigating risks associated with AI but also enhances the overall competency of the workforce in leveraging AI for optimal benefits. Regular updates and refreshers on these topics are essential to keep pace with the rapid advancements in AI technology (Rane, 2023).

Transparency and disclosure have previously also critical components of an effective generative AI policy prior to the availability of platforms such as Microsoft's Co-Pilot. Organizations have stressed the need to clearly define protocols for when and how employees can use AI tools, emphasizing the importance of documenting and disclosing AI use within the workplace. This ensures that all AI-generated outputs are accountable and traceable, which is vital for maintaining the integrity and trustworthiness of the processes enhanced by AI (Rožman et al., 2023). Moreover, policies should address the verification of AI outputs to ensure accuracy, relevance, and compliance with company standards and values, especially concerning intellectual property rights and data privacy (Díaz-Rodríguez et al., 2023). Also, considering the ethical implications and potential biases of generative AI is indispensable. Organizations should implement policies that actively prevent and mitigate bias in AI outputs, protect user privacy, and ensure that AI applications align with ethical standards. This involves continuous monitoring and evaluation of AI tools to safeguard against unintended consequences and maintain regulatory compliance. As generative AI technologies become more embedded in business operations, the dynamic nature of these policies will require regular updates and adjustments to address new challenges and opportunities that arise.

An example of such considerations for institutions and employees can be found at the authors' own institution. The "Use of Generative AI in Employment Policy" at Lindenwood University was designed at time of inception to govern the utilization of generative AI tools by its employees and contractors (LU, 2024) (Table 5.3). The policy is particularly significant given the evolving capabilities of AI to generate creative content such as text, art, and music. As these tools, including popular models like ChatGPT, can process and generate outputs based on extensive datasets, the policy aims to guide their use in a manner that aligns with legal standards and protects both personal and institutional data. As other policies also consider, the scope of the policy is comprehensive, applying to all university employees and contractors, regulating the use of generative AI strictly for university purposes. Personal use of AI for non-university tasks is not covered under this policy, emphasizing a clear demarcation between professional and personal AI use.

Key to the policy is the categorization of AI usage into prohibited, high-risk, medium-risk, and low-risk activities. Each category is defined by the sensitivity of the data involved and the potential risk to the university's privacy, security, and compliance obligations. For example, the policy explicitly prohibits the use of generative AI for processing non-public personal data or confidential university information. High-risk activities, such as drafting

Table 5.3 Use of Generative AI in Employment Policy

Section	*Details*
Purpose	To provide guidelines for the use of generative AI by employees and those performing work for Lindenwood.
Scope	Applies to all employees and those performing work or services for Lindenwood; covers only university-related use.
Policy definitions	Definitions of terms such as "Application," "University," "Legal," "Personal Data," "IT," "Network," "System," and "Users."
Use case dependent	Use of Generative AI depends on the specific use case; requires sound judgment prior to use.
Prohibited processing activities	Includes not using AI for non-public personal data, student info, confidential info, HR processes, and legal documents.
High risk processing activities	Activities like preparing public documents and making significant decisions require written approval and human review.
Medium risk processing activities	Uses not covered by other sections need risk analysis and supervisor approval before proceeding.
Low risk processing activities	Low-risk activities do not require review; include personal use and instructional use within policy limits.
Independent validation	All outputs must be independently validated for accuracy and legality.
Transparency	Use of AI must be disclosed, especially in public documents and communications.
Exceptions	Exceptions may be considered under limited circumstances with prior approval from Legal.
Training	Mandatory ongoing training through the Lindenwood Learning Academy.

public documents or developing new university products, require prior approval and thorough oversight. The policy also mandates regular training for all users, ensuring they remain informed about the capabilities and risks of AI tools. This training is part of a broader strategy to foster a responsible AI use environment that upholds data privacy and protects proprietary information. Regular updates to the policy are anticipated, reflecting the rapid pace of technological development in AI and the corresponding need for adaptive governance frameworks.

The integration of generative AI writing tools into search engines, databases, and word processors through platforms like Microsoft Co-Pilot presents significant challenges to maintaining the accountability outlined in previous AI usage policies. While these tools enhance productivity and accessibility of AI-driven content creation across various platforms, they also complicate the enforcement of strict compliance and data privacy measures that were once more controllable. Despite the technological advances, the fear of litigation and the precedents set by past lawsuits continue to drive the creation of stringent policies. Organizations are prompted to develop these comprehensive guidelines as a protective measure against potential legal actions, highlighting a continued commitment to ethical standards and legal compliance in the face of rapidly evolving AI capabilities.

Over 2022–2023, there has been a notable wave of lawsuits challenging the practices of major AI developers like OpenAI, Microsoft, Stability AI, and others, reflecting deepening concerns over copyright, privacy, and ethical use of AI-generated content. High-profile cases include The New York Times versus Microsoft and OpenAI, where the newspaper alleged copyright infringement for the use of its content to train AI models without permission (Hadero & Bauder, 2023). Similarly, individual authors Nicholas Basbanes and Nicholas Gage pursued action against OpenAI and Microsoft, accusing them of misusing their literary content. In the visual arts sector, Getty Images, and a collective of artists have filed suits against Stability AI for unauthorized use of images, while Universal Music Publishing Group and others have targeted Anthropic over copyright issues in music lyrics (Coulter, 2023).

In response to such litigation, platforms like Microsoft Co-Pilot and Adobe Firefly have incorporated semantic overlays and other mechanisms to address concerns related to copyright infringement and reduce the risk of litigation. Microsoft's Co-Pilot offers a "Copyright Commitment" which provides indemnity against intellectual property infringement claims for users adhering to built-in safety protocols and using the service within the prescribed guidelines. This commitment applies to various intellectual property rights including copyright and trademarks, provided that the use complies with the terms set by Microsoft. Similarly, Adobe Firefly incorporates robust data sourcing and content creation controls to ensure that the AI-generated content does not infringe on copyrights. Adobe offers reimbursement to its enterprise users against copyright lawsuits, signifying confidence in the legality of its data sourcing and the AI's output. This approach is aimed at fostering trust and ensuring that users can rely on the tool for creating content without legal repercussions (Ahmed et al., 2024). Such policies reflect a proactive approach by both companies to safeguard users against potential legal issues while promoting responsible and creative use of their AI technologies.

All things considered, the regulatory landscape for AI, especially GAI, is rapidly evolving as both industry and education sectors grapple with new challenges related to data privacy, intellectual property, and accountability. As these systems increasingly permeate various facets of operations, institutions must navigate a complex array of legal considerations that affect how they deploy these technologies. In the educational realm, policies are increasingly being standardized to incorporate data privacy and intellectual property protections. However, in the industry, the situation is more dynamic. Regulatory bodies in regions like the EU and the United States are intensifying their focus on ensuring that AI deployments are transparent, accountable, and safeguard fundamental rights. For instance, the EU's Artificial Intelligence Act establishes stringent requirements for AI systems, particularly those classified as high-risk, requiring comprehensive risk assessments and adherence to strict transparency obligations (Laux et al., 2024).

Accountability in the use of AI systems is gaining increasing attention as organizations are required to ensure their AI operations are not only effective but also ethical and lawful (Hirvonen, 2024). This encompasses robust mechanisms for human oversight, where individuals monitor AI systems to ensure they function as intended and correct any deviations from expected performance. Moreover, there is a significant push to ensure AI outputs are devoid of biases and discrimination, promoting fairness and equality across all automated decisions. Such initiatives aim to prevent scenarios where AI systems inadvertently perpetuate existing societal biases or introduce new forms of discrimination.

The concept of "privacy by design" is crucial in this context, where privacy considerations are integrated into the development phase of AI systems and maintained throughout their lifecycle. This approach helps in safeguarding sensitive data and adhering to stringent data protection laws like the GDPR, which mandates that data privacy is an integral part of the system design, not an afterthought (Shehzadi, 2024). These practices can improve the changes that organizations build trust among users and stakeholders, ensuring that AI systems respect user privacy and data integrity from the outset. The main consideration is in creating a framework where the functionality of the tools aligns continuously with privacy standards and ethical expectations. Likewise, with the evolving regulatory landscape, organizations must remain vigilant and adaptive. Regulations such as the EU AI Act are setting stringent compliance standards that require regular assessments and transparency in AI operations. Organizations should develop a proactive approach to governance that can handle the complexities of AI technologies, ensuring that ethical considerations are prioritized in every phase of AI implementation (Thelisson & Verma, 2024). These measures can not only act to prevent legal repercussions but also foster a positive public perception, which is crucial for the widespread adoption of AI technologies. By embedding accountability and privacy into the fabric of AI development, organizations can ensure that their AI systems are not only powerful and innovative but also responsible and trustworthy. This balance is essential for harnessing the full potential of AI while respecting the ethical boundaries and legal frameworks that govern its use.

Navigating the shifting regulatory terrain for AI requires organizations to maintain agility and adaptability. Keeping abreast of legal changes and being prepared to quickly adjust policies and practices are crucial as AI technologies evolve and become more integrated into various sectors. This involves a robust framework for continuous monitoring of AI systems, regular updates to governance frameworks, and proactive engagement with emerging legal and ethical standards (Babu, 2024). Implementing such measures helps mitigate risks, fosters trust, and ensures AI technologies are used in a way that aligns with broader societal values and legal requirements.

Regulatory efforts globally are aiming to harmonize approaches to AI, enhancing interoperability at organizational and technical levels, which in turn could bolster trade and enable smaller organizations to scale internationally. The introduction of frameworks like the NIST AI Risk Management Framework, ISO/IEC 42001, and the EU AI Act offers guidelines and standards for managing AI risks and ensuring ethical use (Kshetri, 2024). In addition, international efforts like those of the OECD and other bodies are crucial as they work toward setting global standards for AI that align with local regulations but also facilitate a unified approach across borders. These standards are intended to ensure that AI systems are robust, respect privacy, and are free from bias, thereby fostering a technology landscape that is both innovative and responsible.

In considering the AI policies in education and industry, there is an increasing need to address the diverse needs and concerns of employees, staff, and students. In educational settings, AI policies are centered around promoting equitable learning experiences, integrating AI tools into pedagogy responsibly, and addressing academic integrity. For instance, schools are developing frameworks to utilize AI in ways that support differentiated instruction and enhance teaching strategies while ensuring that all students benefit equitably. This involves creating policies that guide how AI tools are used in lesson planning and teaching, ensuring that these tools do not replace the teacher-student interaction but rather augment it (Dwivedi et al., 2021; Southworth et al., 2023).

In the context of industry, the focus on AI policies is increasingly centered around managing data privacy, intellectual property rights, and ensuring the ethical use of AI technologies in various operations. Companies are deploying comprehensive guidelines to dictate the application of AI within the workplace, with a strong emphasis on transparency, data protection, and accountability of AI systems. The ethical challenges posed by the integration of AI, especially with technologies like the IoT in creative industries, are profound, highlighting concerns over data privacy, security, and intellectual property rights (Sen, 2023). Also, intellectual property rights are significantly impacted by this new technology and its ability to generate content and ideas, leading to a reevaluation of traditional IP frameworks. The legal implications and the need for policy adjustments to accommodate the new dynamics introduced by AI are critically discussed, emphasizing the necessity for an updated approach that considers these tools and their unique capabilities (Zakir et al., 2023).

On the other hand, companies are increasingly aware of the need to train their employees on the ethical implications of AI. This includes understanding potential biases in AI systems, establishing clear usage boundaries, and ensuring that AI applications are in line with organizational goals and compliance standards. Such initiatives are vital for fostering an ethical AI environment within industries, which is crucial for maintaining public trust and legal compliance. The policies that govern the use of AI in industry settings are thus evolving to address these new challenges, focusing on creating a framework that supports innovation while ensuring that all operations are conducted ethically and responsibly. As AI technologies become more embedded in everyday business operations, the importance of these policies will only increase, highlighting the need for continuous evaluation and adaptation to new technological advancements (Li et al., 2024).

Both the educational and industrial sectors are increasingly dedicated to creating ethical AI environments. This commitment is evident in their focus on professional development aimed at integrating AI usage with foundational ethical principles like privacy by design. Initiatives such as these are crucial to ensure that as AI technologies develop, they do so with careful consideration of their potential impacts on privacy and human rights. Furthermore, these sectors are actively crafting AI policies that not only respond to current technological needs but also proactively anticipate future ethical, legal, and social challenges. By doing so, they aim to foster responsible AI ecosystems that uphold stringent ethical standards and promote transparency and accountability in AI applications. This proactive approach reflects a wider trend toward prioritizing sustainable and ethical practices in the fast-evolving technological landscape.

However, it is crucial to recognize that the development of such policies must prioritize enabling the use of AI tools within these sectors. For employees, staff, and students to become accustomed to AI technologies, policies must support, rather than inhibit, their exploration and use. The experience from January 2023, where policies that outright banned the use of AI tools were introduced, serves as a cautionary tale (Yu, 2023). Such prohibitive measures have led to confusion, paranoia, and fear among users, ultimately hindering the successful integration of AI technologies (de Koning, 2024). The authors regularly heard from various employees that they feared using the tools at all for fear that IT was monitoring their work computers and activity and would report them to HR. As such, even with ample training provided, employees avoided it out of fear of lack of administrative support and reprisal from their supervisors. Those employees that did report using generative tools (in confidence) noted increased productivity and a desire to share with other overworked colleagues. Such employees have become known as "secret cyborgs" (Esterman, 2023). With such a culture of uncertainty over what is supported and allowed in the workplace, only micro-efficiencies are possible instead of holistic transformation (Sudirjo et al., 2023).

Considering these previous foils, groundwork must be laid prior to any AI initiative. To foster a conducive environment for the integration of AI technologies, it is imperative that policy frameworks are not only clearly communicated but also actively disseminated, ensuring they explicitly support the supervised use and experimentation with AI tools while taking into account considerations such as data privacy. This support is crucial, without it, even well-designed training may fail to encourage employee engagement with new technologies that could significantly benefit their organizations. The strategy was confirmed by a Director of Employee Development in interviews as they highlighted the transformative role of generative expectations and specialized training sessions during an interview (Hutson & Rains, 2024a). Their recommendations are outlined in Table 5.4.

Table 5.4 Strategic Recommendations for Effective AI Integration in Institutional Settings

Recommendation category	*Description*
Develop clear and supportive policies	Institutions should craft policies that support the use of AI and are flexible enough to adapt to rapid technological changes. These policies should facilitate the adoption and effective use of AI technologies, thus promoting an environment conducive to innovation.
Enhanced communication and training	It is crucial to implement robust communication and training programs that clearly demonstrate how AI tools can add value specific to the institution's context. These programs should aim to ensure that all staff members are well-informed and feel supported throughout the AI integration process.
Address cultural resistance	Institutions must manage cultural resistance to AI, often rooted in traditional attitudes toward innovation. By promoting the benefits of AI and integrating AI education into existing professional development programs, institutions can help shift cultural perceptions and foster acceptance of AI.
Personalized training approaches	Training should be personalized to address the diverse roles and responsibilities within the institution. This ensures that each staff member can smoothly transition to using new AI tools, which are aligned with their specific job functions and workflows.

The senior administrator further elaborated on the broader implications of AI, emphasizing its potential to redefine job roles and responsibilities, and stressed the importance of strategic professional development programs that leverage AI to enhance productivity and decision-making processes. Addressing cultural resistance within the institution, they identified the need for a cultural shift to fully embrace AI technologies. The Director mentioned the challenges of integrating AI into existing workflows and underscored the importance of offering targeted, role-specific training. They pointed out the varied needs for support among staff, stating, "Some people will take a link that you send them and say, "Alright, I've got it." Others need to see it within their context, in their job, for them to actually gravitate to the tool."

Therefore, for the successful integration of these generative tools within institutions, it is essential that employees perceive the relevance of AI in their specific roles. This perception begins with the establishment of clear and supportive policies. Again, the Director emphasized the importance of enabling rather than restricting the use of AI, stating, "Folks will do what they're allowed to do by policy." In addition to clear policies, enhanced communication and training are pivotal in ensuring that all staff members feel supported and well-informed about the benefits of AI. Institutions must implement robust training programs that illustrate how AI tools can be beneficial within their specific frameworks. Managing cultural resistance to new technologies is also critical; institutions should integrate AI education into existing professional development programs to foster acceptance and facilitate a cultural shift toward embracing AI. Furthermore, training should be personalized to meet the diverse needs of various roles within the institution, enabling smoother transitions and greater acceptance of AI technologies. These strategic efforts ensure that AI tools are seen as beneficial additions to the workplace, thereby enhancing productivity and job satisfaction while mitigating fears related to job security.

5.2 Cultivating an AI-Ready Culture

In the rapidly evolving landscape of Industry 4.0, AI significantly impacts every facet of organizational operations. Cultivating an AI-ready culture within educational and business organizations is thus crucial. However, before delving into this cultural transformation, it is essential to establish a clear institutional policy, as discussed earlier. This policy serves as the foundation for all further actions and ensures alignment across the organization regarding the role and use of these new tools.

The readiness to embrace AI involves more than just adopting new technology; it represents a fundamental shift in organizational culture—how members understand, interact with, and implement AI. This transformation is centered around developing a mindset that values innovation, upholds ethical considerations, and actively involves all stakeholders in leveraging AI for strategic benefits. Such a cultural shift does not happen spontaneously but is the result of careful planning and persistent effort. It is underpinned by foundational policies that clearly support and commit to AI integration.

Culture and professional development within an organization keep it aligned with its mission and vision. The prevailing culture is influenced by modern tools and transformations, which can redefine how institutions operate and evolve. As AI technologies become more integrated into everyday activities, they can significantly shape and sometimes challenge the existing cultural norms, prompting organizations to adapt and evolve in ways that align with their core values and strategic goals. This dynamic interaction between culture and technology necessitates continuous professional development and adaptive leadership to guide and sustain the cultural transformation necessitated by AI adoption.

To effectively cultivate such a culture, tools like the EDUCAUSE Higher Education Generative AI Readiness Assessment (2024) serve as valuable starting points. These tools assist organizations in evaluating their current state of AI integration and readiness, identifying areas requiring enhancement, and understanding where to best allocate resources and energy for maximum impact. They guide organizations in developing strategies that align AI initiatives with their broader mission and operational goals while ensuring that the workforce is empowered and equipped with the necessary skills and knowledge. By providing a structured framework for assessment, these tools help pinpoint the most effective approaches to nurturing an AI-ready culture, highlighting the importance of leadership commitment, continuous learning, and an inclusive, collaborative approach to innovation. This strategic, tool-supported approach ensures that the development of an AI-ready culture is both comprehensive and aligned with the organization's long-term objectives, thereby facilitating sustainable growth and resilience in a digitally transformed landscape.

As educational institutions increasingly recognize the importance of AI readiness, the positive response and preparedness of primary and secondary educators serve as a crucial foundation for transitioning into more comprehensive AI integration within higher education environments (Woodruff et al., 2023). The readiness of K-12 educators to embrace AI in their classrooms heralds an optimistic outlook for AI adoption as the incoming generation, often referred to as Generation Alpha, prepares to enter the educational system. A survey involving 4,500 K-12 educators across all 50 states revealed a significant comfort level with technology, indicating a robust groundwork for AI integration. A majority of these educators reported at least some comfort with technology, with 40.77% feeling somewhat comfortable and an encouraging 16.13% reporting extreme comfort. This readiness is critical as these educators are likely to be the first point of contact for Generation Alpha students, who are expected to be even more immersed in technology.

The survey also delved into the technological training that educators received, which varied by age, suggesting a generational divide in exposure and comfort with digital tools. Younger educators, particularly those between 18 and 24 years old, while less comfortable with technology, reported receiving substantial training during their teacher-preparation programs. This training likely equips them with the latest pedagogical advancements, including AI. Most educators expressed openness to learning new technologies, with 56.74% indicating a positive response to adopting new tech tools. This openness is crucial for fostering an AI-ready culture within schools, preparing students for a future where AI is ubiquitous. The educational sector's proactive approach in training teachers and encouraging a positive disposition toward AI adoption reflects a significant shift toward integrating AI into everyday learning and administrative processes, setting a precedent for higher education institutions to follow.

As part of a comprehensive study aimed at assessing institutional readiness for AI adoption, specific instruments, such as that from EDUCAUSE, have been developed to evaluate how well higher education and industry are prepared to integrate AI technologies. These instruments, detailed in the appendix, include surveys tailored to capture the perception, experience, and support structures within various educational units, encompassing faculty, staff, and students. The authors have also created an instrument available here for use in the appendices titled "Institutional Readiness for AI Adoption in Higher Education: Assessing Perception, Experience, and Support Structures" and is designed to gather insights into the factors that affect AI adoption across different segments of educational institutions (Appendix A).

The educational AI readiness survey asks participants to evaluate their comfort with technology, their general perception of AI, and their optimism or pessimism about AI's impact on education. It also explores the specific applications of AI they foresee as beneficial in areas like research, teaching, and service, and their willingness to integrate AI into these areas. Each response is quantitatively measured, contributing to an overall "Institutional Readiness Score," which helps in quantitatively assessing the preparedness of institutions for embracing AI (Table 5.5). The key considerations for readiness outlined in the survey aimed at assessing the integration of AI in higher education and industry include several crucial factors that can provide valuable insights to administration and thought leaders. These considerations revolve around assessing the perception, experience, and support structures related to AI at institutions.

The instrument was used in an institution-wide study conducted in Spring 2024 at a mid-sized, private educational institution, boasting over 7,000 full-time students, provides pivotal insights into the perceptions of AI among faculty, staff, administration, and students (Hutson & Rains, 2024b). The findings

Table 5.5 Key Considerations for Assessing Institutional Readiness for AI Adoption

Consideration	*Description*
Perception of AI	Gauges how participants (faculty, staff, students) perceive AI, whether their attitudes are positive, neutral, or negative. This helps leaders identify areas of resistance or enthusiasm, crucial for framing communication strategies and educational campaigns.
Experience with AI	Assesses prior experience with AI tools and technologies to determine the current level of familiarity and comfort within the institution. This informs where to focus training efforts and how to tailor AI integration strategies.
Support structures	Explores existing support structures within institutions, such as training resources, mentorship programs, and infrastructural readiness. Insights into these areas help understand what support mechanisms are effective and what gaps need filling.
Willingness to integrate AI	Measures the willingness of faculty, staff, and students to integrate AI into their work, whether in research, teaching, or administrative services. This metric helps gauge the readiness of the institution to embrace AI.
Concerns and barriers	Identifies concerns about AI's impact on job security, ethical issues, data privacy, and the quality of education. Understanding barriers like insufficient funding, lack of infrastructure, and training needs can direct resource allocation and policy adjustments.
Strategic actions for improvement	Participants suggest actions that their institution should take to improve AI readiness, providing a grassroots perspective on needed resources, training, and professional development opportunities.
Institutional readiness score	Numeric scores assigned to responses help quantify the overall readiness of the institution to adopt AI. This score serves as a benchmark for measuring progress and comparing readiness across different departments or institutions.

resonate with broader research conducted across various organizations, illustrating a mixed sentiment of optimism tempered by caution toward the growing role of technology in academia and beyond (Abulibdeh et al., 2024; Alhumaid et al., 2023; Filgueiras, 2023; Rodway & Schepman, 2023).

The study reveals a general optimism among both students and faculty/staff regarding the potential of AI within their domains. This optimism, however, is not without its reservations. Ethical considerations, the fear of dependency on AI, and concerns that it might undermine human skills and efforts are prominent. Notably, students display a significant awareness of and engagement with generative AI technologies, pointing toward a shift in how the younger generation perceives and interacts more with it. As well, echoing a broader societal discourse, both groups express apprehensions about the ethical and societal ramifications of AI. Data privacy, job displacement, and the potential for misuse of AI technologies emerge as key concerns. This reflection of wider debates underscores the need for ethical guidelines and robust discussions around the deployment of AI in sensitive contexts.

The engagement with AI technologies is notably high among students, who utilize these tools for academic purposes, personal projects, and entertainment. This contrasts with faculty and staff, who, while also engaging with the tools, predominantly focus on productivity and administrative tasks. As with the variety of uses among the younger generations, the study also highlights the recognition of the group of the diverse applications of the new generative features of AI, from text generation and code creation to the production of original images and art, showcasing an awareness of the technology's transformative potential. As such, a pronounced demand for AI literacy and ethical training emerges from the study, indicating a consensus on the importance of understanding capabilities and limitations. Both students and faculty/staff express a keen interest in learning more about generative AI technologies through courses or workshops.

The call for institutional support in preparing for integration is clear. Training, policy development, and the establishment of ethical guidelines are deemed crucial by both students and faculty/staff. This includes measures to combat plagiarism, enhance AI literacy, and align AI use with educational integrity. Furthermore, there is a widespread belief, especially among students, that AI will significantly influence future careers and fields of study. This anticipation highlights the imperative for educational institutions to prepare their communities for a future where AI plays a central role in the workforce. A full discussion of the study and the data shall follow, but the nuanced perceptions of AI within an educational context, emphasizing a collective enthusiasm for possibilities while recognizing the need for careful consideration of its ethical, societal, and educational implications.

Along with education, industry was considered separately in another survey instrument titled "Industry Readiness for AI Adoption in Firms: Assessing Perception, Experience, and Support Structures" which is designed to gather comprehensive insights on how various industries perceive and engage with these technologies, along with the support structures in place to facilitate AI adoption (Appendix B). This survey plays a crucial role in understanding the current state of AI readiness across different sectors and identifying areas where additional support and resources are needed to accelerate the successful integration of AI in the workplace.

Participants are prompted to reflect on their own experiences, the resources available within their companies, and the broader industry context to provide a nuanced view of AI integration. The survey covers demographic data, AI experience and perception, and the perceived impact of AI on job roles. It queries participants about their optimism or pessimism regarding AI's influence on the industry and explores specific areas where AI could be integrated within their job functions. Furthermore, the survey assesses the willingness of individuals to embrace AI in their workflows and identifies any barriers that might hinder this integration, such as ethical concerns, data privacy issues, or a lack of familiarity with AI tools.

The information gathered is essential for developing targeted strategies and recommendations to improve AI adoption across industries. By examining factors such as leadership support, funding, infrastructure, employee familiarity with AI, and organizational culture, the survey aims to pinpoint critical areas that require attention. Additionally, it explores the availability of AI training programs within organizations and the types of support offered, such as in-house workshops, online courses, or partnerships with external experts. At the same time, the data helps industry leaders, policymakers, and other stakeholders understand the challenges and opportunities surrounding AI adoption. The insights gained are instrumental in facilitating the successful integration of AI technologies across various sectors, enhancing productivity, efficiency, and innovation. The survey's findings are expected to guide strategic decisions and policy formulations, ensuring that industries are well-equipped to navigate the complexities of AI integration and harness its full potential for growth and advancement.

After deploying a readiness assessment tool and analyzing the results, organizations should proceed to the critical phase of formulating their training strategies. This process should begin by examining the anticipated future of work within the industry and identifying the key skills that will be necessary to thrive in this evolving landscape. Understanding these future demands helps tailor training programs that are not only relevant but also proactive in equipping employees with the skills needed to leverage AI effectively. This forward-looking approach ensures that training initiatives are aligned with both the current capabilities and future needs of the workforce, thus fostering a more resilient and adaptable organizational environment. By integrating insights from the readiness assessment, organizations can strategically plan training that closes the skills gap, enhances productivity, and prepares employees for the future dynamics of work influenced by AI advancements.

5.3 Change Leadership and Disruptive Innovation

Part of cultivating an AI-ready culture requires exploring the dynamics of change leadership and disruptive innovation, and the critical roles these elements play within educational and technological industries. Change leadership, characterized by its strategic and proactive nature, is fundamental for guiding organizations through the transformative processes necessary for successful AI integration. This leadership style ensures that the introduction and assimilation of AI technologies align with organizational goals while navigating the associated risks and opportunities effectively. Disruptive innovation, further, challenges traditional business paradigms by introducing groundbreaking methods that significantly alter industry landscapes. For organizations to not only survive but thrive with AI, leaders must foster an environment conducive to innovation and be prepared to redefine the market norms. This includes implementing AI technologies in a manner that is both innovative and in alignment with the organization's strategic vision, ensuring that such advancements genuinely enhance operational capabilities and competitive positioning. The synthesis of change leadership and disruptive innovation creates a robust framework for organizations to manage the complexities of adopting AI. This framework supports not just the technological adoption but also the cultural shifts necessary to maximize the benefits of AI, making it crucial for leaders to be well-versed in both the theoretical and practical aspects of these processes.

Organizational transformation encompasses a broad and complex set of processes that integrate leadership dynamics, organizational culture, established policies, and procedural guidelines. Hechanova et al. (2018) emphasize the critical role these components play in steering complex change mechanisms within an organization. To facilitate the effective implementation of transformational change, various models have been developed, serving as blueprints that guide organizations through the nuanced stages of planning, executing, and sustaining profound changes. Each model addresses specific aspects of transformation, suggesting approaches tailored to the unique cultural and operational characteristics of each organization. The success of organizational transformation hinges on the coherent application of these models, ensuring strategic planning and execution of change initiatives.

One influential model is the Burke–Litwin model, introduced in 1992, which provides a comprehensive framework describing the critical drivers of organizational change (Hechanova et al., 2018). This model identifies 12 key factors (Table 5.6) that influence organizational transformation, divided into transformational and transactional categories. Transformational factors, like culture and leadership, are abstract and challenging to measure, while transactional factors, such as policies and procedures, are more tangible and easier to quantify (Hechanova et al., 2018; Nilsen & Bernhardsson, 2019). These factors range from the external environment, mission and strategy, leadership, organizational culture, to management practices and systems, each playing a pivotal role in shaping the organization's transformation efforts.

Table 5.6 Key Factors Influencing Organizational Transformation: The Burke–Litwin Model

Factor number	*Factor name*	*Description*
1	External environment	Refers to external forces impacting the organization, such as competition, economic conditions, and regulatory changes.
2	Mission and strategy	Pertains to the organization's mission, vision, and strategic goals.
3	Leadership	Involves the quality of leadership, including the ability to inspire, motivate, set clear goals, and provide support.
4	Organizational culture	Consists of the shared values, beliefs, and norms shaping individual behavior within the organization.
5	Structure	Represents both the formal and informal systems of authority, communication, and decision-making within the organization.
6	Management practices	Encompasses the policies and procedures governing the organization's day-to-day operations.
7	Systems	Refers to the technological and information systems supporting the organization's operations.
8	Work climate	Describes the overall atmosphere and working conditions within the organization.
9	Task requirements and individual skills	Refers to the skills and competencies required to achieve the organization's goals.
10	Individual needs and values	Pertains to personal needs, values, and motivations of individuals within the organization.
11	Motivation	Involves the factors that drive individuals to perform at their best, such as recognition, rewards, and growth opportunities.
12	Performance	Measures the overall performance of the organization, including financial, operational, and strategic outcomes.

The Burke–Litwin model's holistic view of organizational change is one of its key strengths, as it considers a wide array of factors that can impact an organization's performance, offering a comprehensive understanding of the dynamics driving change (Falletta, 2013). The model also emphasizes the critical role of leadership in driving transformation, recognizing that effective leadership is essential for meaningful organizational change (Kouzes &

Posner, 2017). The model has been applied across various sectors, including healthcare, education, and government, to guide change initiatives, diagnose organizational problems, and identify areas for improvement (O'Sullivan & Dooley, 2009; Sullivan et al., 2017).

Despite its strengths, the Burke–Litwin model is not without limitations. Critics argue that the model's complexity can make it difficult to comprehend and apply effectively (Howard, 2004). Furthermore, some suggest that it does not adequately consider external factors such as competition or economic conditions that drive organizational change (Schad & Smith, 2019). The model also lacks specific guidance on how organizations can implement the changes it suggests, which can be a significant barrier to practical application (Kaufman & Clark, 1999). To address these gaps, organizational leaders may integrate complementary, prescriptive models like Kotter's Change Leadership, which provides a more actionable approach to forming and guiding change efforts and organizational transformations (Kotter, 1996).

The foundational concepts of organizational change and change leadership, as highlighted by Hechanova et al. (2018), offer a vital perspective on the application of these theories within the realm of organizational leadership. While these concepts are interconnected, a clear understanding of each provides essential context for grasping their synergy and the nuances of their relationship within organizational dynamics. Organizational leadership merges theories of organization, management, and leadership to effectively achieve organizational goals and visions. In contrast, change leadership focuses on strategies, activities, and techniques aimed at addressing the human aspects of significant organizational changes, such as maximizing acceptance and minimizing resistance among members (Griffith-Cooper & King, 2007).

Kurt Lewin, a prominent figure in social psychology, made substantial contributions to change management, developing theories that have laid the groundwork for this field. Notably, Lewin's "Change Management Theory," or the "Unfreeze-Change-Refreeze Model," outlines three critical stages of change: "unfreezing" where existing norms are dismantled; "changing," which involves modifying behaviors and attitudes; and "refreezing," where new behaviors are stabilized within the organization (Burnes, 2004). This model has been extensively recognized and utilized within the disciplines of organizational behavior and management, driving substantial research and practical application (Armenakis & Harris, 2009).

The "unfreezing" stage addresses overcoming organizational resistance to change, necessitating change agents to challenge the status quo and instill a sense of urgency for change (Kotter, 1996). It is a phase where dissatisfaction with the current state is fostered, encouraging an openness to change among employees (Schein, 1996). The "changing" stage focuses on the transition to new behaviors, requiring ample support and training to acclimate employees to new operational methods (Elrod & Tippett, 2002). During this phase, effective communication and collaboration are crucial. The final "refreezing" stage involves solidifying new practices within the organizational culture, thereby establishing them as the new norm. This stage includes reinforcing the changes by celebrating successes and integrating new behaviors into the organizational systems and policies (Kotter, 1996).

While Lewin's model provides a structured approach to change, it is recognized that its simplicity may not fully encapsulate the complexities of modern organizational change, which often requires more adaptive and responsive strategies (Van de Ven & Poole, 1995). As a response, newer models like Kotter's 8-Step Process for Leading Change have built upon Lewin's framework, offering more detailed guidance for executing change in today's dynamic environments. Nonetheless, Lewin's model remains a cornerstone in the study of organizational change, revered for its clarity and enduring relevance in understanding and managing change processes across various organizational settings, including education, healthcare, and government sectors. This enduring legacy highlights the significant impact of Lewin's work on contemporary change leadership research and practice, bridging foundational theories with modern approaches to facilitate effective organizational transformation.

Building on the foundational theories of organizational change, Black's (2014) changing-individuals-changes-organizations model offers a micro-to-macro perspective, emphasizing the gradual nature of building capabilities across an organization. This model suggests that transformation occurs through a scaled transition that might initially face challenges but ultimately leads to significant improvements. Leaders play a critical role in this process by reinforcing the belief that new mental maps and strategies will better align organizational offerings with market demands and lead to improvements. Furthermore, Black (2014) articulates that leaders can effectively motivate their teams by clarifying the organizational vision, enhancing capabilities, and ensuring that team members see positive outcomes from their efforts, thus driving movement toward desirable organizational changes. This approach to change leadership resonates with Kotter's perspective, which centers around the leader's pivotal role in driving and managing change within the organization.

Kotter (1996) argues that clinging to past successes will become increasingly counterproductive as organizations face the necessity to adapt to rapid market changes over the coming decades. He warns against complacency, which often focuses an organization on maintaining the status quo rather than seizing new growth opportunities. This complacency is frequently rooted in past successes, which can reinforce a natural human desire for stability and predictability (Kotter, 2014). The discord between market expectations for swift adaptation and the innate human preference for stability presents a significant challenge, creating organizational dissonance (Kotter & von Ameln, 2019). To address this, Kotter's leading change model proposes a structured method for initiating and managing extensive change efforts, aligning them with the dynamic forces of the market. This model outlines how organizations can become more efficient, resilient, and relevant by balancing the existing structures that support ongoing operations with innovative approaches to new products or markets (Kotter, 2021).

Modern organizations face a near-constant imperative to adapt to rapidly evolving market conditions, driving leadership to validate or invalidate current market assumptions and develop forward-looking strategies (Kotter, 2021, p. 14). Organizational relevance now depends on incorporating agility and innovation within traditional hierarchical structures, which is essential not only for growth but also for survival. Kotter (2021) emphasized that adapting to new market realities necessitates strong core capabilities and swift action, requirements that were previously unheard of. Therefore, the need for accelerated change has never been more critical. To address this, Kotter presented the dual operating system as a model essential for balancing operational and innovation capabilities. Organizations often begin with network structures that allow for minimal constraints, promoting individual contributions and experimentation. This network structure is typically adopted out of necessity in startups, where limited capital and resources compel teams to innovate based on a founder's vision. Such environments foster opportunity-seeking and risk-taking, yielding positive results that are challenging to achieve in hierarchical organizations.

The dual operating system model integrates these network benefits with the stability of hierarchical structures, providing a framework for consistent operations and the agility needed for innovation. In Kotter's (2021) survive/thrive model, the organizational structure consists of two interdependent segments: "survive" (hierarchy) and "thrive" (network). The "survive" segment focuses on identifying and addressing operational threats quickly, facilitating incremental improvements. In contrast, the "thrive" segment emphasizes opportunity-seeking and experimentation to develop innovative products or services that meet evolving customer needs. This dual approach enables organizations to maintain operational consistency while fostering the agility necessary for innovation, supported by Kotter's eight accelerators for change.

Kotter's Accelerate model extends the original 8-step change leadership framework by emphasizing innovation, experimentation, partnerships, data-driven decision-making, and cultivating a culture of agility and adaptability. This model requires a new kind of leadership and approach to change, reflecting the dual operating system's context (Kotter, 2014). The eight accelerators include (a) creating a sense of urgency around a significant opportunity, (b) building and evolving a guiding coalition, (c) forming a change vision and strategic initiatives, (d) enlisting a volunteer army, (e) enabling action by removing barriers, (f) generating and celebrating short-term wins, (g) sustaining acceleration, and (h) instituting change. Each accelerator builds on the previous one, aligning strategies and initiatives with organizational resources, vision, and opportunities.

Creating a sense of urgency around a big opportunity is crucial for successfully executing strategic change initiatives, requiring deliberate leadership action and focus (Kotter, 2014). By developing a compelling opportunity statement that is both rational and exciting, leaders can foster a sense of urgency, purpose, belonging, and commitment within their teams. These elements collectively generate the energy needed to sustain teams through challenging transformations. The big opportunity and change vision must be compelling and memorable to create a lasting impact. The Accelerate model benefits organizations in rapidly changing environments where traditional change management approaches may fall short. Emphasizing a shared vision, aligning the organization around it, and empowering individuals to act on that vision enables organizations to respond swiftly to new opportunities and threats.

Additionally, focusing on short-term wins, consolidating gains, and embedding new approaches into the organizational culture helps ensure that changes are sustainable in the long term. Kotter's Accelerate model has been effectively implemented in various industries, including healthcare, finance, retail, and government, transforming organizations and enhancing performance, innovation, and sustainable growth. Thus, it is an apt model for organizations striving to remain competitive in today's fast-paced business environment. As we now explore Christensen's Disruptive Innovation next, the relevance of these models for change becomes particularly apparent, offering insights into how institutions can navigate transformative changes in response to disruptive innovations.

Christensen's theory of disruptive innovation (1997) provides a profound framework for understanding the impact of modern technologies and evolving business models on established markets and industries. The theory outlines how new entrants can disrupt market leaders by initially targeting underserved or overlooked market segments with simpler and less expensive solutions. Over time, these entrants enhance their offerings, eventually surpassing established firms focused primarily on meeting the needs of their most demanding and profitable customers. This theory distinguishes between sustaining innovations, which enhance existing products for current customers, and disruptive innovations, which create new markets or significantly alter existing ones. Disruptive innovations typically begin in niche markets where customer demands are less stringent, allowing new entrants to gain a foothold without direct competition from more established players. As these innovations evolve, they often expand their market reach, fundamentally changing industry dynamics.

Established companies, according to Christensen (1997), may find themselves ill-prepared to respond to these market shifts due to their focus on high-end customers and their often rigid, complex organizational structures. This makes it challenging for them to adapt swiftly to innovative technologies or business models targeting initially smaller, less lucrative market segments. Christensen's insights into disruptive innovation are particularly pertinent to sectors like technology, healthcare, and education, where rapid changes can redefine competitive landscapes. Despite criticisms that the theory may oversimplify some aspects of innovation or underestimate the adaptability of established companies, it remains a crucial tool for understanding and navigating the forces of disruptive change. This theory also complements other models discussed in the literature, such as Kotter's dual operating system, by providing a structured approach to recognizing and responding to disruptive forces in markets, including the higher education sector where traditional institutions must strategize effectively to address technological advancements, demographic shifts, and increasing competition. The next section will delve deeper into these industry-specific challenges and the strategic adaptations necessary to thrive in an environment marked by continual disruption.

5.4 Skills for the Future: Training and Development

With the evolving state of the world, the discussion surrounding the future of jobs and the necessary skills to thrive in a workplace augmented by AI becomes increasingly pertinent. The rapid integration of these tools and platforms across various sectors prompts a significant transformation not just in job roles but also in the required competencies of the workforce. The future of work will be deeply influenced by these new abilities to automate complex tasks and analyze vast amounts of data, reshaping industries from manufacturing to healthcare. Research indicates that while AI will automate certain tasks, it will also create new job opportunities that require a blend of technical skills and soft skills, such as problem-solving, critical thinking, and interpersonal communication (AlAfnan et al., 2024). Moreover, the evolution of jobs in sectors like architecture, engineering, and construction will demand not only familiarity with AI and robotic automation but also skills in handling augmented and virtual reality tools as part of the workflow (Rane et al., 2023).

The readiness assessments currently being used in various industries aim to identify the gaps between current competencies and those required in an AI-enhanced workplace (Pradhan & Saxena, 2023). These tools evaluate factors such as current AI integration levels, employee perceptions of AI, and the existing support structures like training programs. Insights from these assessments guide the development of targeted training programs tailored to meet the future demands of the job market. Therefore, as organizations contemplate the future of work, it becomes crucial to design training and development programs that not only address the immediate skill gaps but also prepare the workforce for ongoing technological advancements. Such programs should emphasize continuous learning and adaptability, equipping employees with the skills needed to collaborate effectively with AI systems and maximize their potential in an increasingly automated world.

As we delve into the future of work, it is imperative for leaders to understand how generative AI is shaping business landscapes. A recent guide published by IBM in 2024 emphasizes that "Generative AI won't replace people, but people who use generative AI will replace people who don't." This statement encapsulates the transformative role of generative AI in enhancing human capabilities rather than merely automating tasks. As the guide notes, GAI stands apart from previous technological advances by augmenting human skills and streamlining creative processes; it assists in everything from content creation and experience design to the automation of routine tasks like data analysis and code development. For example, customer service agents can leverage generative AI to handle routine inquiries, freeing up time to focus on sales enablement. Similarly, coders can move away from mundane programming tasks to concentrate on enhancing code quality and security. In human resources, specialists can transition from day-to-day operational tasks to more strategic roles such as talent development. The immediate feedback loops enabled by generative AI pave the way for improved business outcomes, making it a crucial tool for competitive advantage.

However, the integration of generative AI into business operations goes beyond mere technological deployment. It requires a fundamental shift in organizational structure and mindset. According to IBM, a significant challenge is the perception of HR as purely administrative, cited by 60% of executives. This view risks undermining the potential benefits of generative AI by limiting HR's role in driving organizational progress. Thus, to effectively harness the benefits of generative AI, CEOs and business leaders are encouraged to adopt strategies that place a strong emphasis on human capital rather than merely focusing on the technological aspects. Recognizing that the key to successfully leveraging generative AI lies in enhancing the capabilities of their workforce, leaders are advised to ensure that their AI strategies are centered around people. This involves viewing employees as central to the technological adoption process, thereby boosting their ability to work alongside advanced AI systems.

A significant aspect of this strategic approach involves transforming the role of HR within the organization. Traditionally viewed as a purely administrative function, HR is poised to become a strategic cornerstone essential for the integration of generative AI into the workplace. This transformation begins with reskilling HR professionals, equipping them with the necessary knowledge and tools to lead the development of a workforce capable of thriving in an AI-enhanced environment. Also, implementing a transparent change management plan is crucial. Such a plan should comprehensively outline the processes of adoption, testing, and integration of generative AI technologies. The report signals that it is important that this plan includes continuous and open communication with employees, sharing insights into the applications, successes, failures, and lessons learned from generative AI. This transparency helps in building trust and ensures that all employees are on board and informed about the changes affecting their work environment.

Additionally, establishing a robust ethical framework for the use of generative AI is essential before its full-scale implementation. Setting clear standards and guidelines helps maintain trust and transparency across the organization, ensuring that all AI initiatives conform to the highest ethical standards. This preparation not only safeguards the organization against potential pitfalls but also reinforces its commitment to responsible AI use. These strategies are intended to allow leaders and their organizations to not just adapt to the changes brought about by GAI but are also poised to thrive.

Such considerations are necessary as industry researchers note the changing nature of jobs in the new Digital Age. Forbes, for instance, outlined twelve new jobs that will emerge (Marr, 2024) (Table 5.7). The new era of human–machine collaboration is giving rise to novel job roles that amalgamate human expertise with artificial intelligence capabilities. While generative AI holds the potential to automate certain tasks, it is paradoxically creating unprecedented opportunities for skilled professionals adept at optimizing these powerful technologies. Rather than purely replacing human workers, generative AI is catalyzing the emergence of a new breed of roles centered around guiding, refining, and interpreting AI systems to achieve optimal outcomes.

On the frontlines are AI Prompt Engineers, language experts meticulously crafting prompts to elicit tailored outputs from AI applications like ChatGPT. With finely tuned communication abilities, acute attention to detail, and deep data proficiency, these prompt engineers ensure generative models deliver relevant, nuanced results aligned with specific objectives. Across creative industries, Generative Design Specialists are pioneering the artistic intersection of human and artificial intelligence. In fields like architecture, product design, and engineering, these specialists leverage AI to conjure a galaxy of design permutations, then critically interpret and steer the AI's outputs to manifest optimal designs.

Stepping into more strategic roles, AI Input/Output Managers oversee the information streams flowing into and out of an organizations' AI systems. This oversight function is paramount, as it addresses critical considerations around data privacy, copyright adherence, AI explainability, and bias mitigation. Closely related are AI Content Reviewers, professional guardians

Table 5.7 Emerging AI-Related Jobs and Required Skills

Future jobs created by AI	*Skills required*
AI prompt engineer	Communication abilities, attention to detail, data proficiency, understanding of prompt engineering techniques (e.g., contextual prompting, parameter tuning)
Generative design specialist	Creativity, ability to interpret and guide AI-generated designs, domain knowledge in fields like architecture, product design, engineering
AI input/output manager	Understanding of data privacy, copyright, AI explainability, bias mitigation, oversight and management skills
AI content reviewer	Critical thinking, ability to assess quality, accuracy, and appropriateness of AI-generated content across different domains
AI trainer	Subject matter expertise, ability to provide training data, fine-tune AI models, ensure model relevance
AI maintenance engineer	Technical skills, ability to update models, optimize system performance, troubleshoot AI infrastructure issues
AI security specialist	Cybersecurity knowledge, ability to defend against AI-enabled threats like phishing, malware, and cyber attacks
AI ethicist	Understanding of AI ethics, ability to establish ethical frameworks and guidelines for responsible AI development and deployment
AI compliance manager	Knowledge of organizational policies and legal regulations related to AI, ability to ensure compliance
AI personality designer	Creativity, understanding of user experience, ability to design engaging personalities for AI assistants and tools
Custom AI solution developer	Domain expertise, ability to develop custom AI solutions tailored to specific industry needs and challenges

tasked with scrutinizing the quality, accuracy, and appropriateness of AI-generated content across written, visual, and analytical domains prior to dissemination or implementation.

In the realm of model refinement, AI Trainers have emerged as essential conduits between human subject matter expertise and machine learning capabilities. These trainers "teach" AI models by providing comprehensive training data, fine-tuning outputs, and ensuring relevance as knowledge domains continuously evolve. Keeping AI systems operating at peak performance are AI Maintenance Engineers, conducting vital technical upkeep like model updates, system optimizations, and issue troubleshooting within complex AI infrastructures.

As AI's disruptive potential magnifies, so too does the need for AI Security Specialists – cybersecurity professionals defending against the malicious exploitation of generative AI technologies. These specialists proactively mitigate emerging threats like AI-enabled phishing, malware, and cyber attacks. Complementing their efforts, AI Ethicists establish frameworks to ensure AI development and deployment occur in a principled, socially responsible manner void of harmful biases and unintended consequences. Enforcing these ethical guardrails are AI Compliance Managers, charged with upholding organizational policies and legal statutes governing AI initiatives as regulations continuously take shape. Underpinning all these roles is the fundamental need for professionals capable of harmonizing human and artificial intelligence toward productive ends.

While LLMs are now often conflated with AI in general, it is noteworthy to discuss how enterprises are using them right now before discussing the skills workers will need moving forward (Surendira, 2023). The advent of large language models is catalyzing a seismic shift across enterprises, with companies rapidly mobilizing to harness the transformative potential of these powerful AI technologies. No longer relegated to the realms of research and experimentation, these models are being operationalized at breakneck speeds as organizations race to stake their claim in this new frontier. At the vanguard of this movement are strategic initiatives meticulously mapping the capabilities of the tools to core business needs. Cross-functional teams are conducting comprehensive feasibility studies, ROI analyses, and competitive benchmarking to lay the foundations for LLM adoption roadmaps. In parallel, organizations are procuring requisite licenses, tools, and establishing robust governance frameworks to guide responsible usage.

Fueling LLM performance is the intensive work of data curation and annotation teams. These professionals are assiduously preparing and labeling domain-specific datasets to fine-tune model outputs for niche applications. Through data anonymization, cleaning, and preprocessing pipelines, they are constructing the high-quality training grounds critical for custom enterprise API. Complementing these efforts, data engineers employ bootstrapping and augmentation techniques to continuously expand datasets. Once data pipelines are established, model development teams spring into action. Leveraging state-of-the-art architectures like GPT-4, LLAMA, Codex, and PaLM, these AI experts build, fine-tune, and optimize LLMs for specialized domains and use cases. Retrieval Augmented Generation (RAG) systems are engineered to enhance accuracy, reduce costs, and imbue models with contextual awareness. Prompt engineering strategies like few-shot learning and chain-of-thought prompting unlock new performance thresholds.

As these customized models take shape, application development teams integrate them into a myriad of AI-powered products and services. From conversational chatbots to question-answering engines, code autocompleters, and text summarization tools, their capabilities are being infused across enterprise software ecosystems via APIs. Organizations are showcasing their prowess through custom demo applications to position themselves as industry leaders. And powering this burgeoning landscape are MLOps teams streamlining training and deployment workflows. They construct scalable GPU training clusters, optimize model inference for speed and cost-efficiency, and containerize models for simplified deployment across cloud platforms. Robust CI/CD pipelines ensure continuous model retraining and deployment as new data streams accumulate. In lockstep with technological advancement is the critical function of LLM explainability and auditing. Specialized teams conduct rigorous privacy testing to safeguard against sensitive data leaks and security red teams work to identify and remediate vulnerabilities. Systematic model audits certify adherence to industry quality standards before high-stakes deployments.

At the bleeding edge, research teams publish pioneering papers advancing the frontiers of natural language algorithms and explore their novel applications spanning fields like multimodal learning and drug discovery. By participating in academic challenges like the GLUE benchmark, they showcase their organizations' capabilities to the world. This multifaceted embrace of large language models across enterprises is poised to reshape workforce dynamics. As their adoption accelerates, a burgeoning ecosystem of new roles and specializations will inevitably emerge to support the ideation, development, deployment, and governance of these AI systems at scale.

As AI capabilities rapidly advance, and the use cases in industry grow, the nature of work is being reshaped in profound ways. To thrive in this new era, Jarrahi et al. (2023) relay that organizations must cultivate a workforce adept at navigating the symbiotic partnership between human and artificial intelligence. Developing the right mix of skills will be paramount for unlocking AI's full potential while allowing humans to retain relevance amid the machine age. At the core of this human-AI synthesis are "cooperative skills"—abilities that enhance collaboration between people and AI systems. Foremost is data literacy, with 83% of successful AI companies citing data skills as a critical capability according to an IDC report. Workers must possess the analytical acumen to interpret AI-generated insights, validate results through methods like A/B testing, and effectively communicate findings across stakeholder groups (Faheem & Dutta, 2023).

Equally vital is attaining AI literacy—an understanding of how algorithms operate, their decision-making processes, inherent biases, and limitations. According to a Deloitte survey, only 32% of companies provide any form of workforce AI training, underscoring the pressing need to equip employees with this foundational knowledge. AI ethicists and governance professionals will take the lead in developing equity-promoting fairness criteria and conducting continuous algorithmic audits. Perhaps the most nuanced cooperative skill is "algorithmic communication"—the capacity to articulate objectives that appropriately leverage an AI's strengths while interpreting system outputs through a contextual human lens. A Harvard Business Review study revealed that improper communication is one of the top failure points in human-AI collaboration (Jarrahi et al., 2023). Emerging practices like prompt engineering, which crafts natural language prompts to elicit desired AI responses, represent a vanguard technique.

In tandem with these cooperative skills, humans must hone abilities that constitute a competitive edge over AI. While machines excel at rapid data processing and pattern detection, emotional intelligence remains a uniquely human capability. As AI customer service assistants proliferate, human agents will be imperative for intuitively recognizing emotions, providing empathetic solutions, and creating resonant personal connections. In fact, a holistic, strategic mindset separates people from the present capabilities of these tools. An Accenture report highlighted that 63% of companies struggle with integrating AI outputs into broader decision-making frameworks (Alexandre & Blanckaert, 2020). Skilled workers adept at contextualizing AI insights within the bigger operational picture will be invaluable. Moreover, the human capacity for imagination, creativity, and out-of-the-box thinking are unmatched by today's AI. While AI can analyze consumer data to identify trends, it is the creative genius of human marketers and product designers that ultimately translates those insights into resonant ad campaigns and innovative offerings.

In all, as AI proliferates across industries, society will increasingly depend on critical thinkers capable of scrutinizing AI decisions and safeguarding ethics. A PwC survey found that 88% of companies face accountability and ethical challenges in operationalizing AI. Governance professionals armed with robust ethical frameworks will fill this need (Mökander & Floridi, 2023). On the AI side of this collaborative paradigm, systems themselves must cultivate capabilities enabling seamless human–machine cooperation. Transparent explainability, providing clear rationales behind outputs, is a necessity—particularly in high-stakes domains like healthcare where inscrutability is untenable. Advances in natural language processing, allowing AI to communicate in natural, context-aware manners akin to human dialog, will further bridge the human-AI divide. Perhaps most critically, next-generation AI must exhibit adaptability and personalization—learning from individual user interactions to tailor subsequent responses. This capacity is exemplified by the current vanguard of "AI assistants" that enhance workplace productivity by analyzing activity patterns and user preferences.

As organizations strive to harmonize these complementary human and AI skill portfolios, pioneering strategies will emerge. By democratizing access to data and analytics, companies can empower their talent to apply uniquely human strategic thinking to AI-derived insights. Accessing on-demand external talent marketplaces and remote work models will become a prerequisite for sourcing the cooperative and competitive skills this new era demands. Ultimately, developing human-AI symbiosis represents the path forward for driving sustained innovation and maintaining relevance amid technological disruption. By thoughtfully cultivating skills that elevate both cooperative human–machine partnerships and competitive advantages, organizations can position themselves for success in an AI-powered future.

Such considerations and recommendations are also made by Craig (2023) in a Forbes article on what skill building in the age of AI includes. As generative AI ascends, the capacity to ask the right questions emerges as arguably the most critical skill. As the adage goes, "A wise man can learn more from a foolish question than a fool can learn from a wise answer." This fairly sums up the state of generative AI—answers are readily available, but questions are everything. Poor question framing, Craig relates, will not produce useful results, making "failure to ask the right questions…a much bigger barrier to our AI-enabled future than hallucinations. Insufficient human questioning-capital could end up bursting AI's bubble." Formulating incisive queries requires a multifaceted skill set that educational institutions must make paramount. Knowing what to ask is founded on deep subject matter expertise—whether it's an understanding of insurance claims processes for those in risk management or familiarity with digital marketing platforms and metrics. As large language models become further specialized, this domain knowledge coupled with real-world experience and pattern recognition will prove indispensable.

However, subject mastery alone is insufficient. The emerging discipline of prompt engineering equips humans with techniques for properly structuring questions to elicit AI's full potential. This skill encompasses methods like providing contextual information, leveraging specific prompting techniques like chain-of-thought prompting, and optimizing output parameters. According to a McKinsey report (2022), 7% of AI-adopted organizations already list prompt engineering capabilities in job requirements—a trend likely to accelerate as the technology proliferates.

Most consequential is developing the "why" capacity—framing inquiries through the lens of overarching objectives and desired outcomes rather than narrow tasks. As former IBM CEO Ginni Rometty emphasized, "I really need [workers] to understand how to work, how to think, how to problem solve…I can give people hard skills, and in the digital world they change every three to five years. It doesn't matter that much." This bedrock of critical thinking fuels the ability to reframe questions iteratively based on results—a core "why" proficiency (Craig, 2023). Moreover, professionals must cultivate timing judgment around AI involvement, knowing precisely when to solicit generative assistance versus relying on human-driven approaches. This discernment stems from extensive on-the-job experience and contextual pattern recognition. Lastly, AI's output is simply input for the next stage—workers must think critically about how to fully synthesize and operationalize the machine's contributions within broader processes and deliverables. Mere AI literacy is insufficient without this crucial "what next?" capacity.

Assessing how well our education system is preparing students for the AI-enabled workforce quickly reveals areas of profound strength and glaring deficiency, Craig argues. In the realm of developing critical thinking capabilities—the foundational "why" skills for formulating overarching objectives and reframing queries—academic institutions have historically excelled. From kindergarten through graduate studies, honing reasoning, analysis, and problem-solving abilities remains a curricular cornerstone. In this vital arena, educators can award themselves a well-earned grade of A. However, mere cognitive development is insufficient for empowering the next generation to thrive amid AI's ascendance. Equally paramount are the experiential "what" skills rooted in subject matter expertise and on-the-job pattern recognition. Yet most education models currently lack substantive mechanisms for integrating real-world work experiences, earning them a middling grade of D in equipping students with this mission-critical capability.

The picture grows increasingly concerning when viewed through the lens of emerging AI skillsets. Institutions get an outright failing grade on prompt engineering—the burgeoning "how" discipline of structuring inquiries to optimize generative AI's potential. With little training available on practices like contextual prompting and parameter tuning, students are being left behind on this essential frontier. A similar shortcoming plagues the development of sound timing judgment around AI utility. Determining "when" to leverage these powerful technologies versus relying on human-driven approaches is inherently contextual—a capacity that flourishes via immersive workplace exposure. Most academic environments fall short here, earning them a middling C grade.

There are glimmers of promise, however, in building "what next?" thinking skills. Project-based and inquiry-based pedagogies help instill the mindset for operationalizing AI outputs and integrating them into broader processes. But these methods remain unevenly implemented, resulting in a decent B grade that still has ample room for improvement. Ultimately, the sobering overall assessment is a C grade for the education system's readiness to equip the AI-empowered workforce. While critical thinking remains a stalwart emphasis, gaping experiential deficits leave graduates lacking the subject matter foundations, contextual decision-making skills, and AI proficiencies increasingly demanded by employers.

Closing this experience chasm requires a wholesale reconceptualization—one where the working world is brought into direct convergence with the classroom. A potent trifecta has emerged as the path forward: work-integrated learning platforms enabling seamless virtual collaboration with employers; a robust ecosystem of third-party providers designing formalized internship programs at scale; and paid apprenticeship pathways that immerse students in robust on-the-job AI training. Rather than treating professional experience as a supplemental nicety, educational institutions must make it a programmatic centerpiece facilitated by specialized workforce intermediaries. In tandem, AI's potential to streamline core academics creates invaluable capacity for this essential experiential emphasis.

The AI age is a make-or-break crucible for the education sector. Failure to prioritize human–machine collaborative skills risks leaving the next generation irreparably underequipped for career sustainability. Conversely, holistic integration of work immersion positions graduates to flourish amid technological disruption. The path forward is clear—academia must evolve in lockstep with the emerging AI paradigm. While academic institutions have historically emphasized critical thinking, their insular nature fails to sufficiently develop the subject matter mastery, contextual decision-making abilities, and synthesizing skills that true workplace immersion provides. The rapid mainstreaming of generative AI will only exacerbate this experience gap.

To bridge this divide, a convergence is required—bringing the working world into the classroom via three integrated pillars:

1 **Work-Integrated Learning**: Platforms like Riipen enabling seamless remote collaboration between students and employers on real projects.
2 **Formalized Internships**: A new ecosystem of third-party intermediaries designing structured internship programs at scale.
3 **Apprenticeships**: Perhaps the gold standard, paid apprenticeships provide robust on-the-job training while embedding AI skills.

Rather than siloing work experience as supplemental, schools must make it a programmatic centerpiece facilitated by specialized intermediaries. Simultaneously, AI offers the tantalizing prospect of streamlining academic learning to free up capacity for this experiential focus. As these technologies become deeply enmeshed within organizational workflows, professionals must cultivate a new comprehensive skillset enabling harmonious human–machine collaboration. On the human side, uniquely cognitive skills like creativity, emotional intelligence, contextual decision-making, and holistic strategic thinking will be paramount. The ability to not just use AI tools, but to prompt them with precise queries, interpret their outputs through a tailored lens, and adjudicate when human judgment should supersede automated recommendations will separate stellar performers from those rendered obsolete.

Recognizing this imperative, visionary industry and academic leaders are already working to bake AI proficiencies and human-centric skills into curricula and upskilling initiatives. Degree programs are integrating AI ethics, governance, and risk modules to produce a workforce capable of deploying these powerful technologies responsibly. Vocational training emphasizes human-AI collaboration through apprenticeships, simulations, and work-integrated learning programs that immerse students in real-world AI workflow scenarios. Courses on prompt engineering, algorithmic communication, and AI explainability are rapidly rising in prominence. With intensifying urgency, human skills like creativity, critical thinking, and adaptive problem-solving are taking center stage through experiential learning approaches. Those organizations and institutions embracing this holistic human–AI skillset development today will lead tomorrow.

5.5 Evaluating Professional Development Initiatives

Identifying the emerging AI-related jobs and the requisite skills to perform them is only the initial step. To truly prepare the workforce for this technological shift, educational institutions and organizations must actively develop and implement comprehensive professional development training programs. Evaluating the effectiveness of these initiatives is paramount to ensure their success and continuous improvement. The crucial need for such professional development efforts was a resounding theme across interviews with experts in the field of generative AI integration (Hutson & Rains, 2024a). For instance, the Director of Employee Development at a mid-sized liberal arts university underscored AI's potential to augment rather than replace human capabilities when properly integrated within institutional frameworks. However, realizing this potential necessitates targeted, role-specific training tailoring AI tools' utilization to diverse job contexts across staff and faculty roles.

Moreover, institutional policies must foster an environment conducive to rapid AI adoption by providing clear guidelines and continuous communication around technology integration. As the director aptly stated, "Folks will do what they're allowed to do by policy." This sentiment highlights policies' pivotal role in smoothing workforce transitions into AI-enhanced operations.

With the substantial investments required for developing and deploying professional AI training programs, rigorously evaluating their effectiveness becomes critical. Such evaluations not only assess current impacts but inform future training efforts' strategic refinement. By continually analyzing professional development initiatives' successes, shortcomings, and evolving needs, organizations can ensure their AI integration realizes intended educational and operational objectives.

In the realm of professional development, these interviews revealed that leaders have been prompted to rethink how they train and prepare their workforce for the evolving demands of the workplace. The insights from a series of in-depth interviews reveal how different institutions are approaching this challenge. A Deputy CIO at a large public doctoral-degree granting institution emphasized the critical role of ongoing learning and professional development in their strategy for integrating AI technologies. The phased approach they adopted, which was aligned with the EDUCAUSE model for digital transformation, was significantly accelerated by the pandemic. This strategy heavily focuses on inclusivity and continuous engagement across the campus, illustrating the importance of professional development in fostering a workforce that is competent and confident in utilizing AI technologies. The Deputy CIO highlighted the importance of training in responsible AI use to avoid unintended consequences, stating,

> how do you make sure that we're using AI responsibly so we don't have unintended consequences so that we minimize the…harm that can be done through certain communities, but it's also taking full advantage of that very powerful technology within the policies and guidelines of the university.

Similarly, a Business Systems Specialist at a large public research university in Ontario discussed the shift in their professional development efforts from merely encouraging technology adoption to managing its integration and governance. The rapid deployment of new technologies, including AI, necessitated a robust approach to change management and risk assessment within the institution. This required a new focus on governance and highlighted the need for ongoing training and support to ensure that staff and faculty are well-prepared to navigate the challenges presented by these technologies.

These narratives illustrate the significant impact of professional development in the successful integration of AI technologies within educational and industry settings. They emphasize the need for strategic approaches that include continuous learning, skill enhancement, and responsible technology use, ensuring that the workforce remains agile and adaptable in an increasingly AI-driven world. Such efforts are critical in not only leveraging AI for operational efficiency and educational outcomes but also in preparing individuals to thrive in the future landscape shaped by rapid technological advancements.

Crucially, these observations nurture a culture of perpetual learning and innovation surrounding AI capabilities—an absolute necessity given the relentless pace of technological progress. Systematic assessment provides a feedback loop guiding curricula updates, resource allocation, and the integration of emerging best practices. Only through this commitment to data-driven program improvement can institutions confidently upskill their workforces for sustained competitive advantages. As new AI-related roles crystallize and skill demands rapidly shift, launching professional development initiatives is not enough. Continuous, rigorous program evaluation enables educational leaders to refine their AI training approaches proactively. By prioritizing this evaluative function, institutions position themselves as catalysts propelling their people into the AI-empowered future of work.

The evaluation of professional development initiatives, particularly those involving GAI, continues to represent a significant area of interest for educational and industry technology professionals. As elucidated by earlier studies such as Merchie et al. (2018), assessing the effectiveness of professional development initiatives requires a robust evaluative framework that can accommodate the dynamic and multifaceted nature of these programs. There area a variety of methods and outcomes associated with professional development, highlighting the need for tailored evaluation strategies that reflect the specific contexts and goals of such initiatives. In the realm of AI, the incorporation of these technologies into professional development requires an understanding not only of their potential to enhance learning and operational efficiency but also of the challenges they present. For instance, Petrovska et al. (2024) discuss the integration of generative AI in software development education, noting the importance of formative and summative assessments that help learners critically evaluate AI output. The approach is crucial in preparing professionals not only to use AI tools but also to understand their limitations and implications, ensuring that AI integration is both effective and ethically sound.

One critical area highlighted in recent studies is the integration of transversal skills necessary to bridge current workplace skills gaps. Morandini et al. (2023) emphasize the significance of helping workers identify essential skills for AI adoption, enhancing existing skills, and developing new capabilities. This approach is essential as AI technologies continue to transform professional landscapes, necessitating ongoing upskilling and reskilling efforts by organizations. These strategies are crucial for preparing employees not only to use AI tools but also to understand their implications and potential biases, ensuring that AI integration is both effective and ethically sound. Furthermore, the application of GAI in specialized job functions is gaining attention. For example, Korinek (2023) discusses how generative AI, particularly LLM like ChatGPT, can assist professionals in fields such as economics by enhancing productivity in ideation, research, data analysis, and other areas. The study provides practical examples of how generative AI can be leveraged to foster innovation and efficiency, illustrating the broad potential of AI to augment professional capabilities.

In multinational corporations, particularly in the IT sector, the necessity for upskilling is highlighted by the rapidly evolving AI landscape.

Jaiswal et al. (2022) identify critical skills for employee upskilling, including data analysis, digital skills, complex cognitive skills, decision-making, and continuous learning. These skills are vital for enabling employees to adapt to and excel in an AI-enhanced workplace, underscoring the importance of targeted training and development initiatives. As well, the productivity benefits of generative AI are demonstrated in the context of customer support through a study by Brynjolfsson, Li, and Raymond (2023). They found that generative AI tools significantly increase productivity, especially among novice and lower-skilled workers. This suggests that generative AI can be a valuable asset in disseminating tacit knowledge and enhancing job performance across various skill levels, making a strong case for its broader adoption in organizational practices.

The importance of specifically tailored educational strategies in PD initiatives involving AI is further highlighted by the need to address the unique challenges these technologies pose, such as rapid technological changes and ethical concerns. The incorporation of AI into professional development programs must therefore be accompanied by rigorous evaluation mechanisms that can assess both the immediate and long-term impacts of these initiatives on professional practice and organizational outcomes. The latest research on best practices for HR, learning academies, and employee development directors in designing and implementing upskilling programs for generative AI highlights many different approaches that encompass strategic planning, personalized learning, and continuous evaluation.

Morandini et al. (2023) emphasize the importance of strategic planning in the implementation of AI technologies within organizations. They highlight the necessity of mapping the transversal skills needed by workers to mitigate the current skills gap in the workplace. Organizations can help workers identify the skills required for AI adoption, enhance current skills, and develop new capabilities. This strategic approach ensures that upskilling programs are aligned with both the immediate needs of the organization and the long-term career goals of employees, thereby fostering a workforce that is adaptable and prepared for future technological advancements. Again, Jaiswal et al. (2022) discuss the critical skills necessary for upskilling in the context of multinational corporations, particularly in the IT sector. They identify key areas such as data analysis, digital skills, complex cognitive skills, decision-making, and continuous learning. By focusing on these areas, HR and development directors can design personalized learning paths that cater to the specific needs of employees, enhancing their ability to work effectively with AI technologies and adapt to rapidly changing work environments.

The need for training programs for the technology extends pre-pandemic. The study by S. Maity (2019), for instance, explored the opportunities for AI in training and development, emphasizing the need for continuous evaluation and adaptation of training programs. Maity suggests that training and development programs should be designed with high employee engagement and involvement, considering factors such as the extent of training transfer to ensure that employees not only learn new skills but are also able to apply them effectively in their roles. This ongoing evaluation helps in adjusting training strategies to meet the evolving needs of the organization and the workforce. These studies collectively provide a robust framework for HR professionals and employee development directors to design and implement effective upskilling programs tailored to the use of generative AI in various job roles. By focusing on strategic skill mapping, personalized learning, and continuous program evaluation, organizations can ensure that their workforce remains competitive and well-prepared to leverage the benefits of AI technologies.

Building upon the general recommendations provided by previous research, the forthcoming section delves into a specific study conducted for this project, which utilized a Professional Learning Community (PLC)—a collaborative group of educators that continuously seeks to improve teaching skills and student outcomes through shared practices, experiences, and professional development activities. The activities (Table 5.8) that took place in the spring of 2024 aimed to identify concrete steps necessary for developing and deploying effective training programs tailored to the use of generative AI across various job functions. The study undertaken by the PLC was specifically designed to outline strategic approaches for determining the types of training required within an organization. The approach thus includes defining clear objectives that align training with the overarching goals of the institution, ensuring that each program is not merely an addition but an integral part of the organizational culture.

Key aspects investigated by the PLC include methods for garnering buy-in from various stakeholders within the organization. Understanding that successful implementation of any new training program depends heavily on support from multiple levels of the organization, the PLC explored strategies to communicate the benefits of proposed training effectively, thereby securing commitment across the board. As well, the study focused on ways to incentivize training participation. Recognizing that motivation can significantly influence the uptake and success of professional development initiatives, the PLC examined various incentive structures to encourage active participation and engagement with the training programs. Finally, the importance of integrating the training initiatives with institutional mission and vision was a critical area of focus. This integration ensures that the training programs support long-term strategic goals and contribute to the sustained growth and evolution of the organization. By aligning the training with institutional objectives, the PLC aims to foster a culture that naturally embraces continual learning and innovation, rather than viewing training as an external addition to regular operations. The targeted approach by the

Table 5.8 Overview of PLC Activities for AI Training Integration

Phase	*Activities*	*Objectives*
Initial setup	• Establishment of PLC under the institutional learning academy. • Leadership by the Director of Faculty Development.	• To create a structured framework for discussing and planning AI training integration. • To align AI training initiatives with institutional educational goals.
Engagement & promotion	• Activities promoted through various weekly distribution channels. • Solicitation of participation from faculty and staff across all areas.	• To ensure broad and inclusive participation. • To gather diverse perspectives on AI training needs and applications.
Utilization of resources	• Leveraging AI Ambassadors from all departments and staff units.	• To utilize existing AI expertise within the institution. • To enrich discussions with specialized knowledge and experiences.
Meeting arrangements	• Offering both in-person and online meeting options. • Scheduling face-to-face sessions at the beginning of each week and online sessions at the end.	• To accommodate varying schedules and preferences. • To maximize accessibility and participation in ongoing discussions.
Content focus	• Alternating focus between awareness and education, and practical application and integration.	• To address both the theoretical underpinnings and practical applications of AI. • To ensure comprehensive understanding and readiness for AI deployment.

PLC is expected to provide a blueprint for effectively implementing generative AI training programs that are not only practical but also embraced by the entire organization as essential components of its developmental fabric.

The first task undertaken by the PLC, building on the foundational efforts of a Presidential Working Group on AI, was to update the employee use policy to reflect the current functionality and integration of Microsoft Co-Pilot accounts within the institution. This revision aimed to clarify the scope of permissible and prohibited activities under the new system, specifically addressing the unique aspects of risk associated with the use of AI tools. By leveraging the protected semantic layer of Co-Pilot, accessible only through a university login, the PLC focused on ensuring that these revisions mitigated potential risks effectively, setting clear guidelines for safe and responsible use of AI technologies by employees. This step was crucial in aligning the policy with the latest technological advancements and maintaining a secure and efficient operational environment.

Following the institution-wide survey on AI readiness for adoption, which was conducted among all employees and students, there emerged significant concerns regarding the use of AI in relation to academic freedom. To address and clarify these concerns, a white paper titled "Addressing Academic Freedom in the Age of AI" was drafted, now available in full in Appendix C. The white paper elucidates the intersection of AI with the principle of academic freedom—a cornerstone of higher education and research institutions worldwide. It articulates that academic freedom ensures scholars the liberty to teach, research, and publish without undue restriction, a principle that is increasingly vital as AI technologies become more ingrained in various academic activities. The paper identifies that while AI offers profound opportunities for enhancing research methodologies and the dissemination of knowledge, it also poses challenges that necessitate a reexamination of the boundaries and responsibilities that define academic freedom in today's digital age.

Specifically, the white paper, drawing on the principles established in the Lindenwood University Academic Freedom Policy, asserts the importance of creating an environment conducive to open, critical thinking where intellectual inquiry and education are central. It emphasizes that academic freedom is accompanied by significant responsibilities, requiring the university to protect the ability of faculty to express ideas and teach concepts relevant to their subjects without interference. Furthermore, the white paper stresses that while academic freedom supports the unfettered expression of views, it does not tolerate disrespect, discrimination, or the infringement of others' freedoms.

The white paper also outlines what academic freedom covers, including the freedom in research and publication, teaching, and expression. It clarifies that academic freedom does not protect unprofessional conduct, shield from criticism, or provide absolute autonomy, particularly in decisions related to teaching modality and student assessments, which are increasingly influenced by digital and AI technologies. Lastly, the challenges introduced by AI—such as concerns over data privacy, intellectual property rights, and the perpetuation of biases—demand a careful reconsideration of how academic freedom is practiced. The white paper advocates for a balanced approach, where innovation in teaching and research is encouraged, but within the framework of institutional responsibilities and collective educational goals. Through addressing these points, the white paper aims to clarify the nuances of academic freedom in the age of AI, ensuring that the principles of open inquiry and expression are maintained and adapted to the evolving technological landscape. The example can be used as an example for discussions across fields.

With the initial considerations addressed, the PLC on AI was strategically housed within the institutional learning academy, an arrangement that underscored the initiative's emphasis on educational innovation and faculty development. The Director of Faculty Development led the PLC, ensuring that the activities aligned with the institution's broader goals for enhancing teaching and learning through technology. To maximize engagement and participation, the PLC's activities were widely promoted across the institution through various weekly distribution channels. This inclusive approach aimed to solicit active participation from faculty and staff from all areas, ensuring a diverse range of perspectives and expertise in the discussions about AI integration and policy development.

Recognizing the existing resources within the organization, the PLC leveraged the AI Ambassadors—a group of specialists in AI from all departments and staff units. These ambassadors played a pivotal role in driving the initiative forward by sharing their specialized knowledge and experiences with AI, facilitating a richer and more informed dialogue among participants. To accommodate varying schedules and preferences among the participants, the PLC offered both in-person and online options for joining the discussions. This hybrid approach was designed to maximize accessibility and participation. Face-to-face sessions were scheduled at the beginning of each week, providing an opportunity for direct interaction and engagement among participants. To complement this, online sessions were held at the end of each week, offering convenience and flexibility for those unable to attend in person. This dual approach ensured that every week of the 16-week term was utilized effectively, allowing for continuous and comprehensive discussions on AI and its implications for the institution.

The meetings covered a comprehensive range of topics, all intricately connected to the integration and utilization of GAI within the institution. These discussions were thoughtfully structured around two pivotal elements that would form the core of the strategic plan to socialize and train the institution on GAI effectively. The first core element focused on *awareness and education*. Recognizing the need to build a foundational understanding of GAI across all levels of the institution, this element aimed to demystify AI and generative AI technologies for both faculty and staff. Discussions under this theme addressed the basic principles of AI, the specifics of generative models, and real-world applications that could resonate with the diverse academic and administrative roles within the university. By elevating the general AI literacy of the community, the PLC sought to foster a common language and understanding, paving the way for more nuanced and informed discussions about potential uses and ethical considerations of AI in various departments.

The second core element revolved around *practical application and integration*. These discussions were geared toward exploring how GAI could be specifically leveraged within different faculties and administrative units to enhance efficiency, creativity, and problem-solving capabilities. The PLC facilitated brainstorming sessions to identify potential projects and areas where AI tools could be integrated into the daily workflows and academic curricula. Emphasis was placed on identifying pilot projects that could serve as test cases for broader AI integration across the campus. This practical approach aimed to illustrate the tangible benefits of AI, reduce hesitancy, and generate enthusiasm for its potential.

Throughout the 16-week term, the PLC systematically designed the meetings to alternate between these two themes, ensuring a balanced focus that addressed both theoretical and practical aspects of AI integration. This dual-focus strategy was instrumental in building both the confidence and competence of the institution's members, equipping them with the necessary knowledge and skills to embrace and advocate for the responsible use of GAI technologies. By the end of the term, these structured discussions had laid a solid foundation for developing a comprehensive training program on GAI, tailored to meet the diverse needs and enrich the unique capabilities of the university community.

Following the conclusion of the PLC meetings for the term, both online and face-to-face, a consensus was reached with the CIO that a minimum use policy for AI training and adoption is essential. This policy is critical for the first phase to ensure that students can freely experiment with the tools provided. This decision aligns with the general arguments laid out in the "AI Minimum Use Policy White Paper," found in full in Appendix D. The white paper proposes a comprehensive framework for integrating artificial intelligence across all curricula at Lindenwood University. The primary objective is to equip students with essential AI competencies necessary for success in a digitally-driven global economy. This initiative synthesizes best practices from leading universities to develop a policy that supports the educational mission of Lindenwood University while adhering to ethical standards and promoting AI literacy.

The policy mandates a minimum level of AI usage in coursework across all departments, ensuring that all students gain valuable experience with AI technologies and concepts. The scope of this policy spans all courses offered at the institution, targeting integration at various levels of the curriculum to ensure comprehensive exposure to AI for every student, regardless of their major. The implementation guidelines specify that all teaching faculties incorporate a minimum level of AI content in their courses. This includes the use of AI-driven tools for educational purposes, the introduction of AI concepts in course materials, and the implementation of AI-focused assignments and projects. By the four-week point in a 15-week course, faculty members must engage students with AI either through a class activity or by allowing them to use AI in developing a course assignment.

Moreover, the policy outlines robust support for faculty development and AI literacy, echoing Harvard's approach. Continuous professional development opportunities will be provided to enhance faculty proficiency in AI technologies. This initiative includes workshops, seminars, and access to essential AI resources, ensuring that faculty can effectively and responsibly guide students in navigating the complexities of AI technologies. Ethical considerations and data privacy are also emphasized, consistent with Columbia University's guidelines. The policy stresses the ethical use of AI, including safeguarding intellectual property and personal information and verifying the accuracy and biases of AI-generated content.

A committee was also proposed to be established to oversee the implementation of this policy, conducting annual audits of course syllabi, instructional methodologies, and faculty development efforts to ensure compliance with the AI usage requirements. This committee will also monitor the effectiveness of AI tools across departments and review the policy biennially to adapt to technological advancements and pedagogical insights, ensuring that the guidelines remain current and effective in fostering beneficial AI practices.

Following the productive discussions and collaborative efforts of the PLC, significant outcomes were achieved, including the development of white papers and the revision of policy language for HR. These efforts culminated in a comprehensive plan that intricately wove together two fundamental themes: *awareness and education*, and *practical application and integration* of GAI across the institution. The final plan emphasized the importance of establishing a broad base of AI literacy within the institution. This involved developing a series of workshops and seminars designed to introduce the fundamental concepts of AI and GAI to the entire university community. Topics included an introduction to AI technologies, understanding GAI and its capabilities, ethical considerations in AI deployment, and potential impacts on privacy and data security. These sessions were aimed not only at demystifying AI but also at fostering an environment where all members felt confident to engage in discussions about how AI could be integrated into their specific roles. Recommendations for this area stressed the need for ongoing education that could adapt to the rapidly evolving AI landscape, ensuring that the institution remained at the cutting edge of technological advancements.

For the practical application and integration aspect of the plan, the PLC focused on identifying and demonstrating specific use cases of GAI within the university's operational and academic frameworks. This component of the plan outlined a phased approach to integrating AI tools into daily workflows, academic research, and classroom instruction. Topics covered in this section included:

1 **Developing** AI-enhanced learning modules that could personalize education and improve learning outcomes.
2 **Integrating** AI into research methodologies to enhance data analysis capabilities and foster innovative research projects.
3 **Employing** AI tools in administrative tasks to improve efficiency in areas such as scheduling, human resources, and student services.

Recommendations for practical application highlighted the need for pilot projects that could serve as models for wider AI adoption across the institution. These projects would not only showcase the benefits of AI integration but also allow for the careful monitoring of challenges and the development of best practices for mitigating potential risks associated with AI usage. Additionally, it was suggested that departments should be encouraged to propose their own AI integration ideas, fostering a sense of ownership and creative engagement with the technology.

The comprehensive plan, enriched by the white papers and revised HR policies, presented a balanced approach that combined a solid foundation of AI knowledge with actionable steps for integration. The strategic blueprint was presented to leadership and aimed to ensure that all members of the institution could effectively and ethically engage with AI technologies, thereby enhancing the institution's mission and broadening its educational and operational horizons. Through this meticulous planning and structured implementation, the university positioned itself to harness the full potential of AI, driving forward both academic excellence and administrative efficiency.

As organizations continue to navigate the complexities of integrating artificial intelligence (AI), the formulation of effective AI use policies, cultivation of an AI-ready culture, development of future-oriented skills, and the evaluation of professional development initiatives are crucial for fostering a sustainable and innovative environment. This chapter has explored these areas comprehensively, offering insights and strategic guidelines that are vital for any institution aiming to leverage AI effectively.

Formulating AI use policies is the foundational step in ensuring that the deployment of AI technologies aligns with organizational values and regulatory standards. Key takeaways from this section emphasize the importance of clear, comprehensive policies that outline permissible uses of AI, data handling practices, and user responsibilities. Best practices suggest involving stakeholders from various levels of the organization in the policy formulation process to ensure broad understanding and acceptance. Recommendations include regular reviews and updates of AI policies to accommodate technological advancements and emerging ethical considerations, ensuring that policies remain relevant and effective.

Cultivating an AI-ready culture is essential for the seamless integration of AI technologies into organizational processes. This section highlighted the necessity of fostering an environment that encourages experimentation and continuous learning. Key takeaways suggest that an AI-ready culture is built on the principles of inclusivity, transparency, and ongoing education. Best practices involve promoting AI literacy across all organizational levels and encouraging open dialogue about the benefits and challenges associated with AI implementation. Recommendations for cultivating such a culture include providing ample resources for learning and adaptation and aligning AI initiatives with the organization's strategic objectives.

The development of skills for the future is critical as AI continues to redefine job roles and industry requirements. This section provided insights into the types of skills that will be increasingly in demand, such as data literacy, AI ethics, and system thinking. Key takeaways include the necessity for organizations to invest in both technical and soft skills training to prepare their workforce for the AI-driven future. Best practices recommended include the design of personalized training programs that address specific skills gaps and the integration of AI-based tools into training modules to enhance learning experiences. Organizations are advised to establish partnerships with educational institutions and technology providers to keep abreast of the latest training methodologies and technologies.

Finally, evaluating professional development initiatives is crucial for determining their effectiveness and identifying areas for improvement. Key takeaways from this section underscore the importance of using robust evaluative frameworks that can measure both the immediate impacts and long-term outcomes of training programs. Best practices involve continuous monitoring and assessment of training initiatives to ensure they meet the evolving needs of the organization and its employees. Recommendations include employing a variety of evaluation methods, such as participant surveys, skill assessments, and performance metrics, to gain comprehensive insights into the efficacy of professional development efforts. As AI technologies continue to evolve and permeate various aspects of organizational operations, the strategies discussed in this chapter provide a structured approach to navigating these changes. By adhering to the outlined best practices and recommendations, organizations can enhance their capacity to adapt, innovate, and thrive in an increasingly digital landscape, ensuring that their culture, policies, and training programs are well-equipped to meet the challenges and opportunities presented by AI.

References

Abulibdeh, A., Zaidan, E., & Abulibdeh, R. (2024). Navigating the confluence of artificial intelligence and education for sustainable development in the era of industry 4.0: Challenges, opportunities, and ethical dimensions. *Journal of Cleaner Production*, 140527, https://doi.org/10.1016/j.jclepro.2023.140527

Ahmed, I., Kajol, M., Hasan, U., Datta, P. P., Roy, A., & Reza, M. R. (2024). ChatGPT versus Bard: A comparative study. *Engineering Reports*, e12890. http://dx.doi.org/10.36227/techrxiv.23536290.v2

AlAfnan, M. A., Dishari, S., & Mohd Zuki, S. F. (2024). Developing soft skills in the artificial intelligence era: Communication, business writing, and composition skills. *Journal of Artificial Intelligence and Technology*. https://doi.org/10.37965/jait.2024.0496

Alexandre, C., & Blanckaert, L. (2020). The Influence of Artificial Intelligence on The Consulting Industry. *Unpublished master's thesis*, Louvain School of Management, Université Catholique de Louvain. http://hdl.handle.net/2078.1/thesis, 24659.

Alhumaid, K., Naqbi, S., Elsori, D., & Mansoori, M. (2023). The adoption of artificial intelligence applications in education. *International Journal of Data and Network Science*, *7*(1), 457–466.

Armenakis, A. A., & Harris, S. G. (2009). Reflections: Our journey in organizational change research and practice. *Journal of Change Management*, *9*(2), 127–142. https://doi.org/10.1080/14697010902879079

Babu, C. S. (2024). Adaptive AI for dynamic cybersecurity systems: Enhancing protection in a rapidly evolving digital landscap. In *Principles and applications of adaptive artificial intelligence* (pp. 52–72). IGI Global.

Black, J. S. (2014). *It starts with one*. Pearson Education.

Brynjolfsson, E., Li, D., & Raymond, L. R. (2023). *Generative AI at work* (No. w31161). National Bureau of Economic Research.

Budhwar, P., Chowdhury, S., Wood, G., Aguinis, H., Bamber, G. J., Beltran, J. R., ... & Varma, A. (2023). Human resource management in the age of generative artificial intelligence: Perspectives and research directions on ChatGPT. *Human Resource Management Journal*, *33*(3), 606–659.

Burnes, B. (2004). Kurt Lewin and the planned approach to change: A re-appraisal. *Journal of Management Studies*. https://doi.org/10.1111/j.1467-6486.2004.00463.x

Chaka, C. (2023). Detecting AI content in responses generated by ChatGPT, YouChat, and Chatsonic: The case of five AI content detection tools. *Journal of Applied Learning and Teaching*, *6*(2). https://doi.org/10.37074/jalt.2023.6.2.12

Chan, C. K. Y. (2023). A comprehensive AI policy education framework for university teaching and learning. *International Journal of Educational Technology in Higher Education*, *20*(1), 38.

Chechitelli, A. (May 23, 2023). AI writing detection update from Turnitin's Chief Product Officer. *Turnitin*. https://www.turnitin.com/blog/ai-writing-detection-update-from-turnitins-chief-product-officer

Christensen, C. M. (1997). *The innovator's dilemma: When new technologies cause great firms to fail*. Harvard Business Press

Coulter, M. (2023) Aiming for fairness: An exploration into getty images v. stability AI and its importance in the landscape of modern copyright law. *DePaul Journal of Art, Technology & Intellectual Property Law*, *34*(1), 124.

Craig, R. (September 8, 2023). Building skills for an age of AI. *Forbes*. Retrieved: https://www-forbes-com.cdn.ampproject.org/c/s/www.forbes.com/sites/ryancraig/2023/09/08/building-skills-for-an-age-of-ai/amp/

Crawford, J., Cowling, M., Ashton-Hay, S., Kelder, J. A., Middleton, R., & Wilson, G. S. (2023). Artificial intelligence and authorship editor policy: ChatGPT, bard bing AI, and beyond. *Journal of University Teaching & Learning Practice*, *20*(5), 1.

Dempere, J. M., Flores, P., & Allam, H. (2023, November). The challenges posed by national artificial intelligence strategies and policies on higher education institutions. In *Dempere, Juan, Flores, Pedro, & Allam, Hesham (2023). The challenges posed by national artificial intelligence strategies and policies on higher education institutions. In Proceedings of the HCT international general education conference (HCT-IGEC 2023)* (pp. 185–200). Dubai, United Arab Emirates.

Díaz-Rodríguez, N., Del Ser, J., Coeckelbergh, M., de Prado, M. L., Herrera-Viedma, E., & Herrera, F. (2023). Connecting the dots in trustworthy Artificial Intelligence: From AI principles, ethics, and key requirements to responsible AI systems and regulation. *Information Fusion*, 99, 101896.

Dwivedi, Y. K., Hughes, L., Ismagilova, E., Aarts, G., Coombs, C., Crick, T., … & Williams, M. D. (2021). Artificial intelligence (AI): Multidisciplinary perspectives on emerging challenges, opportunities, and agenda for research, practice and policy. *International Journal of Information Management*, 57, 101994.

EDUCAUSE (2024). *Higher Education Generative AI Readiness Assessment (EDUCAUSE)*. AI Advisory Boards. Retrieved: https://aiadvisoryboards.wordpress.com/2024/04/09/higher-education-generative-ai-readiness-assessment-educause/

Elrod, P. D., & Tippett, D. D. (2002). The "death valley" of change. *Journal of Organizational Change Management/Journal of Organisational Change Management*, *15*(3), 273–291. https://doi.org/10.1108/09534810210429309

Esterman, M. (2023). Secret cyborgs at school: Opportunities and challenges for teaching history using AI. *Teaching History*, *57*(3), 32–34.

Faheem, H., & Dutta, S. (2023). Artificial intelligence failure at IBM'Watson for oncology'. *IUP Journal of Knowledge Management*, *21*(3), 47–75.

Falletta, S. V. (2013). *Organizational diagnostic models: A review & synthesis*. Leadersphere.

Filgueiras, F. (2023). Artificial intelligence and education governance. *Education, Citizenship and Social Justice*, https://doi.org/10.1177/17461979231160674

Ghimire, A., & Edwards, J. (2024). From Guidelines to Governance: A Study of AI Policies in Education. *arXiv preprint arXiv:2403.15601*.

Gimpel, H., Hall, K., Decker, S., Eymann, T., Lämmermann, L., Mädche, A., … & Vandrik, S. (2023). *Unlocking the power of generative AI models and systems such as GPT-4 and ChatGPT for higher education: A guide for students and lecturers* (No. 02-2023). Hohenheim Discussion Papers in Business, Economics and Social Sciences.

Griffith-Cooper, B., & King, K. (2007). The partnership between project management and organizational change: Integrating change management with change leadership. *Performance Improvement*, *46*(1), 14–20. https://doi.org/10.1002/pfi.034

Hadero, H., & Bauder, D. (2023). New York Times sues Microsoft, Open AI over use of content. *Globe & Mail* (Toronto, Canada), B1-B1.

Hechanova, M. M., Caringal-Go, J. F., & Magsaysay, J. F. (2018). Implicit change leadership, change management, and affective commitment to change: Comparing academic institutions versus business enterprises. *Leadership and Organization Development Journal*, *39*(7), 914–925. https://doi.org/10.1108/LODJ-01-2018-0013

Hirvonen, H. (2024). Just accountability structures–a way to promote the safe use of automated decision-making in the public sector. *AI & Society*, *39*(1), 155–167.

Howard, A. (2004). *Diagnosis for organizational change: Methods and models*. Guilford Press.

Hutson, J. & Rains. T. (2024a). *Qualitative leadership interview study [data set]*. Lindenwood University.

Hutson, J. & Rains. T. (2024b). *Institutional readiness study [data set]*. Lindenwood University.

Ibrahim, H., Liu, F., Asim, R., Battu, B., Benabderrahmane, S., Alhafni, B., … & Zaki, Y. (2023). Perception, performance, and detectability of conversational artificial intelligence across 32 university courses. *Scientific Reports*, *13*(1), 12187.

Jaiswal, A., Arun, C. J., & Varma, A. (2022). Rebooting employees: Upskilling for artificial intelligence in multinational corporations. *The International Journal of Human Resource Management*, *33*(6), 1179–1208.

Jarrahi, M. H., Monahan, K. & Leonardi, P. (June 8, 2023). What will working with AI really require? *Harvard Business Review*. Retrieved: https://hbr.org/2023/06/what-will-working-with-ai-really-require

Kaufman, R., & Clark, R. E. (1999). Re-Establishing performance improvement as a legitimate area of inquiry, activity, and contribution: Rules of the road. *Performance Improvement* https://doi.org/10.1002/pfi.4140380905

Kobeissi, M. M. (2023). Artificial intelligence syllabus statement: Setting expectations. *Nurse Educator*, *48*(5), 275.

de Koning, M. (2024). *The professional project manager: Revolutionizing employee experience through HR-tech synergy*. Business Expert Press.

Korinek, A. (2023). *Language models and cognitive automation for economic research* (No. w30957). National Bureau of Economic Research.

Kotter, J. P. (1996). *Leading change*. Harvard Business School Press.

Kotter, J. P. (2014). *Accelerate*. Harvard Business Review Press.

Kotter, J. P. (2021). *Change*. Harvard Business Review Press.

Kotter, J. P., & von Ameln, F. (2019). Agility, hierarchy, and lessons for the legacy and future ofchange Management. Gruppe. Interaktion. *Organisation. Zeitschrift Für Angewandte Organisationspsychologie (GIO)*, *50*(2), 111–114 https://doi.org/10.1007/s11612-019-00461-5

Kouzes, J. M., & Posner, B. Z. (2017). *The leadership challenge: How to make extraordinary things happen in organizations* (6th ed.). John Wiley & Sons. https://doi.org/10.1002/9781119416809

Kshetri, N. (2024). Economics of artificial intelligence governance. *Computer*, *57*(4), 113–118.

Laux, J., Wachter, S., & Mittelstadt, B. (2024). Three pathways for standardisation and ethical disclosure by default under the European Union Artificial Intelligence Act. *Computer Law and Security Review*, *53*, 105957.

Lau, S., & Guo, P. (2023, August). From" Ban it till we understand it" to" Resistance is futile": How university programming instructors plan to adapt as more students use AI code generation and explanation tools such as ChatGPT and GitHub Copilot. In *Proceedings of the 2023 ACM Conference on International Computing Education Research-Volume 1* (pp. 106–121).

Li, Y., Song, Y., Sun, Y., & Zeng, M. (2024). When do employees learn from artificial intelligence? The moderating effects of perceived enjoyment and task-related complexity. *Technology in Society*, *77*, 102518.

Lindenwood University (LU). (2024). *Use of generative AI in employment policy. Lindenwood University*. Retrieved: https://www.lindenwood.edu/policies/list/use-of-generative-ai-in-employment-policy/

Lund, B. (2023). AI Use Policies in University Syllabi. *Available at SSRN 4518594*.

Maity, S. (2019). Identifying opportunities for artificial intelligence in the evolution of training and development practices. *Journal of Management Development*, *38*(8), 651–663.

Marr, B. (January 23, 2024). 12 new jobs in the generative AI era. *Forbes*. Retrieved: https://www-forbes-com.cdn.ampproject.org/c/s/www.forbes.com/sites/bernardmarr/2024/01/23/12-new-jobs-for-the-generative-ai-era/amp/

McKinsey & Company. (2022). *McKinsey global survey on AI*. McKinsey & Company. https://www.mckinsey.com/capabilities/quantumblack/our-insights/the-state-of-ai-in-2022-and-a-half-decade-in-review

Merchie, E., Tuytens, M., Devos, G., & Vanderlinde, R. (2018). Evaluating teachers' professional development initiatives: Towards an extended evaluative framework. *Research Papers in Education, 33*(2), 143–168.

Mökander, J., & Floridi, L. (2023). Operationalising AI governance through ethics-based auditing: An industry case study. *AI and Ethics, 3*(2), 451–468.

Mollick, E. R., & Mollick, L. (March 17, 2023). Using AI to implement effective teaching strategies in classrooms: Five strategies, including prompts. *Including Prompts*.

Morandini, S., Fraboni, F., Puzzo, G., Giusino, D., Volpi, L., Brendel, H., … & Pietrantoni, L. (2023). Examining the nexus between explainability of AI systems and user's trust: A preliminary scoping review. *Proceedings http://ceur-ws.org ISSN, 1613, 0073*.

New York University (NYU). (2024). *Adapting Assignments to Generative AI*. Retrieved April 25, 2024: https://www.nyu.edu/faculty/teaching-and-learning-resources/teaching-with-generative-tools/adapting-assignments-to-generative-AI.html

Nilsen, P., & Bernhardsson, S. (2019). Context matters in implementation science: A scoping review of determinant frameworks that describe contextual determinants for implementation outcomes. *BMC Health Services Research*. https://doi.org/10.1186/s12913-019-4015-3

O'Sullivan, H., & Dooley, L. (2009). Applying innovation. *Decision Support Systems*, 5(2), 310–323.

Petrovska, O., Clift, L., Moller, F., & Pearsall, R. (2024, January). Incorporating generative AI into software development education. In *Proceedings of the 8th conference on computing education practice* (pp. 37–40). Durham, UK.

Plata, S., De Guzman, M. A., & Quesada, A. (2023). Emerging research and policy themes on academic integrity in the age of Chat GPT and generative AI. *Asian Journal of University Education*, 19(4), 743–758.

Pradhan, I. P., & Saxena, P. (2023). Reskilling workforce for the artificial intelligence age: Challenges and the way forward. In *The adoption and effect of artificial intelligence on human resources management, Part B* (pp. 181–197). Emerald Publishing Limited.

Quinn, R. (April 16, 2024). Annual provost's survey shows need for AI policies, worries over campus speech. *Inside Higher Ed.*. Retrieved: https://www.insidehighered.com/news/tech-innovation/artificial-intelligence/2024/04/16/provosts-survey-shows-need-ai-policies

Rane, N. (2023). Role and challenges of ChatGPT and similar generative artificial intelligence in human resource management. *Available at SSRN 4603230*.

Rane, N., Choudhary, S., & Rane, J. (2023). Integrating Building Information Modelling (BIM) with ChatGPT, Bard, and similar generative artificial intelligence in the architecture, engineering, and construction industry: Applications, a novel framework, challenges, and future scope. *Bard, and similar generative artificial intelligence in the architecture, engineering, and construction industry: Applications, a novel framework, challenges, and future scope (November 22, 2023)*. http://dx.doi.org/10.2139/ssrn.4645601

Rashidi, H. H., Fennell, B. D., Albahra, S., Hu, B., & Gorbett, T. (2023). The ChatGPT conundrum: Human-generated scientific manuscripts misidentified as AI creations by AI text detection tool. *Journal of Pathology Informatics, 14*, 100342.

Rodway, P., & Schepman, A. (2023). The impact of adopting AI educational technologies on projected course satisfaction in university students. *Computers and Education: Artificial Intelligence, 5*, 100150.

Rožman, M., Oreški, D., & Tominc, P. (2023). Artificial-intelligence-supported reduction of employees' workload to increase the company's performance in today's VUCA Environment. *Sustainability*, *15*(6), 5019.

Schad, J., & Smith, W. (2019). Addressing grand challenges' paradoxes: Leadership skills to manage inconsistencies. *Journal of Leadership Studies* https://doi.org/10.1002/jls.21609

Schein, E. H. (1996). *Organizational culture and leadership*. Jossey-Bass.

Sen, P. L. (2023). Digital creativity and ethical challenges: The case of IoT in creative industries. *Journal of Digitainability, Realism & Mastery (DREAM)*, *2*(02), 66–71.

Shehzadi, S. (2024). Privacy by design: Integrating information theoretical privacy in AI development. *Integrated Journal of Science and Technology*, *1*(2).

Southworth, J., Migliaccio, K., Glover, J., Reed, D., McCarty, C., Brendemuhl, J., & Thomas, A. (2023). Developing a model for AI Across the curriculum: Transforming the higher education landscape via innovation in AI literacy. *Computers and Education: Artificial Intelligence*, *4*, 100127.

Sticker, J. K. (December 11, 2023). Reflections on AI policies in higher education: And why first-hand generative AI experience is crucial for leadership. *The Future of Higher Education*. Retrieved: https://jeppestricker.substack.com/p/the-problem-with-ai-policies-in-higher

Sudirjo, F., Ausat, A. M. A., Rijal, S., Riady, Y., & Suherlan, S. (2023). ChatGPT: Improving communication efficiency and business management of MSMEs in the digital age. *Innovative: Journal of Social Science Research*, *3*(2), 643–652.

Sullivan, T. J., Schweiger, W. K., Chermak, G. M., & Julien, R. (2017). Applying the Burke-Litwin model as a diagnostic framework for assessing organizational effectiveness. *International Journal of Management & Applied Research*, *4*(1), 52–61. https://doi.org/10.18646/2056.41.17-005

Surendira, S. (October 7, 2023). 7 ways enterprises are adopting LLMs. *LinkedIn*. Retrieved: https://www.linkedin.com/pulse/7-ways-enterprises-adopting-llms-siva-surendira/

Temple University (TU). (2024) *A faculty guide to A.I. Center for the Advancement of Teaching*. Retrieved April 25, 2024: https://teaching.temple.edu/teaching-technologies/faculty-guide-ai

Thelisson, E., & Verma, H. (2024). Conformity assessment under the EU AI act general approach. *AI and Ethics*, *4*(1), 1–9. http://dx.doi.org/10.1007/s43681-023-00402-5

Van de Ven, A. H., & Poole, M. S. (1995). Explaining development and change in organizations.*Academy of Management Review*, *20*(3), 510–540.

WCET (January 7, 2023). Developing institutional level AI policies and practices: A framework. *WECETFrontiers*.Retrieved:https://wcet.wiche.edu/frontiers/2023/12/07/developing-institutional-level-ai-policies-and-practices-a-framework/

Woodruff, K., Hutson, J., & Arnone, K. (2023). Perceptions and barriers to adopting artificial intelligence in K-12 education: A survey of educators in fifty states. In Mistretta, S. ed., *Reimagining education - the role of E-learning, creativity, and technology in the post-pandemic era*. IntechOpen. https://doi.org/10.5772/intechopen.1002741

Xiao, P., Chen, Y., & Bao, W. (2023). Waiting, banning, and embracing: An empirical analysis of adapting policies for generative AI in higher education. *arXiv preprint arXiv:2305.18617*.

Yu, H. (2023). Reflection on whether Chat GPT should be banned by academia from the perspective of education and teaching. *Frontiers in Psychology*, *14*, 1181712.

Zakir, M. H., Khan, S. H., & Saeed, Z. (2023). The impact of artificial intelligence on intellectual property rights. *International Journal of Human and Society*, *3*(4), 312–319.

6 Conclusion

Embracing the AI Future

6.1 Reflecting on AI's Unmet Expectations

The rapid development, deployment, and adoption of new generative technologies has been unprecedented and unpredicted. In fact, predictive models prior to 2022 significantly misjudged the speed and impact of AI development, often underestimating the rapid advancements and market penetration of AI technologies (Ulloa-Cazarez, 2020). This misalignment calls for a reassessment of AI's developmental trajectory, emphasizing the need for new models that accurately reflect the current and future landscape of artificial intelligence. Reflecting on AI's unmet expectations, it's evident that the anticipation surrounding the AI "gold rush" of 2023 was profound. The financial sector expected massive returns from AI technologies, especially after notable investments in AI companies surged, painting a promising picture of exponential growth. For instance, the generative AI market was forecasted to reach a valuation of $1.3 trillion by 2032, driven by significant investments and the development of new AI applications (Saintvilus, 2023).

However, despite these optimistic projections, the tangible returns in the first fiscal quarter following these investments fell short of expectations for many. The enthusiasm for potential market-altering AI technologies led to significant investments, as seen in cases like OpenAI's staggering $10 billion funding from Microsoft and other hefty funding rounds in the AI sector. These investments reflected a widespread belief in the transformative potential of AI (Zhang, 2023). Yet, the reality that emerged was more tempered. The market performance of major AI-driven companies, although positive, did not always match the high expectations set early on. For example, while companies like Microsoft and Nvidia saw substantial stock increases due to their AI developments, the overall returns were more modest than the initially projected transformative impacts (Lango, 2024). The discrepancy between expectation and outcome highlights the complexity and unpredictability of integrating cutting-edge technologies into the market and serves as

DOI: 10.4324/9781003512813-6

a reminder of the inherent risks involved in high-stakes investment sectors, particularly those as dynamic and rapidly evolving as artificial intelligence.

Over the past two years, the high expectations surrounding the transformative capabilities of AI have not always translated into tangible returns, revealing a variety of obstacles. Key among these challenges are regulatory concerns, which have begun to see more structured responses with emerging data privacy regulations necessitating rigorous impact assessments for AI technologies. Such regulations often require documentation detailing the training data, logic, and evaluations of AI systems to ensure accuracy, fairness, and lack of bias (Feltz, Peretti, & Austin, 2022).

Additionally, data privacy issues have become increasingly prominent as the volume and sensitivity of data processed by AI systems grow. This raises significant concerns about the misuse of personal information and the potential for privacy intrusions, which are exacerbated by AI's capability to make inferences at an unprecedented scale and speed (Kerry, 2020; Lee et al., 2024). The need for internal expertise in developing proprietary AI models also remains a crucial hurdle. Many organizations lack the specialized knowledge required to create and manage effective AI systems, often leading to ineffective implementations, as exemplified by the costly development failures like Bloomberg's, which became obsolete with the release of "off-the-shelf" solutions via an API like ChatGPT 4 (Ahmed, 2021; Easterbrook, 2024).

Given the significant challenges and complexities involved in developing proprietary AI models, such as regulatory compliance and data privacy concerns, it is advisable to reconsider the strategy of training one's own AI model unless there are extraordinary circumstances justifying such an approach. Instead, organizations should consider leveraging new closed models, like Co-Pilot, which are designed with robust data privacy features to ensure that sensitive data does not leak. These models provide the dual benefits of advanced AI capabilities without the inherent risks associated with data management and compliance in creating proprietary systems.

However, leaders should maintain realistic expectations regarding the capabilities of AI tools like Co-Pilot moving forward and should budget time for employee training, even for tools promoted as easy to use. Our pilot study of the advanced features of Microsoft Co-Pilot demonstrates that merely launching new tools does not immediately enhance productivity. Instead, we have observed only micro-efficiencies. The pilot involved a select group of 17 participants with diverse roles within the institution (Hutson & Rains, 2024). This demographic and departmental diversity provides a comprehensive view of how different segments of the institution interact with and perceive the new AI tool.

The participants included six administrators (35.29%), such as department chairs, deans, and provosts, highlighting strong engagement from institutional leadership. Faculty members, including professors, lecturers, and adjuncts, constituted 17.65% (three participants), indicating the reach of the tool into the academic faculty. The largest group was staff members, including support staff and IT, who made up 47.06% (8 participants), reflecting significant usage among operational personnel. Notably, there were no entries under "Other," suggesting a targeted selection of roles for the pilot. The distribution across departments was equally telling about the pilot's scope. Academic Affairs, Admissions, and Arts and Humanities were well-represented, each accounting for about 17.65% and 23.53% of participants respectively. These areas often deal directly with both the academic and administrative applications of such tools, which could explain their higher representation. Fiscal Affairs and Science, Technology, and Health each had two representatives (11.76%), while Financial Aid, Executive Office, and Information Technology each had one (5.88%). This spread across various departments underscores the tool's broad potential application across different functional areas of the institution.

Participants were then asked to identify a range of tasks they typically handle within their functional areas, revealing significant insights into their daily workloads and potential areas for AI integration. Composing and managing emails emerged as the most frequent task, reported by 18.67% of participants, reflecting the heavy reliance on communication tools within their roles. This was closely followed by the creation of presentations and PowerPoint slides, noted by 13.33% of participants, which underscores the importance of visual communication in their tasks. As well, participants also engage in a variety of other critical tasks such as grading and providing feedback on assignments (6.67%), conducting financial analysis and reporting (10.67%), and undertaking research and development activities (13.33%). Strategic planning and policy development were also significant, involving 12% of the participants, while administrative tasks and project management were reported by 16%, indicating a broad spectrum of responsibilities that could potentially benefit from AI enhancements.

The study highlighted the ubiquity of Microsoft 365 Apps in their daily routines, with 100% of participants using these tools daily. Outlook is especially pivotal, predominantly used for managing emails, which aligns with the high percentage of participants engaged in email-related tasks. Other frequently used tools included Word, Excel, and PowerPoint, with their usage statistics reflecting their roles in document creation, data handling, and presentation development respectively. Challenges faced by participants included time-consuming processes (22.22%), a lack of automation features (16.67%), and integration issues with other software (11.11%). These challenges point to significant areas where AI tools like Co-Pilot could offer improvements, such as enhancing efficiency and streamlining workflows.

In the evaluation phase of the pilot, the familiarity and reception of the tools among participants varied. About 43.75% of participants indicated they were moderately familiar with the Co-Pilot AI tools, such as Insights for Excel and PowerPoint Designer, while 31.25% were only slightly familiar. A smaller segment, 18.75%, reported being very or extremely familiar, suggesting a learning curve that could impact initial usability and adoption. Participants generally felt positive about using the Co-Pilot AI tools, with 47.06% expressing somewhat positive feelings and 23.53% feeling extremely positive. However, 17.65% remained neutral, and 11.76% had somewhat negative reactions, highlighting varied individual experiences and possibly the challenges of integrating new technologies into existing workflows.

Expectations for benefits from using Co-Pilot AI tools were optimistic, with many anticipating improvements in efficiency and productivity, enhanced creativity and design capabilities, each cited by 14.43% of respondents. Other expected benefits included streamlined workflows, automated routine tasks, and better data analysis, suggesting that participants see potential in AI tools to enhance a broad spectrum of activities. Yet, despite the optimism, several concerns were noted regarding the adoption of Co-Pilot AI tools. The largest concern was integration with current workflows (36.36%), followed by dependability and accuracy (30.30%), and the learning curve required for adaptation (21.21%). These concerns reflect typical challenges faced when integrating new technologies and underscore the need for effective training and support.

In terms of commitment to learning the new tools, a majority (52.94%) were willing to invest 1-3 hours per week during the pilot program, indicating a significant but manageable investment in time to adapt to the AI tools. Preferred methods for learning varied, with 35.29% favoring online tutorials and another 35.29% preferring trial and error, suggesting a desire for hands-on, flexible learning options that accommodate different learning styles and schedules.

The pilot group also expressed concerns about usability and accuracy, which are crucial for successful integration and adoption. Feedback indicated that the user interface and user experience (UI/UX) of Co-Pilot are not as intuitive or user-friendly as those of other tools. For instance, tasks such as finding and attaching a reference file in "draft with copilot" were described as extremely problematic, likened to a "royal nightmare." This highlights significant issues in the tool's design and functionality that could hinder efficient workflow integration. Additionally, participants noted that the accuracy of Co-Pilot in delivering desired results was not on par with other AI tools like Gemini. There were complaints that Co-Pilot often provided explanations on how to perform tasks rather than executing them directly. This kind of response mechanism can lead to frustration among users who expect direct action and results, rather than guidance on processes. As such, effective integration often requires a series of tailored examples for each operational area and standard operating procedures to get started. To facilitate this, it is beneficial to distribute short instructional videos regularly, offer optional drop-in sessions for face-to-face training, conduct virtual training sessions, and provide formal certifications. These steps help ensure that all team members are proficient and can fully leverage the new technology to its fullest potential.

Identifying and leveraging internal expertise through a train-the-trainer model is a strategic approach that can significantly enhance organizational capability in utilizing new AI tools. By pinpointing key personnel who already possess a foundational understanding or show an aptitude for AI technology, organizations can cultivate a core group of internal trainers. These trainers can then be upskilled, either through external training programs or dedicated in-house sessions, to deepen their proficiency in specific AI applications. Investing in such training not only builds out an internal knowledge base but also ensures that expertise is distributed throughout the organization more effectively. Once trained, these internal experts can support their colleagues, leading training sessions and helping integrate AI tools into daily workflows. This peer-led training approach can be more relatable and directly applicable, addressing specific challenges and questions that arise in the context of the organization's unique operational environment.

Furthermore, bringing in external trainers or investing in specialized courses for key personnel can introduce fresh perspectives and advanced skills to the internal team. After completing such programs, these employees can return to act as multipliers, disseminating new knowledge and practices across the organization. This method helps to create a sustainable learning culture that adapts continuously as AI technologies evolve.

Establishing a permanent internal group dedicated to artificial intelligence can significantly enhance an organization's ability to stay at the forefront of technological advancements. This group should consist of individuals from various departments, each bringing a unique perspective and expertise in different AI domains. Their collective task would be to continuously scan the technological horizon, keeping up to date with the latest developments and trends in AI. Such a team would serve as the organization's central hub for AI knowledge, responsible for disseminating this information across different units, aiding in strategic decision-making and ensuring that the organization remains competitive in a rapidly evolving landscape. This group's ongoing mission would involve not only monitoring new technologies but also evaluating potential AI applications for their relevance and impact on the organization's goals.

By integrating insights from diverse fields—ranging from data science and engineering to ethics and regulatory compliance—the group can provide a holistic view of the AI landscape. This enables the organization to make well-informed decisions about adopting new technologies, optimizing existing AI systems, and anticipating future trends that could affect their industry. This proactive approach ensures that the organization not only keeps pace with technological change but is also prepared to leverage AI innovations for strategic advantage.

6.2 Leadership for the Next Technological Frontier

The next step for leaders is to look ahead to the horizon. The advent of these tools has ushered in a new era of technological advancement, which has already begun reshaping various industries and aspects of our lives. It will certainly change how we complete daily tasks and what our expected outputs will be. Such integrations have the potential to add up to $4.4 trillion to the global economy annually (McKinsey, 2023). This substantial economic impact is attributed to its ability to perform tasks that typically require human intelligence, such as decision-making, problem-solving, and natural language processing. One of the primary areas where GAI is expected to have a profound impact is knowledge work, particularly activities involving decision-making and collaboration (Manyika, 2022). Professionals in fields like education, law, technology, and the arts will likely see parts of their jobs automated sooner than anticipated, due to the capacity of these tools to predict patterns in natural language and utilize it dynamically. This automation will not only enhance productivity but also free up professionals to focus on higher-value tasks that require creativity, empathy, and critical thinking (Kaur & Singh, 2024).

The deployment of GAI will have varying impacts on different industries, with some experiencing more significant gains than others, the McKinsey report highlights. High tech and banking, for instance, will benefit substantially from the potential to accelerate software development, while marketing and sales functions across industries will see the most significant gains. This disparity in impact underscores the need for organizations to understand the specific applications and benefits of gen AI in their respective domains.

Yet, despite the promising potential, most organizations have yet to harness its capabilities, with 60% of marketing and sales leaders admitting that their organizations rarely or never use GAI or ML for commercial activities (Hemachandran & Rodriguez, 2023). This lag in adoption is surprising, given that 90% of marketing and sales leaders believe their organizations should be using gen AI or machine learning for commercial activities at least "often." Bridging this gap between awareness and adoption will be crucial for organizations seeking to remain competitive in an increasingly AI-driven landscape (Deveau, Griffin, & Reis, 2023). In fact, the enthusiasm for the technology is palpable among marketing and sales leaders, with lead identification, marketing optimization, and personalized outreach being the most anticipated use cases (McKinsey, 2023). These applications have the potential to revolutionize marketing and sales strategies, enabling organizations to target customers with unprecedented precision and personalization. As gen AI continues to evolve, it is likely that new use cases will emerge, further expanding its impact on marketing and sales.

The efficiency of software engineering is also poised to receive a significant boost from the tools' assistance (First et al., 2023). Developers using gen AI-based tools were more than twice as likely to report overall happiness, fulfillment, and a state of flow, indicating a substantial improvement in their experience. By automating routine tasks and providing developers with more time to focus on creative and high-value tasks, gen AI has the potential to increase productivity and job satisfaction within the software engineering community.

As well, the momentum for adoption is building among workers, with the vast majority having tried gen AI tools at least once, whether in or outside work (McKinsey, 2023). Notably, baby boomers report using gen AI tools for work more than millennials, highlighting the appeal of gen AI across age groups. As gen AI becomes more pervasive, it is essential for organizations to develop the necessary infrastructure and training programs to support workers in harnessing its capabilities effectively. However, the increasing adoption of gen AI also raises concerns about the need for more gen AI-literate employees (Manyika, 2022). As organizations begin to set gen AI goals, they are developing a need for more workers with the skills to effectively utilize and manage gen AI systems. The gap between supply and demand for skilled workers remains wide, emphasizing the importance of investing in education and training programs that address this need.

Thus, GAI has the potential to substantially increase labor productivity across the economy, leading to a more sustainable and inclusive world (Manyika, 2022). However, this will require workers whose jobs are affected to shift to other work activities that allow them to at least match their 2022 productivity levels. Supporting workers in learning new skills and, in some cases, changing occupations will be essential for reaping the benefits of this productivity boost. Given these reports, AI represents a significant breakthrough in artificial intelligence, poised to revolutionize various industries and aspects of our lives. Its potential to add up to $4.4 trillion to the global economy annually, automate knowledge work, and enhance software engineering efficiency makes it an exciting and promising technology. However, its adoption must be accompanied by caution and investment in education and training programs.

At the same time, leaders should also directly engage with these emerging technologies. Hands-on experience with AI tools is essential for leadership, as it provides a concrete understanding of their capabilities and limitations. This firsthand knowledge is crucial for making informed decisions that will shape long-term strategic and financial planning. Without this direct engagement, leaders may find their perspectives limited, leading to potentially myopic or misinformed decisions that could impact the organization's adaptability and competitiveness in the AI age. One important reason for getting hands-on is that the stakes in the AI age are exceptionally high, requiring leaders to not only understand but also anticipate how AI will transform their industries and the broader economy. The situation demands a proactive approach to leadership development and employment strategies, ensuring that top executives are not only aware of but proficient in leveraging AI technologies. This proficiency allows them to foresee and navigate the complex dynamics AI introduces into marketplaces and workplaces, ensuring that their organizations remain at the cutting edge of innovation and effective adaptation.

As Kitt.AI CEO Robert Talebi notes, "AI won't replace people, but people who use AI will replace people who don't." Institutions failing to prioritize skills for effective human-AI collaboration risk leaving graduates underequipped for the new world of work. By holistically integrating professional experience, our education systems can pave pathways to AI-empowered career sustainability. At the same time, leaders hiring for the future face a pivotal strategic inflection point. The first question that always arises is "Will I lose my job?" The question is right to be asked as the discussion of profits associated with reducing human overhead and automating tasks is a reality fast approaching. But rather than myopically fixating on AI's potential to reduce headcount through automation, forward-thinking leaders are reframing the conversation. The paramount question is not "Who can AI replace?" but rather "How can we scale our operations and amplify our talent by incorporating AI capabilities?"

This mindset shift reflects an understanding that generative AI represents not a threat to the human workforce, but a force-multiplier elevating our collective potential. Pioneering organizations are asking "What longstanding challenges or ambitious projects have we shelved due to resource constraints? How can AI's computational prowess and analytical scale empower us to finally pursue those opportunities?" This expansive thinking unlocks new frontiers rather than perpetuating zero-sum trade-offs. Moreover, an AI-enabled enterprise frees its people to become more creative, experimental, and innovative in their plans and strategies. Relieved of the mundane through intelligent automation, professionals can redirect their passion and mental bandwidth toward ideation, problem-solving, and reinvention. The question then becomes "How can AI augment and turbocharge our human ingenuity?" catalyzing breakthroughs previously unimaginable.

Approaching AI through this conscientious, human-centric lens is the hallmark of authentic leadership - one rooted in holistic vision, emotional intelligence, and genuine care for an organization's lifeblood: its people. These "leaders with heart" appreciate that beyond any balance sheet impacts, human capital appreciation is the surest path to enduring growth and marketplace resilience. In this light, rather than reducing headcounts, organizations should explore opportunities to elevate existing employees through comprehensive AI enablement and skill development initiatives. Investing in work-integrated learning programs, immersive AI training, and the cultivation of uniquely human competencies like strategic thinking, emotional intelligence, and creativity will position the workforce for sustained excellence.

This is the clarion call sounding for businesses and academic institutions alike. Colleges and universities must integrate professional experiences, apprenticeships, and hands-on AI skill development into their core curricula. Doing so equips graduates with the contextualized knowledge and applied proficiencies that AI cannot replicate, empowering success amid technological disruption. For companies, following this human-centric ethos means prioritizing internal talent mobility and upskilling over indiscriminate hiring and firing cycles. It means developing AI collaboration capabilities across roles and levels. It means establishing robust governance and cross-functional stewardship to bake ethical AI principles into the organizational psyche. The transformative potential of GAI hinges on our willingness to harmonize human and machine capabilities. Enterprises simply offloading human capital expose themselves to the risks of miscalibrated, uncontrolled, or unintended AI impacts. Conversely, those fusing human intellect with artificial intelligence open exponential gateways to innovation, sustainable growth, and future-proof competitiveness. The path forward is one of conscious, holistic augmentation - scaling operations and potential by empowering the human core with AI's complementary strengths. It is a path that rejects false trade-offs, uniting human-centered leadership with technological advancement. For those committed to this symbiosis, the possibilities are boundless.

References

Ahmed, H. S. A. (October 6, 2021). Challenges of AI and data privacy- and how to solve them. ISACA. Retrieved: https://www.isaca.org/resources/news-and-trends/newsletters/atisaca/2021/volume-32/challenges-of-ai-and-data-privacy-and-how-to-solve-them

Deveau, R., Griffin, S. J., & Reis, S. (2023). AI-powered marketing and sales reach new heights with generative AI. *McKinsey–2023*. https://www.mckinsey.com/capabilities/growth-marketing-and-sales/our-insights/aipowered-marketing-and-sales-reach-new-heights-with-generativeai

Easterbrook, G. (February 14, 2024). How financial services firms can build a generative AI assistant. *Forbes*. Retrieved: https://www.forbes.com/sites/granteasterbrook/2024/02/14/how-financial-services-firms-can-build-a-generative-ai-assistant/?sh=18eccfb577a0

Feltz, D., Peretti, K. K., & Austin, A. (December 9, 2022). Privacy, cyber & data strategy advisory: AI regulation in the U.S.: What's coming, and what companies need to do in 2023. *Alston & Bird*. Retrieved: https://www.alston.com/en/insights/publications/2022/12/ai-regulation-in-the-us

First, E., Rabe, M., Ringer, T., & Brun, Y. (2023, November). Baldur: Whole-proof generation and repair with large language models. In *Proceedings of the 31st ACM joint European software engineering conference and symposium on the foundations of software engineering* (pp. 1229–1241). San Fransisco, CA.

Hemachandran, K., & Rodriguez, R. V. (Eds.). (2023). *Artificial intelligence for business: An implementation guide containing practical and industry-specific case studies*. CRC Press.

Hutson, J. & Rains, T. J. (2024). *Microsoft co-pilot adoption study [data set]*. Lindenwood University.

Kaur, J., & Singh, K. A. (2024). The human-robot collaboration paradox: Finding harmony in the workplace of the future. In *Robo-advisors in management* (pp. 212–230). IGI Global.

Kerry, C. (February 10, 2020). *Protecting privacy in an AI-driven world.* Brookings. Retrieved: https://www.brookings.edu/articles/protecting-privacy-in-an-ai-driven-world/

Lango, L. (January 10, 2024). Is this the best way to invest in the AI gold rush? *Investor Place*. Retrieved: https://investorplace.com/hypergrowthinvesting/2024/01/is-this-the-best-way-to-invest-in-the-ai-gold-rush/

Lee, H. P. H., Gao, L., Yang, S., Forlizzi, J., & Das, S. (2024). "I don't know if we're doing good. I don't know if we're doing bad": Investigating how practitioners scope, motivate, and conduct privacy work when developing AI products. In *USENIX security symposium*. Seattle, WA.

Manyika, J. (2022). Getting AI right: Introductory notes on AI & society. *Daedalus*, *151*(2), 5–27.

McKinsey & Company. (August 25, 2023). *What's the future of generative AI? An early view in 15 charts*. McKinsey & Company. Retrieved: https://www.mckinsey.com/featured-insights/mckinsey-explainers/whats-the-future-of-generative-ai-an-early-view-in-15-charts

Saintvilus, R. (November 28, 2023). *The AI gold rush: Profiting from picks and shovels*. NASDAQ. Retrieved: https://www.nasdaq.com/articles/the-ai-gold-rush-profiting-from-picks-and-shovels

Ulloa-Cazarez, R. L. (2020). *Joseph E. Aoun: Robot-proof: Higher education at the age of artificial intelligence*: MIT Press, 2018, pp 216, ISBN: 978-0-262-53597-7.

Zhang, M. (April 16, 2023). AI's winning streak: Crushing the venture capital slump. *Artisana*. Retrieved: https://www.artisana.ai/articles/ais-winning-streak-crushing-the-venture-capital-slump

Appendices

A Survey Instrument: Institutional Readiness for AI Adoption in Higher Education: Assessing Perception, Experience, and Support Structures

This survey aims to assess the readiness of educational institutions to adopt generative AI across various units, considering faculty, staff, and students. Your responses will help us understand the factors affecting AI adoption and inform strategies to promote the effective use of AI in higher education. Participation in this survey is voluntary and your responses will remain confidential.

Please note that some questions in this survey have an assigned numeric score. These scores will be used to calculate an Institutional Readiness Score at the end of the survey.

Section 1: Demographics 1.1 Age group:

- 18–24
- 25–34
- 35–44
- 45–54
- 55–64
- 65+

1.2 Gender:

- Male
- Female
- Non-binary
- Prefer not to say

1.10 Race/Ethnicity (Select all that apply):

- White
- Black or African American
- Hispanic or Latino
- Asian
- Native American or Alaska Native
- Native Hawaiian or Pacific Islander
- Other (please specify)
- Prefer not to say

1.3 Type of institution (Carnegie Classification):

- R1: Doctoral Universities (Highest research activity)
- R2: Doctoral Universities (Higher research activity)
- Master's Colleges and Universities
- Baccalaureate Colleges
- Associate's Colleges
- Other (please specify)

1.4 Size of institution:

- 100–1,000 students
- 1,001–5,000 students
- 5,001–10,000 students
- 10,001–20,000 students
- 20,001–30,000 students
- 30,001+ students

1.5 Institution type:

- Public
- Private

1.6 Tenure granting?

- Yes
- No

1.7 Your role (Select one):

- Administrator (e.g., department chair, dean, provost)
- Faculty (e.g., professor, lecturer, adjunct)

- Staff (e.g., support staff, IT, administration)
- Student (e.g., undergraduate, graduate, doctoral)
- Other (please specify)

1.11 If you selected "Faculty" in question 1.7, please identify your rank:

- Senior Professor
- Professor
- Associate Professor
- Assistant Professor
- Lecturer or Instructor
- Adjunct Faculty
- Other (please specify)

1.8 Please select your school, college affiliation, or department from the list below or provide the specific name if not listed:

- Arts and Humanities
- Business and Economics
- Education
- Engineering and Technology
- Health and Medicine
- Law
- Natural Sciences
- Social Sciences
- Interdisciplinary Programs
- Other (please specify)

Section 2: AI Experience and Perception 2.1 Rate your comfort with technology (1 = Not comfortable at all, 5 = Very comfortable): [Score: 1–5]

1.9 Based on your response to question 1.8, how closely do you feel your discipline/department/major aligns with artificial intelligence (AI) with regards to the field? (1 = Not aligned at all, 5 = Very closely aligned): [Score: 1–5]

2.2 General perception of artificial intelligence:

- Positive [Score: 3]
- Neutral [Score: 2]
- Negative [Score: 1]

2.11 How optimistic or pessimistic do you feel about the impact of AI on education? (1 = Very pessimistic, 5 = Very optimistic): [Score: 1–5]

2.2a How do you believe AI will impact the future of teaching and learning? (Select one)

- Replace human teachers/staff altogether [Score: 1]
- Slightly augment the activity of teaching and learning [Score: 2]
- Co-bots used with humans as mentors and coaches [Score: 3]
- No impact at all [Score: 4]
- Unsure [Score: 5]

2.3 Have you used AI tools before?

- Yes [Score: 2]
- No [Score: 1]

2.4 If yes, please select the types of AI tools used previously (Select all that apply):

- Machine learning algorithms (e.g., regression, classification, clustering)
- Natural language processing tools (e.g., sentiment analysis, summarization)
- Computer vision tools (e.g., image recognition, object detection)
- Speech recognition and synthesis tools (e.g., transcription, text-to-speech)
- AI-powered analytics platforms (e.g., data visualization, predictive analytics)
- Intelligent tutoring systems and virtual teaching assistants
- AI-based automation tools (e.g., robotic process automation, workflow automation)
- AI-enhanced collaboration and communication tools (e.g., chatbots, smart email)
- AI-driven decision support systems
- Other (please specify)

2.5 Where do you see AI as appropriate for use? (Select all that apply)

- Research
- Teaching
- Service

2.6 Willingness to integrate AI into these three areas (1 = Not willing at all, 5 = Very willing): [Score: 1–5]

2.7 If unwilling to integrate AI into teaching, please state why: (Select all that apply)

- Concerns about AI's impact on the quality of education
- Ethical concerns surrounding AI use
- Data privacy and security concerns
- Lack of familiarity with AI tools and technologies
- Insufficient support and training resources
- Perception that AI is not relevant to my discipline or subject area
- Belief that AI cannot replace or improve human teaching methods
- Fear of job displacement or reduced human interaction
- Time and effort required to learn and implement AI tools
- Other (please specify)

Please complete the following sections based on your responses to question 2.5:

2.5a If you selected "Research" in question 2.5, please select the ways in which you believe AI is most useful for research (Select all that apply):

- Data analysis and statistical modeling
- Natural language processing and text analysis
- Image and video analysis
- Predictive modeling and forecasting
- Automating repetitive tasks and processes
- Discovery of patterns and relationships in large datasets
- Assisting with literature reviews and information retrieval
- Enhancing research collaboration and interdisciplinary projects
- Simulation and modeling of complex systems
- Other (please specify)

Please provide examples for the selected options:

2.5b If you selected "Teaching" in question 2.5, please select the ways in which you believe AI is most useful for teaching (Select all that apply):

- Personalized learning and adaptive course content
- Automated grading and assessment
- Intelligent tutoring systems and virtual teaching assistants
- Enhancing student engagement and motivation
- Facilitating collaboration and group work

- Supporting students with special needs or learning differences
- Providing real-time feedback and recommendations
- Developing critical thinking and problem-solving skills
- Identifying and addressing learning gaps
- Other (please specify)

Please provide examples for the selected options:

2.5c If you selected "Service" in question 2.5, please select the ways in which you believe AI is most useful for service (Select all that apply):

- Automating administrative tasks and processes
- Enhancing communication and information dissemination
- Supporting decision-making with data-driven insights
- Improving resource allocation and optimization
- Streamlining student advising and support services
- Enhancing community engagement and outreach
- Facilitating interdisciplinary collaboration
- Supporting diversity, equity, and inclusion initiatives
- Improving campus safety and security
- Other (please specify)

Please provide examples for the selected options:

Section 3: Institutional Readiness 3.1 Rate your institution's overall readiness to adopt AI (1 = Not ready at all, 5 = Very ready): [Score: 1–5]

3.2 What do you believe are the key factors that influence your institution's readiness to adopt AI? (Select all that apply)

- Leadership commitment and support
- Funding and resource allocation
- Infrastructure and technological capacity
- Faculty, staff, and student familiarity with AI technologies
- Collaboration and partnerships with external organizations
- Institutional culture and attitudes toward AI
- Training and professional development opportunities
- Integration of AI into curriculum and research activities
- Support services for AI implementation
- Other (please specify)

3.3 Rate your institution's current level of AI integration (1 = No integration, 5 = Full integration): [Score: 1–5]

3.4 Does your organization already have AI training programs in place for employees? (Select one)

1 Yes
2 No
3 In development/planned
4 Unsure

3.4a If you answered "Yes" to question 3.4, please select the types of AI training and support available within your organization (Select all that apply):

5 In-house training courses/workshops
6 Online courses (e.g., MOOCs, e-learning platforms)
7 External workshops or conferences
8 Partnerships with educational institutions or industry experts
9 Mentorship or coaching programs
10 Access to AI-related resources (e.g., articles, books, videos)
11 Support for employees to pursue AI-related certifications or degrees
12 Regularly scheduled knowledge-sharing sessions or presentations
13 Other (please specify)

3.4 What barriers do you believe exist to integrating AI at your institution? (Select all that apply)

- Lack of awareness or understanding of AI technologies
- Resistance to change or negative perceptions of AI
- Insufficient funding or resources
- Inadequate infrastructure or technological capacity
- Limited training and professional development opportunities
- Concerns about data privacy and security
- Ethical concerns surrounding AI use
- Fear of job displacement or reduced human interaction
- Difficulty in aligning AI with institutional mission or goals
- Other (please specify)

3.5 What actions do you believe your institution should take to improve AI readiness? (Select all that apply)

- Increase awareness and understanding of AI technologies
- Secure funding and allocate resources for AI initiatives
- Invest in infrastructure and technological upgrades
- Provide training and professional development opportunities
- Foster collaboration and partnerships with external organizations

- Integrate AI into curriculum and research activities
- Address ethical concerns and establish guidelines for AI use
- Develop support services for AI implementation
- Address data privacy and security concerns
- Other (please specify)

Thank you for completing this survey. Your responses will contribute to a better understanding of the factors affecting AI adoption in higher education and inform strategies to promote its effective use. Your Institutional Readiness Score will be calculated based on your responses to questions with assigned numeric scores. Please press "Submit" to finalize your participation.

Scoring Rubric: Institutional Readiness for AI Adoption in Higher Education

To create a verifiable scale for institutional readiness, we can calculate a composite score based on selected questions from the survey. We can assign scores to each answer option and calculate the average score for each section. The higher the score, the higher the institutional readiness for AI adoption.

Section 2: AI Experience and Perception (Questions 2.1, 2.11, 2.6, 2.8)

- Assign a score of 1–5 for each answer option, with higher scores indicating more positive perceptions, greater experience, and willingness to integrate AI.

Section 3: IT and Technical Training Support (Questions 3.1, 3.2)

- Assign a score of 1–5 for question 3.1, with higher scores indicating better IT and technical training support.
- For question 3.2, assign one point for each selected option, with a maximum score of 9.

Section 4: Challenges and Needs (Questions 4.1, 4.2a)

- For question 4.1, assign one point for each challenge NOT selected, with a maximum score of 9 (indicating fewer perceived challenges).
- For question 4.2a, assign one point for each selected option, with a maximum score of 9 (indicating greater support for resources and initiatives to address challenges).

Calculate the total score by summing the scores from Sections 2, 3, and 4. Normalize the score on a scale of 0–100 by dividing the total score by the maximum possible score (in this case, 32) and multiplying by 100.

$$\text{Institutional Readiness Score} = (\text{Total Score} / 32)^{*} 100$$

This Institutional Readiness Score will provide a quantifiable metric to assess an institution's readiness to adopt generative AI across various units.

Scoring Rubric:

Section 2: AI Experience and Perception (Questions 2.1, 2.11, 2.6, 2.8)

Question	Score
2.1	1–5
2.11	1–5
2.6	1–5
2.8	1–5

Section 3: IT and Technical Training Support (Questions 3.1, 3.2)

Question	Score
3.1	1–5
3.2	0–9

Section 4: Challenges and Needs (Questions 4.1, 4.2a)

Question	Score
4.1	0–9
4.2a	0–9

Institutional Readiness Score Calculation:

1 Calculate the total score by summing the scores from Sections 2, 3, and 4.
2 Normalize the score on a scale of 0–100 by dividing the total score by the maximum possible score (in this case, 32) and multiplying by 100.

$$\text{Institutional Readiness Score} = (\text{Total Score} / 32)^{*} 100$$

This Institutional Readiness Score will provide a quantifiable metric to assess an institution's readiness to adopt generative AI across various units.

B Survey Instrument: Industry Readiness for AI Adoption in Firms: Assessing Perception, Experience, and Support Structures

This survey aims to gather information on how various industries perceive and engage with artificial intelligence (AI) technologies, as well as the support structures in place to facilitate AI adoption. Your participation in this survey will help us better understand the current state of AI readiness across different industries and identify areas where further support and resources may be needed to accelerate the successful integration of AI in the workplace.

As you complete the survey, please consider your own experiences, your company's resources, and your industry's broader context. All responses will remain confidential and will only be reported in aggregate form. Your valuable input will contribute to the development of strategies and recommendations for improving AI adoption across industries.

Section 1: Demographics 1.1 Age group:

- 18–24
- 25–34
- 35–44
- 45–54
- 55–64
- 65+

1.2 Gender:

- Male
- Female
- Non-binary
- Prefer not to say

1.10 Race/Ethnicity (Select all that apply):

- White
- Black or African American
- Hispanic or Latino
- Asian
- Native American or Alaska Native
- Native Hawaiian or Pacific Islander
- Other (please specify)
- Prefer not to say

1.3 Industry sector (please specify):

1.4 Size of the firm (number of employees):

- 1–10
- 11–50
- 51–200
- 201–500
- 501–1000
- 1001–5000
- 5001–10000
- 10001+

1.5 Firm type:

- Public
- Private

1.6 Your role (Select one):

- C-level executive (e.g., CEO, CFO, CIO)
- Director or manager
- Specialist or analyst
- IT support
- Other (please specify)

1.7 Please select your department from the list below or provide the specific name if not listed:

- IT and technology
- Research and development
- Sales and marketing
- Operations
- Human resources
- Finance
- Customer service
- Administration
- Other (please specify)

1.8 Years with the firm:

- Less than 1 year
- 1–2 years
- 3–5 years
- 6–10 years

- 11–15 years
- 16–20 years
- 21–25 years
- 26+ years

Section 2: AI Experience and Perception 2.1 Rate your comfort with technology (1 = Not comfortable at all, 5 = Very comfortable): [Score: 1–5]

2.1 How closely do you feel your discipline/department/job aligns with artificial intelligence (AI) with regards to the job function? (1 = Not aligned at all, 5 = Very closely aligned): [Score: 1–5]

2.2 General perception of artificial intelligence:

- Positive [Score: 3]
- Neutral [Score: 2]
- Negative [Score: 1]

2.3 How optimistic or pessimistic do you feel about the impact of AI on industry? (1 = Very pessimistic, 5 = Very optimistic): [Score: 1–5]

2.4 How do you believe AI will impact the future of work and job roles in your industry? (Select one)

- Replace human workers/staff altogether [Score: 1]
- Slightly augment the activities and tasks of workers [Score: 2]
- Co-bots used with humans as collaborators and support [Score: 3]
- Not impact at all [Score: 4]
- Unsure [Score: 5]

2.5 Have you used AI tools before?

- Yes [Score: 2]
- No [Score: 1]

2.6 If yes, please select the types of AI tools used previously (Select all that apply):

- Machine learning algorithms (e.g., regression, classification, clustering)
- Natural language processing tools (e.g., sentiment analysis, summarization)
- Computer vision tools (e.g., image recognition, object detection)
- Speech recognition and synthesis tools (e.g., transcription, text-to-speech)

- AI-powered analytics platforms (e.g., data visualization, predictive analytics)
- Intelligent tutoring systems and virtual teaching assistants
- AI-based automation tools (e.g., robotic process automation, workflow automation)
- AI-enhanced collaboration and communication tools (e.g., chatbots, smart email)
- AI-driven decision support systems
- Other (please specify)

2.7 Where do you see AI as appropriate for use in your industry? (Select all that apply)

- Research and Development
- Operations and Production
- Customer Service and Support
- Supply Chain Management
- Human Resources
- Decision-Making and Strategy
- Market Analysis
- Other (please specify)

2.8 Willingness to integrate AI into these three areas (1 = Not willing at all, 5 = Very willing): [Score: 1–5]

2.9 If unwilling to integrate AI into your industry operations, please state why: (Select all that apply)

- Concerns about AI's impact on the quality of work or services
- Ethical concerns surrounding AI use
- Data privacy and security concerns
- Lack of familiarity with AI tools and technologies
- Insufficient support and training resources
- Perception that AI is not relevant to my department or job function
- Belief that AI cannot replace or improve human work methods
- Fear of job displacement or reduced human interaction
- Time and effort required to learn and implement AI tools
- Other (please specify)

Please complete the following sections based on your responses to question 2.7:

2.5a If you selected "Research and Development" in question 2.5, please select the ways in which you believe AI is most useful for research and development (Select all that apply):

- Data analysis and statistical modeling
- Natural language processing and text analysis
- Image and video analysis
- Predictive modeling and forecasting
- Automating repetitive tasks and processes
- Discovery of patterns and relationships in large datasets
- Assisting with information retrieval and knowledge extraction
- Enhancing research collaboration and interdisciplinary projects
- Simulation and modeling of complex systems
- Other (please specify)
- Please provide examples for the selected options:

2.5b If you selected "Operations and Production" in question 2.5, please select the ways in which you believe AI is most useful for operations and production (Select all that apply):

- Personalized automation and adaptive processes
- Automated quality control and assessment
- Intelligent monitoring systems and virtual assistants
- Enhancing worker engagement and motivation
- Facilitating collaboration and group work
- Supporting workers with special needs or differences
- Providing real-time feedback and recommendations
- Developing critical thinking and problem-solving skills
- Identifying and addressing operational gaps
- Other (please specify)
- Please provide examples for the selected options:

2.5c If you selected "Customer Service" in question 2.5, please select the ways in which you believe AI is most useful for customer service (Select all that apply):

- Automating customer support tasks and processes
- Enhancing communication and information dissemination
- Supporting decision-making with data-driven insights
- Improving resource allocation and optimization
- Streamlining customer relationship management
- Enhancing customer engagement and outreach
- Facilitating collaboration across departments

- Supporting diversity, equity, and inclusion initiatives
- Improving service quality and response times
- Other (please specify)
- Please provide examples for the selected options:

Section 3: Institutional Readiness 3.1 Rate your institution's overall readiness to adopt AI (1 = Not ready at all, 5 = Very ready): [Score: 1–5]

3.2 What do you believe are the key factors that influence your company's readiness to adopt AI? (Select all that apply)

- Leadership commitment and support
- Funding and resource allocation
- Infrastructure and technological capacity
- Employee familiarity with AI technologies
- Collaboration and partnerships with external organizations
- Organizational culture and attitudes toward AI
- Training and professional development opportunities
- Integration of AI into operational and strategic activities
- Support services for AI implementation
- Other (please specify)

3.3 Rate your institution's current level of AI integration (1 = No integration, 5 = Full integration): [Score: 1–5]

3.4 Does your organization already have AI training programs in place for employees? (Select one)

1 Yes
2 No
3 In development/planned
4 Unsure

3.4a If you answered "Yes" to question 3.4, please select the types of AI training and support available within your organization (Select all that apply):

5 In-house training courses/workshops
6 Online courses (e.g., MOOCs, e-learning platforms)
7 External workshops or conferences
8 Partnerships with educational institutions or industry experts
9 Mentorship or coaching programs

10 Access to AI-related resources (e.g., articles, books, videos)
11 Support for employees to pursue AI-related certifications or degrees
12 Regularly scheduled knowledge-sharing sessions or presentations
13 Other (please specify)

3.4 What barriers do you believe exist to integrating AI at your institution? (Select all that apply)

- Lack of awareness or understanding of AI technologies
- Resistance to change or negative perceptions of AI
- Insufficient funding or resources
- Inadequate infrastructure or technological capacity
- Limited training and professional development opportunities
- Concerns about data privacy and security
- Ethical concerns surrounding AI use
- Fear of job displacement or reduced human interaction
- Difficulty in aligning AI with institutional mission or goals
- Other (please specify)

3.5 What actions do you believe your institution should take to improve AI readiness? (Select all that apply)

- Increase awareness and understanding of AI technologies
- Secure funding and allocate resources for AI initiatives
- Invest in infrastructure and technological upgrades
- Provide training and professional development opportunities
- Foster collaboration and partnerships with external organizations
- Integrate AI into curriculum and research activities
- Address ethical concerns and establish guidelines for AI use
- Develop support services for AI implementation
- Address data privacy and security concerns
- Other (please specify)

Thank you for completing the Industry Readiness for AI Adoption in Firms: Assessing Perception, Experience, and Support Structures survey. Your insights are essential in understanding the current state of AI readiness within various industries and will contribute to the development of strategies and recommendations for accelerating AI adoption.

We appreciate your time and effort in providing this valuable information. The findings from this survey will be used to better inform industry leaders, policymakers, and other stakeholders about the challenges and opportunities surrounding AI adoption in the workplace. By identifying key factors that influence AI readiness and addressing existing gaps, we hope to facilitate the successful integration of AI technologies across industries, ultimately leading to increased productivity, efficiency, and innovation.

Scoring Rubric: Industry Readiness for AI Adoption in Firms: Assessing Perception, Experience, and Support Structures

To create a verifiable scale for institutional readiness, we can calculate a composite score based on selected questions from the survey. We can assign scores to each answer option and calculate the average score for each section. The higher the score, the higher the institutional readiness for AI adoption.

Section 2: AI Experience and Perception (Questions 2.1, 2.11, 2.6, 2.8)

- Assign a score of 1–5 for each answer option, with higher scores indicating more positive perceptions, greater experience, and willingness to integrate AI.

Section 3: IT and Technical Training Support (Questions 3.1, 3.2)

- Assign a score of 1–5 for question 3.1, with higher scores indicating better IT and technical training support.
- For question 3.2, assign one point for each selected option, with a maximum score of 9.

Section 4: Challenges and Needs (Questions 4.1, 4.2a)

- For question 4.1, assign one point for each challenge NOT selected, with a maximum score of 9 (indicating fewer perceived challenges).
- For question 4.2a, assign one point for each selected option, with a maximum score of 9 (indicating greater support for resources and initiatives to address challenges).

Calculate the total score by summing the scores from Sections 2, 3, and 4. Normalize the score on a scale of 0–100 by dividing the total score by the maximum possible score (in this case, 32) and multiplying by 100.

$$\text{Institutional Readiness Score} = (\text{Total Score} / 32)^{*} 100$$

This Institutional Readiness Score will provide a quantifiable metric to assess an institution's readiness to adopt generative AI across various units.

Scoring Rubric:

Section 2: AI Experience and Perception (Questions 2.1, 2.11, 2.6, 2.8)

Question	Score
2.1	1–5
2.11	1–5
2.6	1–5
2.8	1–5

Section 3: IT and Technical Training Support (Questions 3.1, 3.2)

Question	Score
3.1	1–5
3.2	0–9

Section 4: Challenges and Needs (Questions 4.1, 4.2a)

Question	Score
4.1	0–9
4.2a	0–9

Institutional Readiness Score Calculation:

1 Calculate the total score by summing the scores from Sections 2, 3, and 4.
2 Normalize the score on a scale of 0–100 by dividing the total score by the maximum possible score (in this case, 32) and multiplying by 100.

$$\text{Institutional Readiness Score} = \left(\text{Total Score} / 32\right)^{*} 100$$

This Institutional Readiness Score will provide a quantifiable metric to assess an institution's readiness to adopt generative AI across various units.

C Addressing Academic Freedom in the Age of AI

In the era of rapid technological advancements, the intersection of artificial intelligence (AI) and academic freedom presents both opportunities and challenges. Academic freedom, a fundamental principle of higher education and research institutions worldwide, ensures that scholars have the liberty to teach, discuss, conduct research, and publish their findings without undue restriction or fear of repression. However, as AI technologies evolve and permeate various aspects of academia, from research methodologies to the dissemination of knowledge, it becomes crucial to reexamine and clarify the boundaries and responsibilities that define academic freedom today.

Lindenwood University Academic Freedom Policy (adopted 2007)

https://www.lindenwood.edu/academics/support-resources/academic-freedom/

Lindenwood University is committed to the idea that universities are centers of intellectual growth, exploration, creativity, and expression. It is incumbent upon the university, therefore, to create an atmosphere that is conducive to open, critical thinking. Central to that duty is the freedom to formulate and express ideas that advance the process of intellectual inquiry and education. Therefore, freedom of thought and word within the confines of higher education is central to effective education of the whole person.

Academic freedom also carries profound responsibilities. The university itself must take all precautions to protect the ability of faculty to express ideas and teach concepts that are germane to their respective subjects in research and publication as well as the classroom; the ability to do so without interference must remain unfettered. Some subjects of intellectual inquiry cause discomfort to some or all students and faculty members, yet failure to explore those topics would be to deny our responsibility as educators. Rather, the open exchange of ideas between faculty and students must be conducted in an atmosphere of mutual civility, respect, and attention toward the greater good of the university and its members.

Faculty members should neither be censored for expression of their views nor engage in self-censorship out of fear of recrimination; similarly, students should know that they have the right to express their views as well but will be held to the same standard of defense of those views. Academic freedom in no way implies a tolerance of disrespect, of bigotry, or of discrimination regarding age, race, national origin, religion, sexual orientation, or gender, nor should the academic freedom of one person interfere with the freedom of another.

Academic freedom also includes the right to freedom in research and publication. Faculty members are free to select topics, obtain data, and report findings in a manner that is scientifically and academically sound in one's field without censorship. Work that produces monetary gains will be based on standard practices and shall not be linked to nature of the research.

The freedom to associate, to speak, and to write are central to the republic itself. Therefore, it shall be the policy and practice of the university to permit a faculty member's exercise of the basic right of freedom of speech when outside the university itself and to be involved in community activities.

Definition of Academic Freedom

Academic freedom is the right of faculty members and researchers in institutions of higher learning to pursue knowledge wherever it may lead, without undue or unreasonable interference. It encompasses several core components:

1. **Freedom in Research and Publication**: Scholars are free to select their research topics, conduct their studies, and publish their findings without external censorship or disciplinary action for their views.
2. **Freedom of Teaching**: Educators have the liberty to develop and deliver their curriculum, choose teaching methods, and discuss their subject matter freely in the classroom, as long as these are aligned with professional standards and the educational objectives of their institution.
3. **Freedom of Expression**: Academic staff and students have the right to express their views, both inside and outside the classroom, on issues related to their professional expertise, without fear of institutional censorship or retaliation.
4. **Freedom from Institutional Censorship**: While academic freedom protects scholars and educators, it also requires institutions to refrain from interfering with or limiting the intellectual independence of their academic staff.

What Academic Freedom Covers

1. **Exploratory Research**: The freedom to explore new areas of inquiry and adopt unconventional methodologies without immediate practical applications.
2. **Diverse Perspectives**: The encouragement of a variety of viewpoints, fostering a culture where debate and dissent are valued components of the academic process.
3. **Academic Integrity**: Upholding the principles of honesty, transparency, and rigor in research and teaching, even in the face of external pressures to compromise these values.

What Academic Freedom Does Not Cover

1. **Freedom from Criticism**: While academic freedom protects scholars' rights to express their views, it does not shield them from criticism or academic scrutiny from their peers.
2. **Unprofessional Conduct**: Academic freedom does not excuse behavior that falls below the professional standards of the academic community, such as plagiarism, falsification of research, or discrimination against students or colleagues.
3. **Absolute Autonomy**: Academic freedom exists within the context of the responsibilities and goals of the academic institution. It does not grant

individuals the right to ignore institutional regulations that are in place to ensure the proper functioning and integrity of the educational mission.

4 **Selection of Teaching Modality**: Academic freedom does not grant instructors the right to choose the modality through which a course is taught. Decisions regarding whether a course will be delivered in-person, online, or through a hybrid format often depend on broader institutional policies, resources, student needs, and strategic objectives. Especially in an era where digital platforms and AI technologies are reshaping educational delivery, the choice of teaching modality may be influenced by considerations of accessibility, efficacy, and institutional capacity rather than individual instructor preference.

5 **Determination of Student Achievement of Objectives and Assessments**: While instructors have the freedom to set learning outcomes for their courses, the methods by which students are assessed and demonstrate their achievement of these outcomes are not solely at the discretion of the instructor. Assessment strategies and tools may be institutionally mandated, particularly where standardized measures are required for accreditation, quality assurance, and external reporting purposes. These constraints ensure that evaluations of student performance are consistent, fair, and aligned with the educational standards of the institution and accrediting bodies.

Challenges in the Age of AI

The introduction of artificial intelligence (AI) into the academic realm poses nuanced challenges to the concept of academic freedom, particularly in the areas of data privacy, intellectual property rights, the risk of perpetuating biases through AI-driven research, and the evolution of student-teacher dynamics within digital platforms. While AI technologies are becoming essential tools for research and pedagogy, their integration demands a careful reconsideration of traditional academic freedoms. Specifically, while instructors retain the freedom to determine the content of their courses and the learning outcomes they aim to achieve, the advent of AI necessitates a more collaborative approach in deciding how these outcomes are met and assessed. This adjustment reflects a broader understanding that, although academic freedom encompasses the liberty to design and deliver curriculum, it does not extend to unilateral decisions on assessment methodologies or meeting learning objectives, particularly in an era where technology-driven tools and platforms could influence these processes. As the academic landscape evolves with AI, it is critical for the academic community to uphold the core values of academic freedom by fostering an environment where innovative teaching methods are encouraged, yet balanced with the collective responsibility to ensure that educational outcomes are met in a fair, transparent, and equitable manner.

Conclusion

Academic freedom is a cornerstone of higher education, enabling the pursuit of knowledge free from undue constraint. As we navigate the age of AI, it is imperative to reassess and reaffirm the principles of academic freedom, ensuring they are robust enough to withstand new challenges while flexible enough to embrace the opportunities presented by technological advancement. By doing so, the academic community can continue to foster an environment of inquiry, innovation, and intellectual growth.

D AI Minimum Use Policy White Paper

Executive Summary

This white paper proposes a comprehensive AI Minimum Use Policy aimed at integrating artificial intelligence (AI) across all curricula at Lindenwood University. The objective is to equip students with essential AI, GAI, ML, and/or NLP competencies necessary for success in a digitally-driven global economy. This document synthesizes best practices from leading universities to develop a framework that not only supports the educational mission of Lindenwood University but also adheres to ethical standards and promotes AI literacy.

1 **Introduction**

The integration of AI into higher education curricula is becoming a critical element in preparing students for the workforce of the future. This policy mandates a minimum level of AI usage in course work across all departments, ensuring that all students gain valuable experience with AI technologies and concepts.

2 **Policy Framework**

Purpose

The purpose of this policy is to institutionalize the use of artificial intelligence within the curriculum, thereby ensuring that all students acquire essential competencies in AI as part of their academic development. By setting a minimal usage requirement, the institution commits to producing graduates who are proficient in AI technologies and methodologies, equipping them with the skills necessary for success in a digitally driven economy.

Scope

This policy applies to all courses offered at the institution, across all departments and faculties. The policy targets integration at various levels of the curriculum, ensuring that every student, regardless of their major, is exposed to AI concepts and applications.

3 **Policy Statement**
The institution requires that all teaching faculties incorporate a minimum level of AI content in their courses. This includes but is not limited to the use of AI-driven tools for educational purposes, the introduction of AI concepts in course materials, and the implementation of AI-focused assignments and projects.

4 **Implementation Guidelines**

Educational Tools
In line with practices at the University of Texas, AI tools should support various phases of academic work, including research, drafting of content, and revision (Duke Learning Innovation, 2023). Faculties must employ at least one AI-based educational tool or platform. These could range from AI-driven data analysis tools to machine learning environments and adaptive learning technologies.

Graduate Attributes
Each graduate attribute will be revised along with the RISE program to integrate and foreground AI literacy and proficiency. The policy mandates the revision of program and course learning outcomes to include competencies in the use of General AI (GAI), ensuring that these skills are reflected comprehensively across the curriculum.

Curriculum Integration
AI concepts must be integrated into at least ONE activity per course, with additional applications in specialized courses. All courses should feature an assessment mechanism to gauge student proficiency in AI-related skills. This could involve projects, exams, or practical implementations of AI technologies.

Minimum AI Usage Requirement: To ensure that all students have hands-on experience with AI technologies, every faculty member must meet the following requirement:

By the 4-week point in a 15-week course, faculty must either:

a) Involve students in the use of AI for a class activity, OR
b) Allow students to use AI in the development of a course assignment.

Faculty who feel they lack expertise in teaching AI can fulfill this requirement by allowing students to experiment with AI independently for either option a) or b).

Faculty Development and AI Literacy

Echoing Harvard's approach, faculties will be provided with ongoing training to use AI tools effectively and responsibly, ensuring that they can guide students in navigating the complexities of AI technologies (Harvard University, 2023). The institution will facilitate continuous professional development opportunities aimed at enhancing faculty proficiency in AI technologies. This initiative will include workshops, seminars, and access to essential AI resources.

Ethical Considerations and Data Privacy

Consistent with Columbia University's guidelines, the policy emphasizes the ethical use of AI, including safeguarding intellectual property and personal information, and verifying the accuracy and biases of AI-generated content (Columbia University, 2023). See Use of Generative AI in Employment Policy (https://www.lindenwood.edu/policies/list/use-of-generative-ai-in-employment-policy/) for details on data privacy.

Monitoring and Compliance

A committee will be established to oversee the implementation of this policy. This body will conduct annual audits of course syllabi, instructional methodologies, and faculty development efforts to ensure alignment with the stipulated AI usage requirements. The committee will monitor the implementation of AI tools across departments, like the AI Policy Hub at UC Berkeley, which supports the development of policy frameworks for AI (UC Berkeley, 2023).

Review and Adaptation

The policy will be reviewed biennially to adapt to technological advancements and pedagogical insights, ensuring that Lindenwood University's guidelines remain current and effective in promoting beneficial AI practices.

References

Duke Learning Innovation. (2023). Artificial Intelligence Policies: Guidelines and Considerations https://learninginnovation.duke.edu

Harvard University. (2023). Guidelines for Using ChatGPT and Other Generative AI Tools at Harvard https://provost.harvard.edu

Columbia University. (2023). Generative AI Policy https://provost.columbia.edu

UC Berkeley. (2023). AI Policy Hub https://cltc.berkeley.edu

Index

Pages in *italics* refer to figures and pages in **bold** refer to tables.